SPECTRUM MULTIVIEW BOOKS

EVANGELICAL THEOLOGICAL METHOD

FIVE VIEWS

EDITED BY STANLEY E. PORTER
and STEVEN M. STUDEBAKER

CONTRIBUTIONS BY

Sung Wook Chung, John R. Franke, Telford C. Work,
Victor Ifeanyi Ezigbo, *and* Paul Louis Metzger

IVP Academic

An imprint of InterVarsity Press
Downers Grove, Illinois

InterVarsity Press
P.O. Box 1400, Downers Grove, IL 60515-1426
ivpress.com
email@ivpress.com

InterVarsity Press® is the book-publishing division of InterVarsity Christian Fellowship/USA®, a movement of students and faculty active on campus at hundreds of universities, colleges, and schools of nursing in the United States of America, and a member movement of the International Fellowship of Evangelical Students. For information about local and regional activities, visit intervarsity.org.

Cover design: David Fassett
Interior design: Jeanna Wiggins
Image: Radachynskyi/iStock/Getty Images Plus

ISBN 978-0-8308-5208-6 (print)
ISBN 978-0-8308-8600-5 (digital)

Printed in the United States of America ∞

InterVarsity Press is committed to ecological stewardship and to the conservation of natural resources in all our operations. This book was printed using sustainably sourced paper.

Library of Congress Cataloging-in-Publication Data
Names: Porter, Stanley E., 1956- editor.
Title: Evangelical theological method : five views / edited by Stanley E.
  Porter and Steven M. Studebaker.
Description: Downers Grove : InterVarsity Press, 2018. | Series: Spectrum
  multiview book series
Identifiers: LCCN 2018012253 (print) | LCCN 2018017744 (ebook) | ISBN
  9780830886005 (eBook) | ISBN 9780830852086 (pbk. : alk. paper)
Subjects: LCSH: Theology—Methodology. | Evangelicalism.
Classification: LCC BR118 (ebook) | LCC BR118 .E87 2018 (print) | DDC
  230/.0462401—dc23
LC record available at https://lccn.loc.gov/2018012253

P 29 28 27 26 25 24 23 22 21 20 19 18 17 16 15 14 13 12 11 10 9 8 7 6 5 4 3 2 1

Y 43 42 41 40 39 38 37 36 35 34 33 32 31 30 29 28 27 26 25 24 23 22 21 20 19 18

Contents

Preface

STANLEY E. PORTER AND
STEVEN M. STUDEBAKER

This volume directly emerges from the kinds of discussions that theologians of all affiliations should be having among themselves and with their students regarding questions of theological method. The editors are thankful to the McMaster Divinity College faculty for providing an atmosphere in which we are able both to be reminded (sometimes gently and sometimes not so gently) of the importance of theological method and to test various methods and witness their vital role in the theological task as we discuss projects together. We also wish to thank our numerous students, who through the years have responded to our constant exhortations regarding method as they prepare their thesis and dissertation proposals and then execute this important work. We firmly believe that having an appropriate theological method is essential to the theological task. In fact, we believe that having a viable method is the first step in helping to ensure that one can determine what counts as evidence and that one has a means of evaluating this evidence to form coherent theological findings. Without a method, it is only an accident if one arrives at important or viable conclusions (and how would you know anyway?). There have been many theological accidents that we hope this book will help to correct.

Besides our colleagues and students at McMaster Divinity College, we wish to thank the contributors to this volume for their willingness to participate. One of the great strengths of a multiple-views book is that it enlists the participation of those who hold to the various positions represented, rather than depending on a single author to put forward a range of differing and even contradictory positions with equal plausibility. Even within the evangelical theological world, there are sufficiently diverse opinions to merit and support a book with a number of strikingly different methodological positions. In such a book, however, there is also heightened risk of something going wrong, as one puts forward one's best ideas with both boldness and temerity in light of the possible responses that it will garner. In fact, in this book each proposal solicits numerous responses. We are thankful that our five different theological methodologists have more than risen to the occasion and produced essays that have well captured each method and have withstood the scrutiny of their peers. Their responses make clear that there is justifiable critical appreciation among the participants. We thank all of them for their efforts toward this project.

We are grateful to InterVarsity Press for recognizing the value of this project and supporting it, and to David McNutt for his editorial work throughout the process.

On behalf of all of the contributors, ourselves included, we wish to thank our supporting academic and other institutions for providing theological homes for us to do our collective and individual theological work. We also wish to thank those people closer to us even than our colleagues—our spouses and friends—who also have provided encouragement in all of our theological endeavors. We trust that the results in this volume will provide both intellectual and academic challenge and useful methodological insights in our common theological cause.

Method in Systematic Theology

AN INTRODUCTION

STANLEY E. PORTER AND
STEVEN M. STUDEBAKER

This volume is born out of the realities of actual academic experience. One of the regular tasks of faculty members at most graduate-level institutions, including seminaries that support thesis and dissertation research, is the review of dissertation and thesis proposals. Such review is a regular part of McMaster Divinity College faculty meetings. Discussions of proposals from systematic theology students invariably revolve around issues of methodology. What method is this student using? What is the procedure for gathering and assessing the data? What counts for evidence that supports the thesis being argued? Who are the key representatives of this method, and how does this project contribute to, use and/or challenge the approach?

When such proposals have been discussed at McMaster Divinity College, most of these questions have come from biblical studies colleagues. Although never rancorous (or at least hardly ever), the ritual regularity of these conversations grew vexatious for everyone involved. The concerns confronting the faculty as they reviewed theology proposals came down to three questions. *What* is the task of theology? *Why* does one do theology—is theology our attempt to understand God and his revelation, our response to God, or maybe both? *How* does one do theology? Most proposals in theology focus on the "what" and "why" of theology but give less attention to the "how" of theology. In other words, they often do not address questions of theological method.

The "what" and "why" questions are vital, but the "how" question is no less so. This book addresses all three questions in respect to method in evangelical theology. It provides both a practical guide to the major approaches to theological method among evangelical theologians and a useful resource for students, theologians and professors that illustrates the application of these methods. Accordingly, this book presents five methods of doing theology in the global, pluralistic and postmodern landscape of contemporary evangelical theology in North America. Each author has been assigned three tasks: first, to describe *what* their theological method is; second, to explain *why* their orientation to theology is important; and third, to show *how* to do their approach to theology. Each essay outlines the application of its method to the theological topic of Christology and thus provides a concrete example of what the model looks like in action.

Before introducing the five theological methods detailed in this volume, we first consider: (1) the meaning of the term *evangelicalism*, (2) the problem of theological method, (3) the history of theological method in evangelical theology, (4) the contemporary state of theological method, and (5) the sources of theology.

WHAT IS EVANGELICALISM?

Evangelicalism is notoriously difficult to define and appears to be getting more difficult all the time. In this volume, *evangelicalism* describes a movement in North American Protestant Christianity that is the heir to New England Puritanism, the revival movements of the eighteenth and nineteenth centuries, fundamentalism of the early twentieth century, and neo-evangelicalism that emerged in the mid-twentieth century.[1] During the

---

[1]Evangelicalism includes movements in British Protestant Christianity as well. Through the nineteenth century evangelicalism in North America and the UK were more or less common movements, sharing leaders such as John Wesley, George Whitefield and D. L. Moody, and enjoying widespread popular support. In the twentieth century, however, the movements began to diverge. During the twentieth century, evangelical Christianity in the United States became an increasingly popular form of Christianity, whereas in Britain it did not. For the evangelical movement in Britain, see David W. Bebbington, *Evangelicalism in Modern Britain: A History from the 1730s to the 1980s* (London: Unwin Hyman, 1989).

latter half of the twentieth century, evangelicalism's chief public representative was probably Billy Graham. More contemporary iconic public figures include Tim Keller, Max Lucado and Rick Warren. Key graduate educational institutions in the movement are Fuller Theological Seminary, Trinity Evangelical Divinity School and Gordon-Conwell Theological Seminary, as well as undergraduate schools such as Wheaton College, Westmont College and Bethel University. The National Association of Evangelicals is the public and political voice of evangelicalism's myriad constituencies, and the Evangelical Theological Society is the chief scholarly professional society for evangelicals.

Influential evangelical theologians of this time period include Francis Schaeffer (1912–1984), Carl F. H. Henry (1913–2003), Bernard Ramm (1916–1992), John Stott (1921–2011), J. I. Packer (1926–), Millard Erickson (1932–), Clark Pinnock (1937–2010) and Stanley J. Grenz (1950–2005). Some of the common beliefs that typically characterize many (though certainly not all) evangelicals are the deity and virgin birth of Christ, the Trinity, the authority (i.e., inerrancy or infallibility) of the Bible, the importance of a personal conversion experience and relationship with Jesus Christ, and premillennial eschatology.[2] Culturally, evangelicalism for the most part has avoided the shrillness and separatism of fundamentalism. Evangelicals are "postfundamentalists," according to Roger E. Olson. Theologically, evangelicalism rejects liberal theology and maintains traditional evangelical theology. In this respect, it is "conservative."[3]

Although sharing a common theological and religious heritage, evangelicals are far from being monochromatic. Today, two groups vie for the title of "the theological leaders of evangelicalism." According to Olson, the conservatives seek to define the boundaries in terms of a "fairly aggressive form of Reformed theology." Key figures in the neo-Reformed conservative camp are D. A. Carson, John Piper, R. C. Sproul and Bruce Ware. The

---

[2]For accounts of evangelicalism, see Garry J. Dorrien, *The Remaking of Evangelical Theology* (Louisville: Westminster John Knox, 1998); George M. Marsden, *Understanding Fundamentalism and Evangelicalism* (Grand Rapids: Eerdmans, 1991); Mark A. Noll, *American Evangelical Christianity: An Introduction* (Oxford: Blackwell, 2001); and Roger E. Olson, *The Westminster Handbook to Evangelical Theology* (Louisville: Westminster John Knox, 2004). For a comprehensive and detailed history, see the four-volume History of Evangelicalism series by InterVarsity Press.

[3]Olson, *Westminster Handbook to Evangelical Theology*, 56.

second group is what Olson calls—and counts himself among—the post-conservatives. This group is diverse. It includes Arminian and Wesleyan evangelicals. Many Pentecostals would also identify with this trajectory within evangelicalism. It consists, moreover, not only of emerging church leaders, such as Brian McLaren, Doug Pagitt, Tony Jones and Eddie Gibbs, but more importantly of theologians such as Stanley Grenz, Clark Pinnock and John Franke.[4] However, the theological landscape of evangelicalism is probably even more complex than Olson's bifurcation indicates. The diversity of perspectives on theological method presented by the five authors in this book indicates that this binary paradigm of evangelicalism is becoming unstable, if it were ever representative. Although diverse in many respects, evangelicals share an emphasis in their theology and spirituality on the Bible, a reconciled relationship with God based on Jesus Christ's atoning work on the cross, personal conversion and dynamic spiritual formation facilitated by the Holy Spirit, and service and ministry to others.[5]

DEFINITIONS AND ORIENTATIONS, BUT WHITHER THEOLOGICAL METHOD?

Returning to the faculty discussion of dissertation proposals, over several years the chasm between biblical and theological studies on the issue of method has seemed to widen. Biblical studies has defined and developed methods in a way that theology has not. Methodology often drives dissertations in biblical studies. Indeed, they often consist in showing how the application of a different method to a text yields new insights. Method is front and center. For instance, one of our students wrote a thesis that argued that a Ricoeurean reading of Job provides insight not found in alternative approaches and interpretations of Job. Another student developed a complex theory of metaphor drawing on cognitive linguistics, classical studies and systemic functional linguistics to examine various metaphors for kingship in the Bible, especially Jesus as king in John's Gospel. Yet another student utilized cognitive frame theory to describe the interaction between Jesus

---

[4]Roger E. Olson, *Reformed and Always Reforming: The Postconservative Approach to Evangelical Theology* (Grand Rapids: Baker Academic, 2007), 7-31.

[5]Timothy Larsen, "Defining and Locating Evangelicalism," in *The Cambridge Companion to Evangelical Theology*, ed. Timothy Larsen and Daniel J. Treier (New York: Cambridge University Press, 2007), 1-14.

and his disputants in Mark's Gospel. Other examples could easily be provided. Church history seems to fall somewhere between theological and biblical studies. In some respects, with its application of "secular" or "scientific" methods to historical documents and contexts, it is closer to biblical than theological studies.

Theological studies are altogether different. This is not to say that theology is without method. Biblical theology, historical theology, systematic theology, constructive theology and theological ethics are all different ways that theologians practice their craft. None of these methods, however, reaches the precision of the methods applied by their Old Testament and New Testament colleagues. Many students and scholars, for example, study the theology of Thomas Aquinas. But have you ever heard of anyone applying the linguistic method of discourse analysis to yield a new and improved understanding of Aquinas's thought? Applying the method of canonical criticism, for instance, would not illuminate Augustine's thought, especially as Augustine's thought changed and developed in significant ways over time. Reading it as a consistent and progressive whole would distort it. Yet these sorts of procedures are the stock in trade of biblical studies. This book is not a call to colonize the field of theology with the programs and methods of biblical studies. Theology is a distinct discipline from biblical studies. Theology, nevertheless, can achieve more clarity and intentionality in its use of methods. The essays in this volume are an attempt to help reach that goal.

Theological method is—at least as it currently stands—murky. In fact, most theological methodology is not method at all. Theological methods usually offer orientations to theology, not precise procedures for working out theology. What counts as theological method frequently articulates the "what" and "why" but not the "how" of theology. Reinhard Hütter raises this concern as well. In *Suffering Divine Things: Theology as Church Practice*, he laments that "an increasing lack of clarity also attaches to the question of what it means to engage in 'theology' in the first place, or, expressed in what has become the virtually 'canonical' expression in American English, 'how to do theology.'"[6] Hütter's vision that theology is a response to the Spirit that draws on Scripture and the tradition of Christian dogma in order to

---

[6]Reinhard Hütter, *Suffering Divine Things: Theology as Church Practice*, trans. Doug Stott (Grand Rapids: Eerdmans, 2000), 2.

serve the church is superb. It does not, however, articulate a method for *doing* theology. It sets forth a theology of theology. It describes what theology is. It defines theology. Theology is a Spirit-shaped reflection on church doctrine and practice. Beyond the broad orientation and approach of developing theology in light of doctrine and tradition, Hütter's proposal does not develop a theological method.

Consider two more examples. Radical orthodoxy endeavors to reinterpret the domains of human thought and life through Christian theological categories without kneeling before the reigning "secular" orthodoxies.[7] An excellent agenda, but beyond basic methodological movements (critique and *ressourcement* are detailed below), it does not lay out a pathway for Christian leaders to consider theological questions and their relationship to life and ministry, a student to write a paper or a scholar to write an essay in theology. Theological interpretation of Scripture is another case in point. It wants to recover and read the Bible as the Word of God. In place of the (ostensive) lab-like sterility of modern biblical studies and the ideological self-projection of postmodern biblical interpretation, theological interpretation takes Scripture as a theological text. Scripture is a collection of writings about God, God's work in the world, and the way people should live in relationship with God and one another.[8] In the end, however, it provides more of an inspiring orientation to various ways of reading the Bible than it does a theological method.[9] Highlighting its self-conscious diversity, J. Todd Billings points out that theological interpretation is not a "discrete method or discipline."[10]

The recurring problem is that proposals on theological method, though strong on defining what theology is and why it is important, are weak on

---

[7]James K. A. Smith, *Introducing Radical Orthodoxy: Mapping a Post-Secular Theology* (Grand Rapids: Baker Academic, 2004), 63-80.

[8]Kevin J. Vanhoozer, "Introduction: What Is the Theological Interpretation of the Bible?," in *Dictionary for Theological Interpretation of the Bible*, general ed. Kevin J. Vanhoozer (Grand Rapids: Baker Academic, 2005), 19-23.

[9]Wesley Hill's trinitarian reading of Paul is an important advance in developing the methodology of theological interpretation. See Hill, *Paul and the Trinity: Persons, Relations, and the Pauline Letters* (Grand Rapids: Eerdmans, 2015).

[10]J. Todd Billings, *The Word of God for the People of God: An Entryway to the Theological Interpretation of Scripture* (Grand Rapids: Eerdmans, 2010), xii. For a critique of some of these recent efforts, see Stanley E. Porter, "What Exactly Is Theological Interpretation of Scripture and Is It Hermeneutically Robust Enough for the Task to Which It Has Been Appointed?," in *Horizons in Hermeneutics: A Festschrift in Honor of Anthony C. Thiselton*, ed. Stanley E. Porter and Matthew R. Malcolm (Grand Rapids: Eerdmans, 2013), 234-67.

saying how to apply the method. They do not say how it is that a student or theologian should perform the theological task. They may provide a theory of theology, but they do not stipulate how to apply their theological method in concrete terms for others to examine and possibly emulate. Kevin Vanhoozer's *The Drama of Doctrine*, for instance, may be an excellent presentation of his canonical-linguistic theory, but *why* would one want to take this approach? What does it look like to employ this method when actually doing theology? How is a pastor, a seminarian, a thesis writer or a professor to apply this method? How does one *do* canonical-linguistic theology on a particular topic such as Christology? Moreover, books on theological hermeneutics and method often advance a particular approach (e.g., Hütter's *Suffering Divine Things*) or examples from within a theological genre (e.g., Vanhoozer's *The Cambridge Companion to Postmodern Theology*), but they neither provide students and professors with a more comprehensive orientation to the field of theological method nor give specific guidance on the application of their particular theological approach.[11]

This problem is endemic in the literature on theological method. How did we get here? The following section briefly charts the history of modern theological method and its loss of clear methods.

THEOLOGICAL METHOD IN THE MODERN EVANGELICAL TRADITION

The theological methods that dominated the evangelical mind for most of the twentieth century were evangelical propositionalism, the various forms of liberal theology, and the vision of theology articulated by Karl Barth, called neo-orthodoxy.[12] The primary influence of Barth on evangelical theology, however, was not so much to impart a method but to shape basic discussions about theology. This grew out of the belief that all good theology derives directly from the Bible and is Christocentric, along with being suspicious of anything that smacks of natural theology. Although Barth and neo-orthodoxy were central to twentieth-century theology, they

---

[11]Kevin J. Vanhoozer, ed., *The Cambridge Companion to Postmodern Theology* (New York: Cambridge University Press, 2003).

[12]A number of these approaches are placed within their wider hermeneutical context in Stanley E. Porter and Jason C. Robinson, *Hermeneutics: An Introduction to Interpretive Theory* (Grand Rapids: Eerdmans, 2011).

were not readily embraced by mainstream evangelical theology. Donald
Bloesch and Bernard Ramm drew on Barth, but they were exceptions.
Neo-orthodoxy arose in mainline church circles as a self-critical form of
liberal theology (e.g., H. Richard Niebuhr and Reinhold Niebuhr). Many
evangelicals, moreover, although appreciating Barth's critique of liberal
theology and focus on Christ, remained apprehensive about his view
of the Bible as the Word of God. This section, therefore, outlines the
two primary influences on twentieth-century evangelical theology—
propositional and liberal theology.

Propositional theology. Charles Hodge (1797–1878) is the father of evangelical propositionalism.[13] A nineteenth-century theologian at Princeton
Theological Seminary, Hodge articulated a modern adaptation of the older
scholastic method of theology. Theology is a science, Hodge believed. The
Bible is to the theologian what the world is to the scientist. The Bible is a field
of data waiting to be scrutinized and understood. The Bible is the theologian's
"store-house of facts," according to Hodge.[14] Theology is a science because it
follows an inductive, investigative approach that yields indubitable facts and
statements that one must believe. The task of theology, therefore, is to collect
the biblical data and formulate theological principles from these data.

Contemporary and influential evangelical theologian Wayne Grudem
carries on Hodge's theological method. He delineates three steps for doing
systematic theology. First, find and assemble all the relevant passages on
the selected topic of study. Second, read, study and articulate the teachings
of these passages. Third, summarize the teachings into theological statements and correlate them with the other teachings of Scripture on the

---

[13]Notwithstanding different emphases within the spectrum of evangelicalism, Hodge's theology
shaped the method of theology from the fundamentalists to the Wesleyan-Holiness and Pentecostal movements in the twentieth century. Widely popular Wesleyan theologian H. Orton Wiley
takes Hodge as a paradigm for his systematic theology: *Christian Theology*, 3 vols. (Kansas City,
MO: Beacon Hill, 1940–1943). For the influence of the propositional approach to theology on
Pentecostalism, see L. William Oliverio Jr., *Theological Hermeneutics in the Classical Pentecostal
Tradition: A Typological Account* (Leiden: Brill, 2012).

[14]Charles Hodge, *Systematic Theology* (repr., Peabody, MA: Hendrickson, 2003), 1:10, cf. 1-17. Still
used is the similar theology of Louis Berkhof, *Systematic Theology* (Grand Rapids: Eerdmans, 1939).
The method is well displayed in his *Summary of Christian Doctrine* (Grand Rapids: Eerdmans,
1938). Exemplifying the neo-evangelical movement and the propositional approach to theology
of the mid- and late twentieth century is Carl F. H. Henry's *God, Revelation, and Authority*, 6 vols.
(Waco, TX: Word, 1976–1983).

topic.[15] Theology is a process of gathering information and evidence from the Bible and articulating these data in doctrinal statements. This approach is called "propositional" because it believes that the task of theology is to expound the doctrinal content of Scripture. Theology articulates the teachings of the Bible in propositions or doctrines. Theology relates to the data of the Bible the way theory and data do in other fields of science. A Christian doctrine is, therefore, the theological equivalent of Newton's theory of gravity. A doctrine is a theological proposition derived from the field of biblical data.

Why do theology in the propositional way? Answering this question gets to the basic assumption of the propositional method about the nature of Christianity and a person's relationship with God. Propositional theology believes that authentic Christianity consists in doctrinal fidelity. Hodge's differentiation from nonpropositional theologian Friedrich Schleiermacher makes this point clear:

> Religion (subjectively considered) is the reception of certain doctrines as true, and a state of heart and course of action in accordance with those doctrines. The Apostles propounded a certain system of doctrines; they pronounced those to be Christians who received those doctrines so as to determine their character and life. They pronounced those who rejected those doctrines, who refused to receive their testimony, as antichristian; as having no part or lot with the people of God. . . . Those who deny Theism as a doctrine are atheists. Those who reject Christianity as a system of doctrine, are unbelievers. They are not Christians.[16]

Hodge does not deny the importance of the "heart" (orthopathy) and "action" (orthopraxy), but he insists that believing the right doctrines (orthodoxy) is the essence of true Christian faith. Today, few evangelical theologians would put the case in terms as starkly as Hodge did. Nevertheless, proponents of propositional theology still place primacy on right doctrine.[17] Criticizing the propositional method for uncritically

---

[15]Wayne Grudem, *Systematic Theology: An Introduction to Biblical Doctrine* (Grand Rapids: Zondervan, 1994), 36-37. For the same but more detailed articulation of this method, see Millard J. Erickson, *Christian Theology* (Grand Rapids: Baker, 1985), 59-80.

[16]Hodge, *Systematic Theology*, 1:176-77.

[17]David K. Clark, *To Know and Love God: Method for Theology* (Wheaton: Crossway, 2003), 232, 221-32.

adopting a modernist approach to Scripture (i.e., a Baconian or inductive scientific method) and a rationalist view of theology and faith is
fashionable today.[18] This method's strength, however, is the possession of
a clear method.[19]

Liberal theology. Friedrich Schleiermacher (1768–1834) is the "father" of
liberal theology. Paul Tillich (1886–1965) and David Tracy (1939–) are representatives of twentieth-century liberal theology.[20] The task of liberal theology was to reinterpret Christian belief within the cultural values and intellectual trends of modernism. It has two basic commitments. On the one
hand, liberal theology explicitly embraces the rational and scientific assumptions of modernism. On the other hand, liberal theology retains allegiance
to Christianity. Schleiermacher designed his *On Religion: Speeches to Its
Cultured Despisers* (1799) to resuscitate, not impugn, Christianity. Irre-
spective of the way evangelicals regard his influence, his intention was to
promote the cause of the Christian faith.[21]

Like its twentieth-century evangelical counterpart, liberal theology assumes
universal principles. Instead of in Scripture and metaphysical doctrines, it lo-
cates these fundamentals in the realm of human experience.[22] Making theology
the rational description and interpretation of human religious experience gives
it legitimacy as a science, or at least as a social science. Theology is not a metaphysical flight of fancy but an investigation dealing with the world of human
experience, just as are other scientific disciplines. Whether in terms of Schleiermacher's "God-consciousness" or Paul Tillich's "ultimate concern," theology
and religion reduce to expressions of an underlying and essential reality of
human experience. The chief project of the liberal tradition, whether in its

---

[18]For a sustained critique of and creative alternative to propositionalism, see James K. Smith, *Desiring the Kingdom: Worship, Worldview, and Cultural Formation*, vol. 1 of *Cultural Liturgies* (Grand
Rapids: Baker Academic, 2009).

[19]A fine survey of the history of fundamentalist and evangelical theology is Dorrien's *Remaking of
Evangelical Theology*.

[20]Although this discussion focuses on key features of liberal theology's method, especially as it relates to twentieth-century evangelical theology, it also recognizes the diversity of approaches
within the larger movement. For the history of liberal theology and its varied figures and emphases, see Gary Dorrien's three-volume work *The Making of American Liberal Theology* (Louisville:
Westminster John Knox, 2001–2006).

[21]Friedrich Schleiermacher, *On Religion: Speeches to Its Cultured Despisers*, trans. John Oman (New
York: Harper & Row, 1958). See also his *Brief Outline of Theology as a Field of Study*, 3rd ed., trans.
Terrence N. Tice (Louisville: Westminster John Knox, 2011).

[22]John Macquarrie, *Principles of Christian Theology* (New York: Charles Scribner's Sons, 1966), 5-7.

modern or postmodern form, is to correlate "philosophical reflection upon the meanings present in common human experience and meanings present in the Christian tradition."[23] Theology is essentially religious psychology.

The purpose of liberal theology is to explore and understand human religious experience. Doctrine is not important as such, but the underlying religious experience that it expresses is. For example, the Calvinist doctrines of God's glory and predestination are not true per se for liberal theology. The notion that an omnipotent deity decrees all things to glorify itself does not describe anything in or even about God (at the least in any direct sense). These doctrines do, however, express the common human religious experience or spiritual sense that a benevolent God watches over the world and individual lives.

Though criticized by many evangelicals for compromising the Christian faith, theological liberals believe they are correlating Christianity with modern life, science and society.[24] They endeavor to reconcile the values and intellectual claims of modernism and Christianity. Philip Clayton's *Transforming Christian Theology: For Church and Society* is a recent example of how to do liberal theology. Calling for a new theology that transcends the bipolar thought world of liberal and conservative theology, Clayton nevertheless uses the liberal theological method of correlation. He calls denominational leaders to embrace the need to change their organizational structures and to do so in light of the "best practices" of the latest change managers. He cites a canon of contemporary managers of change in support of his call.[25] Clayton's call for denominational leaders to consult the theories of change management is probably good advice. But it is not a new approach to theology. It is traditional liberal theology endeavoring to correlate Christianity with the leading edge of modern society

---

[23]David Tracy, *Blessed Rage for Order: The New Pluralism in Theology* (New York: Seabury, 1975), 34; for a full account of Tracy's revisionist model, which he describes as a continuation of the liberal tradition for a postmodern context, see 43-56. This program is continued in Tracy's *The Analogical Imagination: Christian Theology and the Culture of Pluralism* (London: SCM Press, 1981) and *Plurality and Ambiguity: Hermeneutics, Religion, Hope* (New York: Harper & Row, 1987).

[24]Paul Tillich, *Reason and Revelation, Being and God*, vol. 1 of *Systematic Theology* (Chicago: University of Chicago Press, 1951), 59-66.

[25]Philip Clayton, *Transforming Christian Theology: For Church and Society* (Minneapolis: Fortress, 2010), 49-50. For change managers, see John Hayes, *The Theory and Practice of Change Management* (London: Palgrave, 2002), and Esther Cameron and Mike Green, *Making Sense of Change Management: A Complete Guide to the Models, Tools and Techniques of Organizational Change* (London: Kogan, 2004).

and culture. In the case of Clayton, adapting church leadership practices to the latest insights from the field of institutional leadership is the correlational goal.

Both evangelicals and liberals have sought the same results—timeless truths. The difference between them lies in what they have taken as foundational. Evangelicals mine Scripture for timeless doctrines.[26] Using the tools of grammar and historical analysis, they endeavor to extract the doctrinal deposit of Scripture. David K. Clark describes the method this way: "Principlizing sees doing good theology as a process of abstracting from the Bible certain general theological truths called 'principles.'"[27] Rather than the Bible, liberals start with human religious experience. Their goal is to strip away the historical husk of the biblical stories and identify their transcendent truths.[28] According to Adolf Harnack, "There are only two possibilities here: either the Gospel is in all respects identical with its earliest form, in which case it came with its time and has departed with it; or else it contains something which, under differing historical forms, is of permanent validity. The latter is the true view."[29] Harnack wanted to discover the kernel of truth that spoke across time and space to the common religious dimension of human life. Essential religious truths were evangelicals' and liberals' shared goal. Both groups also used fairly straightforward methods. Evangelicals endeavored to collate encyclopedias of biblical doctrines. Liberals sought to correlate the Bible and Christian doctrines with the universal phenomena of human experience and the various fields of modern science.

THE STATE OF CONTEMPORARY THEOLOGICAL METHOD

Up to the midpoint of the last century, liberal theology, evangelical propositionalism (even if ignored by mainstream liberal theologians), and neoorthodoxy were the major theological methods. By the end of the century, that was no longer the case. In the 1981 publication of *The Shattered*

---

[26]Erickson, *Christian Theology*, 64, 73.

[27]Clark, *To Know and Love God*, 91.

[28]This approach would evolve into Rudolf Bultmann's project of demythologizing, which sought to capture the existential meaning of the gospel for modern people. See Bultmann, "New Testament and Mythology," in *Kerygma and Myth: A Theological Debate*, ed. Hans Werner Bartsch, trans. Reginald H. Fuller (London: SPCK, 1953), 1-44 (a lecture originally delivered in 1941) and his later *Jesus Christ and Mythology* (New York: Charles Scribner's Sons, 1958).

[29]Adolf Harnack, *What Is Christianity?*, trans. Thomas Bailey Saunders (Philadelphia: Fortress, 1986), 13-14.

Spectrum: A Survey of Contemporary Theology, Lonnie D. Kliever assessed the situation: "The revered traditions and towering giants of the theological past have been supplanted by a bewildering variety of theological programs and pundits."[30] At the close of the century, Hütter issued a similar lament, describing the contemporary theological landscape as an "increasingly . . . expanding 'market of possibilities.'"[31] Feminist, womanist, *mujerista*, ecological, political, analytic, philosophical, postmodern, postcolonial, transcendental, liberation, narrative, process and progressive theologies are some of the new players in that market. The more or less binary (or trinary) world of modern theology is gone. Not only have types of theology proliferated, but ways of doing theology have as well. The following describes the major approaches to theological method that have influenced and shaped contemporary evangelical theology.

Postliberal theology. Postliberal theology (also called "the Yale School" and narrative theology) was the first to break open the world of modern theology. Of the panoply of postmodern theologies to emerge in the past several decades, it is also the most relevant for discussing theological method in the evangelical tradition. George A. Lindbeck's *The Nature of Doctrine* is the foundational source for this theological approach.[32]

Postliberalism understands doctrine in terms of a cultural-linguistic system. Culture delineates appropriate ways to live in society. Grammar imparts proper ways to speak. In a similar fashion, doctrines are cultural-linguistic systems. Doctrines teach people how to practice the faith of a religious community.[33] Doctrines, like liturgies, provide the objective structures for individual religious experience. Religion and doctrine, therefore, are not primarily about believing things. They are about life. They show a way to live. They provide a guide to being religious within a specific tradition of Christianity.

---

[30]Lonnie D. Kliever, *The Shattered Spectrum: A Survey of Contemporary Theology* (Atlanta: John Knox, 1981), 1.

[31]Hütter, *Suffering Divine Things*, 2.

[32]George A. Lindbeck, *The Nature of Doctrine: Religion and Theology in a Postliberal Age* (Philadelphia: Westminster, 1984). Also formative for this movement are Hans W. Frei, *The Eclipse of Biblical Narrative: A Study in Eighteenth and Nineteenth Century Hermeneutics* (New Haven, CT: Yale University Press, 1974), and Stanley Hauerwas, *The Community of Character* (Notre Dame, IN: Notre Dame University Press, 1981).

[33]Lindbeck, *Nature of Doctrine*, 33-35.

Whereas evangelical propositionalism takes the Bible as foundational and liberal theology takes religious experience as foundational, the community of faith is the foundation of postliberal theology. Postliberal theology is "post" liberal because the objective realities of religion (e.g., doctrines and liturgies), not subjective religious experience, are fundamental. Liberal theology assumes that doctrines reflect and address religious concerns common to humanity. Doctrine derives from religious experience. Theology moves from doctrine to experience. Theology shows how doctrine expresses and answers human religious questions. Postliberal theology sees theology the other way around. Doctrine shapes and provides the structure for individual religious experience. Postliberal remains "liberal" because the field of study is anthropological, not theological. The beliefs and practices of the Christian community, not God per se, are the subject matter of theological reflection. Where liberal theology is religious psychology, postliberal theology is religious sociology. In contrast to the propositional method, arriving at essential or timeless truth, therefore, is not the task of theology. Articulating the religious beliefs and values of a particular Christian community or tradition and interpreting the world in light of those beliefs and values is the postliberal theological agenda.[34]

Postconservative theology. Postconservative theology is a style of evangelical theology that emerged in the 1990s. Clark Pinnock, John Franke, Stanley Grenz and Roger Olson represent this movement.[35] The postconservative view on the nature and method of theology is very similar to the postliberal approach.[36] Given that, what gives it its distinctive character?

Postconservative and postliberal theologies are the postmodern heirs of their modern theological parents. Postliberal theologians are, or have their background, in the liberal theological tradition. Postconservative theologians come from the evangelical tradition. Since they were never liberals, calling them *postliberal* does not recognize their theological heritage.

---

[34]Ibid., 32-39, 117.

[35]Olson provides a detailed description of postconservative evangelical theology in *Reformed and Always Reforming*.

[36]Two seminal sources in the development of the postconservative approach to theology are Stanley J. Grenz and John R. Franke, *Beyond Foundationalism: Shaping Theology in a Postmodern Context* (Louisville: Westminster John Knox, 2001), and John R. Franke, *The Character of Theology: An Introduction to Its Nature, Task, and Purpose* (Grand Rapids: Baker Academic, 2005).

Postconservatives remain evangelicals but reject the traditional conservative evangelical way of doing theology—i.e., propositional theology. They reject the modernist assumption of objectivity that supports the propositional approach to the Bible—i.e., a field of data waiting for the theologian-scientist to discover and convert to doctrinal and theological truths. Yet they are not radical post-modernists; they do not cast off all restraints and descend into relativism. They remain committed to the authority of Scripture, orthodox doctrine and Christian tradition. *Post* also indicates a different ethos from what defined conservative evangelicalism. Postconservatives want to transcend the categories of "right" and "left," liberal and conservative, and instead embrace an irenic and ecumenical style, and avoid contentious and defensive apologetic strategies.

Postconservative and postliberal theologies share the cultural-linguistic assumptions about the nature of theology. They recognize the role that social context and location within a historical tradition play in reading the Bible and understanding the Christian faith. Propositional theology sees doctrine and theology arising almost directly from the pages of Scripture. Theological statements are expositions of the teachings of the Bible. Although formally not equivalent to the Bible, these statements have the same functional authority. Theological disagreements, therefore, become matters not of biblical interpretation but of fidelity to the faith and the authority of the Bible. Tradition and cultural context do not play an explicit role in propositional theology, though propositional theology clearly reads Scripture in a particular tradition of Protestant Christianity and from a conservative cultural context of North American society.

Theology is explicitly more complex and dynamic for postconservatives. Theology is critical commentary on the community of faith's understanding and practice of the Christian faith. This commentary is not free floating but shaped by and embedded in the context of the specific tradition of Christian faith—for example, evangelicalism, Methodism and Lutheranism. Theology is, therefore, a second-order discipline. It interprets the first-order elements of the faith—Scripture, tradition and practices. The interpretive and contextual nature of the theology means that it is also dynamic. Theology does not broker timeless truths. It brings the community of faith's understanding of the gospel into critical conversation with Scripture, Christian tradition and the contemporary cultural setting.

Canonical-linguistic approach. Kevin Vanhoozer, a leading evangelical theologian, proposes his canonical-linguistic approach as an alternative to evangelical propositional theology and postliberal theology. Propositionalism is too narrow, according to Vanhoozer. Its focus on right thinking misconstrues the nature of Scripture and theology. Scripture is not a trove of facts about God and the Christian life that theology categorizes into an encyclopedia of Christian beliefs. The purpose of theology is to help people live the life of faith, not just believe certain things. Vanhoozer affirms the linguistic insight of postliberal theology but rejects the cultural aspect. With its emphasis on the community of faith, postliberal theology becomes religious sociology. The community of faith and the way it interprets Scripture is primary. In contrast, Vanhoozer makes the Bible—hence, "canonical"—the principal source of theology.[37]

Vanhoozer's canonical-linguistic approach is a postmodern version of the classical Protestant doctrine of *sola Scriptura*. The Bible remains the foundation of theology. The Bible is the product of the theo-drama—the triune God's economic mission of redemption. Scripture is the narrative of this theo-drama.[38] Moreover, its inspiration is one of the divine performances in the theo-drama. The Bible remains the primary source of theology because it both narrates the drama of God's redemptive activity and is itself one of the dramatic acts in the narrative of redemption.[39]

The purpose of Scripture is performative, not propositional. It describes God's narrative of redemption and provides the plot lines, but not a tight script, for the performance of the Christian faith. The theological task finds completion when the story of God told in the Bible becomes the script for Christian life and ministry.[40]

Valuable for emphasizing the authority of Scripture in theology and the Bible as a guide to discipleship and not only belief, the canonical-linguistic approach nevertheless carries on the trend initiated by postliberal theology.

---

[37]Kevin Vanhoozer, *The Drama of Doctrine: A Canonical-Linguistic Approach to Christian Theology* (Louisville: Westminster John Knox, 2005), 16. Vanhoozer's theological progression to theo-drama is seen in his *Is There a Meaning in This Text? The Bible, the Reader, and the Morality of Literary Knowledge* (Grand Rapids: Zondervan, 1998) and *First Theology: God, Scripture, and Hermeneutics* (Downers Grove, IL: InterVarsity Press, 2002).

[38]Vanhoozer, *Drama of Doctrine*, 70.

[39]Ibid., 63-67.

[40]Ibid., 22, 59, 71.

It defines what theology is and why it is important. It is less clear on how to do theology. What, for example, exactly is the canonical-linguistic approach? What are the steps to writing on ecclesiology according to this approach? It is less a theological method than a theological account of theology.[41]

Radical orthodoxy. A theological movement that began among a group of Christian thinkers at Cambridge University—John Milbank, Catherine Pickstock and Graham Ward—in the 1990s, radical orthodoxy is now a popular form of contemporary theology.[42] James K. A. Smith is probably the most prominent and prolific representative of the movement in North America.[43] Less a method than a theological sensibility, Smith suggests, "the label Radical Orthodoxy is effective in naming a certain spirit of theologically driven cultural engagement."[44] Cultural engagement is the key agenda of radical orthodoxy, but to accomplish that task it draws on resources in the Christian tradition and postmodern philosophy and contemporary theology.[45]

Radical orthodoxy uses contemporary postmodern thought and language to critique both postmodernism and modernism and to advocate the interpretation of the world in terms of Christian theology. Exposing and stripping away the secular myths, whether modern or postmodern, that shape the subject area of investigation—e.g., politics, architecture and art—is the first step of the method.[46] Postmodern philosophy, with its exposure of the assumptions and its critique of modernism, provides a useful tool in this task. Although it draws heavily on postmodern thinkers, radical orthodoxy does not seek to reinterpret Christianity in terms of postmodernism. Thus, it does not carry on liberal theology's attempt to correlate Christianity with current cultural assumptions and values.

Returning to the roots of Christian thought is the second step in this theological approach. Inspiration for this methodological move comes from

---

[41]See Porter and Robinson, *Hermeneutics*, 258-69, esp. 262-65.

[42]Some of their key contributions are: John Milbank, *Theology and Social Theory* (Oxford: Blackwell, 1990); Catherine Pickstock, *After Writing: On the Liturgical Consummation of Philosophy* (Oxford: Blackwell, 1998); and Graham Ward, *Cities of God* (New York: Routledge, 2003).

[43]For example, see his *Introducing Radical Orthodoxy* and his series The Church and Postmodern Culture, published by Baker Academic, which publishes initiatives in radical orthodoxy.

[44]Smith, *Introducing Radical Orthodoxy*, 67.

[45]For a detailed description of radical orthodoxy, see ibid., 25-122.

[46]For example, Graham Ward examines late capitalist and postmodern urban life in *Cities of God*.

Catholic theologian Henri de Lubac and a movement in Catholic theology called *nouvelle théologie*.[47] Radical orthodoxy reaches back to ancient sources of Christian thought (*ressourcement*). This return to the roots is the meaning of its use of the term *radical*. Drawing on early church, medieval and other premodern sources enables radical orthodoxy thinkers to attempt to recover Christian thought free of modern assumptions and corruptions.

De Lubac and the *nouvelle théologie* also gave radical orthodoxy a key theological commitment. Like the *nouvelle théologie*, radical orthodoxy also rejects the dualism of nature and grace, and secular and sacred. In its place, it emphasizes a theology of participation. The Christian doctrine of creation means that every dimension of life participates in God; there is no secular space. Radical orthodoxy, however, does not spiritualize participation. Participation means that creation mediates the grace of God. Life is liturgical. Every area of life is the arena for participating in and embodying God's grace.[48] The theology of participation is the reason for this method's overall agenda of cultural engagement.

Cultural engagement is the reinterpretation of the world and the domains of human understanding—e.g., economics—from an overt Christian perspective that does not pay homage to the reigning "secular" orthodoxies.[49] Cultural engagement can be called the third step in radical orthodoxy's theological orientation. After deconstructing the secular way of understanding an area of study—e.g., democracy—it articulates a Christian vision for this area of life most often by drawing on a premodern theological source—e.g., Augustine and Aquinas.[50] Yet, cultural engagement is more than a methodological step. It is the basic theological task of radical orthodoxy. It is the "what" of theology. The "how" or method of theology

---

[47]John Milbank, *The Suspended Middle: Henri de Lubac and the Debate Concerning the Supernatural* (Grand Rapids: Eerdmans, 2005).

[48]For example, see James K. A. Smith's three-volume *Cultural Liturgies*, published by Baker Academic: vol. 1, *Desiring the Kingdom: Worship, Worldview, and Cultural Formation* (2009), vol. 2, *Imagining the Kingdom: How Worship Works* (2013), and vol. 3, *Awaiting the King: Reforming Public Theology* (2017).

[49]On economics, see D. Stephen Long, *Divine Economy: Theology and the Market* (New York: Routledge, 2000), and Daniel M. Bell Jr., *The Economy of Desire: Christianity and Capitalism in a Postmodern World* (Grand Rapids: Baker Academic, 2012).

[50]For example, see Graham Ward's proposal for postmaterial citizens as an alternative to the dominant Western ideologies and values that support its postmodern vision of democracy, globalization and postsecularity—*The Politics of Discipleship: Becoming Postmaterial Citizens* (Grand Rapids: Baker Academic, 2009).

is the critique of secular ideologies and reinterpretation of the world from a Christian perspective by resourcing premodern Christian thought.

Cultural engagement distinguishes radical orthodoxy from liberal theology, propositional theology and the canonical-linguistic approach. The difference is one of emphasis. In contrast to liberal theology, radical orthodoxy desires neither to correlate Christianity with contemporary assumptions nor to reinterpret Christianity in terms of modern philosophical assumptions. Contrary to fundamentalism, it does not ghettoize by retreating from culture. It does not follow the neo-evangelical effort to defend traditional Christian beliefs on the assumptions of modern philosophy, as does, so it argues, much of evangelical theology in the twentieth century—for example, the work of Carl F. H. Henry. Because creation is the place where human beings participate in the life and grace of God, radical orthodoxy strips away the unquestioned secular ideologies that distort life in this world, and casts and reinterprets life in a Christian frame of reference.

THE SOURCES OF THEOLOGY

The topic of theological method invariably leads to the question of sources. What are the sources of theology? What has come to be called the Wesleyan quadrilateral of Scripture, tradition, reason and experience is a common list of sources. But which one is primary? With which one does theology start, or does it matter?[51] "The single greatest challenge in theology is *finding the right place to start*," according to Michael Jinkins.[52] The "starting point" is what theology takes as foundational or most important. For instance, in liberal theology, a universal category of religious experience

---

[51]According to Albert Outler, who coined the term *quadrilateral*, Scripture is the preeminent source of revelation for Wesley. Tradition and reason help interpret the Bible. Experience, though listed in the quadrilateral, is not a source of biblical understanding. Rather, Outler argues, "experience refers to Wesley's conviction that genuine faith is always vital faith or the reception of biblical revelation in the heart (e.g., Wesley's emphasis on 'heart religion') in contrast to mere doctrinal orthodoxy." This view of the relationship between doctrine and experience is consistent with an evangelical one. For resources on the Wesleyan quadrilateral, see Albert C. Outler, "The Wesleyan Quadrilateral in John Wesley," *Wesleyan Theological Journal* 20 (1985): 7-18; W. Stephen Gunter et al., *Wesley and the Quadrilateral: Renewing the Conversation* (Nashville: Abingdon, 1997); and Donald A. D. Thorsen, *The Wesleyan Quadrilateral: Scripture, Tradition, Reason, and Experience as a Model of Evangelical Theology* (Grand Rapids: Zondervan, 1990), 98-100.

[52]Michael Jinkins, *Invitation to Theology* (Downers Grove, IL: InterVarsity Press, 2001), 43 (emphasis original).

is fundamental—e.g., the experience of the holy.[53] Evangelical theology starts with the Bible.

The authority of the Bible is a distinct feature of evangelical theology. For the propositional method, theology, at a functional level, has one source—the Bible. Obviously, traditional evangelicals drew on the sources of tradition—e.g., the Protestant Reformation theology of Martin Luther and John Calvin—but the method of propositional theology makes the Bible—if not absolutely, then nearly—the exclusive source of theology. Wayne Grudem's definition of theology articulates the traditional evangelical approach: *"Systematic theology is any study that answers the question, 'What does the Bible teach us today?' about any given topic."*[54]

Lampooned for an uncritical assumption of Enlightenment foundationalism and naive belief that it reads the text objectively, traditional evangelical theology's emphasis on the Bible is, nevertheless, basically right.[55] Postconservatives recognize the Bible as the "norming norm" of theology.[56] Indeed, in a stroke of irony, the insistence that the Bible is the source of theology reveals the influence of the Christian tradition on evangelical theology. Evangelicalism is heir to the Protestant doctrine of *sola Scriptura*—Scripture alone.

Sola Scriptura means that the Bible is the primary and the final source and authority for theology. It does not dismiss the value of Christian tradition, but it rejects conflating tradition with Scripture.[57] Furthermore, it does not mean that other traditions of Christian theology do not value the Bible. Nevertheless, the Bible plays a unique role in evangelical theological method relative to other traditions of Christian theology. The "Battle for the Bible," after all, took place among North American evangelicals, not Irish Catholics, Swedish Lutherans or English Methodists.[58]

Why is the Bible so important to evangelicals? Because they believe it is the Word of God. Not only does the Bible contain the Word of God or testify to the revelation of God in Jesus Christ, though it clearly does, but

---

[53]John Macquarrie, drawing on Rudolf Otto, proposes that the experience of the holy is the common denominator of all religions: see *Principles of Christian Theology*, 6-7, 78-79.

[54]Grudem, *Systematic Theology*, 21 (emphasis original).

[55]Especially the epistemology of Scottish common-sense realism associated with Thomas Reid.

[56]Grenz and Franke title chapter three "Scripture: Theology's 'Norming Norm'" in *Beyond Foundationalism*, 57-92.

[57]Vanhoozer, *Drama of Doctrine*, 233.

[58]Harold Lindsell, *The Battle for the Bible* (Grand Rapids: Zondervan, 1978).

evangelicals maintain that the *text is* the Word of God. The *book* is the revelation of the identity and work of God. Not only a testimony to the revelation of God, it *is* the revelation of God. This emphasis on the text neither turns the Bible into an idol (Emil Brunner infamously accused the fundamentalists of having a "paper-pope" and committing "bibliolatry") nor diminishes the revelation of God in Jesus Christ.[59]

This theological view of the Bible is found across the spectrum of evangelical theology. On the one hand, consider Kevin Vanhoozer's description of the Bible: "*Inspiration,* to reframe it in theo-dramatic terms, *is a matter of the Spirit's prompting the human authors to say just what the divine playwright intended.*"[60] He clarifies further that "*Canonization is a matter of the theodrama's authoritative articulation, of the theo-drama's coming to speech, and of the church's acknowledgment of Scripture as its authoritative script.*"[61] On the other hand, here is propositional theologian David Clark describing the Bible: "For evangelical theology, it is God's act of inspiration that grounds the Bible's status as God's revelation. . . . The ontological ground of authority, lies rooted in the objective reality of the triune God speaking through the Spirit's inspiration."[62] For both theologians, the Bible, the text itself, is the product of the Spirit's inspiration and, therefore, the primary authority for theology. God is ultimately the ground of the authority of Scripture. The Bible is the inspired self-revelation of God and of God's redemptive work.

The way evangelicals view the Bible shapes the role they give it in their theological method. Whether evangelical theologians call the Bible inerrant, infallible or something else, they affirm that it is the revelation of God, of God's redemptive work and of God's design for life in this world.[63] It is, therefore, the primary source of theology. John G. Stackhouse's remark that "Indeed, truly evangelical thinking about any subject will always privilege scriptural interpretation and never willfully contradict what the Scripture at

---

[59]Emil Brunner, *Reason and Revelation: The Christian Doctrine of Faith and Knowledge* (Philadelphia: SCM Press, 1946), 11, 120.

[60]Vanhoozer, *Drama of Doctrine*, 227 (emphasis original).

[61]Ibid., 229 (emphasis original).

[62]Clark, *To Know and Love God*, 65.

[63]Representing biblical infallibility and inerrancy, respectively, are Jack B. Rogers and Donald K. McKim, *The Authority and Interpretation of the Bible: An Historical Approach* (San Francisco: Harper & Row, 1979), and John D. Woodbridge, *Biblical Authority: A Critique of the Rogers/McKim Proposal* (Grand Rapids: Zondervan, 1982).

least *seems* to say," captures the authoritative place of the Bible in evangelical theology.[64] Considered from the perspective of their theological methods, for example, Wayne Grudem and Kevin Vanhoozer are worlds apart. On the role of the Bible in theology, however, they share a common commitment. They take the Bible as the revelation of the identity and work of God. Despite the different ways evangelicals approach the Bible, read it and use it for theological purposes, the Bible is the primary source in their theological methods.

The doctrinal debates within evangelicalism illustrate the importance of the Bible for the movement. The disputes over eschatology—the timing of the rapture relative to the second coming of Christ and the nature and duration of the millennium—and the gender role debates are more fundamentally arguments about the Bible.[65] If one believes in an inerrant Bible and that God inspired every word, jot and tittle (verbal plenary inspiration), the meanings of *millennium* and *head* are matters of eternal truth and import. Whatever else animates conservative evangelical theology, reverence for the Bible is paramount.

That evangelicals emphasize the Bible does not mean that they disregard other sources. Millard Erickson, a leading figure in the propositional approach to theology, recognizes that Christian tradition and nonbiblical disciplines—e.g., psychology and sociology—have a place in theology.[66] Stanley Grenz and John Franke make tradition and culture, along with Scripture, the three sources of theology.[67] In recent years, a turn to tradition has been part of the explicit embrace of multiple theological sources among evangelicals. Evangelicals have begun to investigate the historical resources in their own tradition. The interest in Jonathan Edwards and other Puritan theologians among evangelical scholars illustrates this trend.[68] But the turn

---

[64]John G. Stackhouse Jr., "Evangelical Theology Should Be Evangelical," in *Evangelical Futures: A Conversation on Theological Method*, ed. John G. Stackhouse Jr. (Grand Rapids: Baker, 2000), 47.

[65]For background on the millennium, see Stanley J. Grenz, *The Millennial Maze: Sorting Out the Evangelical Options* (Downers Grove, IL: InterVarsity Press, 1992).

[66]Erickson, *Christian Theology*, 70-72.

[67]Grenz and Franke, *Beyond Foundationalism*.

[68]For examples, see Douglas J. Sweeney's work on Edwards as well as the broader history of North American evangelicalism—e.g., *Nathaniel Taylor, New Haven Theology, and the Legacy of Jonathan Edwards* (New York: Oxford University Press, 2003) and *Jonathan Edwards and the Ministry of the Word: A Model of Faith and Thought* (Downers Grove, IL: IVP Academic, 2009)—and Kelly M. Kapic's recovery of John Owen's theology in *Communion with God: The Divine and the Human in John Owen's Theology* (Grand Rapids: Baker Academic, 2007).

to tradition has also led evangelical theologians to engage the wider traditions of Christian theology. The key catalyst for this undertaking was Thomas Oden's three-volume presentation of "paleo-orthodoxy."[69] The effort now, however, is widespread among evangelical theologians.[70] During this same time, evangelicals have become more willing to listen to ecumenical voices in contemporary theology.[71] They have also engaged in integrative and interdisciplinary fields of study.[72] Scripture remains the primary and final source of evangelical theology. It is not, however, the only one. Today evangelical theology explicitly draws from many streams of research, which in turn leads to a variety of evangelical theological methods.

FIVE EVANGELICAL THEOLOGICAL METHODS

This book presents five methods of doing theology in the global, pluralistic and postmodern landscape of contemporary evangelical theology. The essays have three broad goals: first, to define and detail the rationale for a specific theological method within evangelical theology; second, to explain the importance of their orientation to theology; and third, to show how to apply the method to the theological topic of Christology and thus provide a concrete example of what the model looks like in action. This last goal is vital to this book. Theological method too often defines the nature of theology but not the steps and procedures for doing theology. This volume, therefore, not only defines but also presents five ways of doing evangelical theology.

---

[69]Thomas C. Oden, *The Living God* (San Francisco: HarperSanFrancisco, 1987); Oden, *The Living Word* (San Francisco: HarperSanFrancisco, 1989); Oden, *Life in the Spirit* (San Francisco: HarperSanFrancisco, 1992).

[70]Roger E. Olson, *The Mosaic of Christian Belief: Twenty Centuries of Tradition and Reform* (Downers Grove, IL: InterVarsity Press, 1999); Robert Webber, *Ancient-Future Faith: Rethinking Evangelicalism for a Postmodern World* (Grand Rapids: Baker, 1999); D. H. Williams, *Retrieving the Tradition and Renewing Evangelicalism: A Primer for Suspicious Protestants* (Grand Rapids: Baker, 1999). InterVarsity Press's Ancient Christian Doctrine series, Ancient Christian Commentary series, Ancient Christian Texts series, and three-volume *Encyclopedia of Ancient Christianity* show the continued interest in Christian tradition among evangelicals.

[71]Veli-Matti Kärkkäinen's work represents this trend—e.g., *Christology: A Global Introduction* (Grand Rapids: Baker Academic, 2003)—and more recently Brad Harper and Paul Louis Metzger's *Exploring Ecclesiology: An Evangelical and Ecumenical Introduction* (Grand Rapids: Brazos, 2009).

[72]Examples of interdisciplinary projects are F. LeRon Shults and Steven J. Sandage, *The Faces of Forgiveness: Searching for Wholeness and Salvation* (Grand Rapids: Baker Academic, 2003), and Jack O. Balswick, Pamela Ebstyne King and Kevin S. Reimer, *The Reciprocating Self: Human Development in Theological Perspective* (Downers Grove, IL: InterVarsity Press, 2005).

Bible doctrines/conservative theology: Codifying God's Word. A popular and enduring form of evangelical theology, this method of doing theology sees the theological task as the identification, compilation and coherent explication of the relevant biblical passages on a particular theological topic. The task of systematic theology here is a form of biblical theology carried out from the perspective of doctrinal topics and theological themes. This method endeavors to systematize the theological themes of Scripture into doctrinal categories or propositions. This method of doing theology has been practiced for years, if not centuries, and continues to be a popular method for doing evangelical theology, to the point of being associated with the theological task in many people's minds. Sung Wook Chung presents a contemporary account of the Bible doctrines or propositional approach to theological method. He argues that the immediate goal of theology is to grow in the knowledge of God and that the way to achieve that goal is a systematic and topical investigation of the Scripture. Successful theology ultimately enables the Christian to glorify God through a life of loving faithfulness. Applying this method to Christology, Chung identifies and interprets the relevant passages of Scripture. He then recommends bringing the biblical data related to Christology into conversation with the wider field of biblical scholarship and historical contributions and developments of the doctrine. The process concludes with summarizing doctrinal statements and applying the doctrine of the Christ to contemporary Christian life and ministry.

Missional theology: Living God's love. This theological method recognizes the postmodern insight that context shapes the questions and answers articulated by the theological task, while also conducting theology within a recognized tradition of Christian theology. The Bible is the key source for this theology. It rejects, however, the "Bible doctrines" approach that conceives of theology as a more direct expression of the doctrinal deposit of Scripture. It does not reject doctrine but gives greater attention to the community of faith, both past and present, in the task of theology than does the Bible doctrines method. This method also seeks to articulate theology in terms of its own concerns and not external philosophical assumptions. It endeavors to construct theology on the basis of the concerns of the Christian community and then reinterpret the world from this vantage point. This approach is also sometimes seen as a form of narrative theology and intentionally resourcing postliberal theology. Narrative theology endeavors to interpret the contemporary nature of Christian life and ministry primarily in terms of the narrative of God's redemptive revelation in Scripture. The interpretation of the biblical story in the context of the community of faith, however, is also a central procedure of this theological method.

John Franke's chapter presents this model in the form of missional theology. Theology, according to Franke, participates in the mission of the triune God. Navigating the dynamic relationships among God, gospel and culture is the task of theology. Enabling faithful mission in the world for God is the goal of missional theology. Turning to Christology, Franke begins by noting that traditional Christology not only privileges ontological and metaphysical categories but also assumes and reflects the cultural context of Christendom. Missional Christology, however, recovers a vision of Christ based on the life and ministry of Jesus. The mission of Jesus Christ informs missional Christology. Based on the diverse accounts of Jesus in the New Testament, Franke affirms that particular expressions of Christology are always contextual, and the way Christian communities embody their faith in Christ will reflect cultural context. Living in the way of Jesus by the presence of the living Christ, not technical doctrinal confession, is the purpose of missional Christology. Forming Christian communities in the way of Jesus should be the primary focus of Christology.

Interdisciplinary theology: Framers and painters. This method seeks to respect the evangelical tradition and to move beyond its traditional categories and discussions. The distinctive feature of this method is its constructive nature. It engages issues that are vital to contemporary Christian life, thought and ministry. This method takes the historical evangelical tradition as a point of orientation. It does not, however, remain within this tradition. It draws on the wider Christian tradition as well as ecumenical and global theological resources in order to develop creative solutions to the issues under consideration. This method also has an interdisciplinary element. It draws Christian theology into conversation with other fields of scholarship—e.g., neuroscience, psychology, sociology and politics—to reconceive traditional Christian doctrines and to open new areas for theological reflection. This method also may serve an apologetic purpose by showing how different fields are mutually beneficial and compatible. An example is the recent popularity of projects on the dialogue between science and religion. The interdisciplinary strategy affirms that dialogue across disciplinary lines expands the insights of one field based on those of another. In his approach to interdisciplinary theology, Telford Work shows that interdisciplinary theological method reflects the approach of Scripture and apostolic sensibility. He develops the paradigm of framers and painters to articulate a model for disciplining theology in light of tradition, but also for encouraging creative adaptations of the Christian faith. He concludes by showing that an interdisciplinary approach to theology can bring the christological categories of the Foursquare Gospel to bear on the church's response to homosexuality.

Contextual theology: God in human context. This theological method consciously articulates theology within a specific cultural context. All theology is contextual, but often only in an implicit way for most theologians and methods. Contextual theology both recognizes the cultural context of the theological enterprise and crafts theology in terms of the concerns and categories of its context. It has many forms in contemporary theological practice. Examples include black, feminist, Hispanic/Latino and postcolonial theology. Projects that address the nature of the Christian's relation to the state in the post-Christian West also exhibit this approach. The chief characteristic of this method is dialogue and/or critique of a cultural reality from a particular theological and cultural perspective.

Victor Ifeanyi Ezigbo defines and describes the method of contextual theology. Applying this method, he begins with the cultural context of Nigerian Christianity. In Nigeria, Christianity is both popular and integrated with indigenous religious beliefs and practices. While recognizing the legitimacy of the spiritual aspirations and concerns that arise among Nigerians, Ezigbo draws on biblical and historical christological categories of Jesus as revealer of divinity and humanity to resolve them. Focusing on points of doctrinal belief per se, however, is not the goal. Showing that Christian beliefs about Jesus Christ speak to the human concerns that arise in particular cultural contexts is the goal of contextual Christology.

Trinitarian dogmatic theology: Confessing the faith. Dogmatic theology works from a clear commitment to a Christian confessional tradition and works with the primary doctrines of the Christian faith—e.g., Christology. Karl Barth and the Reformed tradition are popular examples of forms of dogmatic theology within contemporary theology. The historic confessions of the Christian church also provide important parameters for this approach to theology. The goal of theology is the contemporization and in some cases reinterpretation of historic doctrinal creeds, such as the Westminster Confession, for current generations. Contemporary dogmatic theology is an effort to find an alternative to the accommodation of theological liberalism and the proliferation of postmodern theologies, which are often trendy but unhinged from any meaningful connection with traditional Christian doctrines. Dogmatic theology endeavors to articulate a Christian vision of God and the gospel of Jesus Christ that both reflects a clear theological tradition of biblical interpretation and speaks to the church and society of today's world.

Paul Louis Metzger's essay is an example of dogmatic theology. Drawing on Karl Barth and the Reformed tradition, he proposes a theological method shaped by the doctrine of the Trinity. Applying this method to the doctrine of Christ, Metzger makes three christological contributions from the domain of pneumatology. First, the role of the Holy Spirit in the life of Jesus gives historical grounding for his messianic consciousness that stands in continuity with the later christological dogmas developed in the creeds— e.g., Chalcedon. Second, pneumatology also provides a way to affirm both the uniqueness of Jesus as the union of the Son of God with human nature and the continuity of his Spirit-conditioned life with all human life in this world. Third, the Holy Spirit mediates the incarnate life of Christ to the church, which shapes the christological identity of the church without conflating Christ and church.

In the essays that follow, each of these theological methods is robustly presented, defended and exemplified as we have outlined above. Each of the proponents of these methods is then offered the opportunity to respond to the presentations of the others. We believe that the interaction between the proponents and those of opposing—or at least differing—theological methods will help to define more clearly these various theological methods. These emerging definitions should help us to see the strengths, weaknesses, points of agreement and areas of dispute among these varying methods. The field of evangelical theology continues to become increasingly diverse and complex, and our hope is that these essays will help to promote clarity in the ensuing discussion as well as provide a resource for ways of doing evangelical theology in the church and academy.

PART ONE

FIVE VIEWS OF EVANGELICAL THEOLOGICAL METHOD

1

Bible Doctrines/ Conservative Theology

CODIFYING GOD'S WORD

SUNG WOOK CHUNG

INTRODUCTION

This chapter explores the theological method of conservative and traditional evangelicalism, which is characterized by systematizing and codifying God's Word according to its topics and themes. This approach presupposes that the Scripture of sixty-six canonical books is inspired (*theopneustos*, God-breathed) by the Holy Spirit. This affirmation entails that the ultimate author of the Bible is God and thus it is the inerrant and infallible revelation of the triune God. As the Westminster Confession of Faith (1647) affirms, the Holy Scripture as the Word of God written is "the rule of faith and life."[1]

On the basis of this foundational insight, conservative evangelical theologians have endeavored to formulate Christian doctrines from the Holy Scripture. Codification or systematization of what the Bible teaches about crucial doctrinal topics has defined the task of their theological work. In other words, the topical and thematic approach has traditionally been the central character of the task of doctrinal systematization from the perspective of conservative evangelical theology. So in the conservative evangelical tradition, doing systematic theology has been identified with organizing God's Word into a system of doctrines in accordance with essential topics of biblical instruction. *Conservative* stands in relation to progressive evangelicals, who have

---

[1] Philip Schaff, ed., *The Creeds of Christendom* (Grand Rapids: Baker, 1985), 3:602.

critiqued the propositional approach to theology. This essay generally uses the shorthand term *evangelical theology* to denote the conservative approach to theology, although it recognizes that the evangelical tradition includes diverse approaches to theology.

The process of codifying God's Word usually takes several steps, from biblical exegesis to writing catechisms, confessions, creeds and works of systematic theology. Before explicating this approach in more detail, I will draw a historical sketch of this traditional method of theology.

HISTORICAL SKETCH

The Bible and topical approaches. First of all, it is very important to appreciate that the canonical books of Holy Scripture employ a topical and thematic approach in giving us divine instructions. I believe that we should rediscover and reemphasize this insight. Above all, Jesus Christ made the best use of topical approaches in his teaching and preaching ministry. The best example of Jesus' topical approach is the Sermon on the Mount, found in Matthew 5–7. According to Matthew's account of the Sermon on the Mount, Jesus taught and preached about major topics and themes including the law (Mt 5:17-20), murder (Mt 5:21-26), adultery (Mt 5:27-30), divorce (Mt 5:31-32), oaths (Mt 5:33-37), love for enemies (Mt 5:38-48), giving to the needy (Mt 6:1-4), prayer (Mt 6:5-16), fasting (Mt 6:16-18) and so on. The Sermon on the Mount exemplifies the topical and thematic organization of divine truths.

Several biblical authors also adopt topical and thematic approaches. The apostle Paul is the best model for this. For example, in 1 Thessalonians, Paul uses the phrase "about a [certain topic]." In 1 Thessalonians 4:9, Paul states, "Now *about your love for one another* we do not need to write to you, for you yourselves have been taught by God to love each other" (NIV). In 1 Thessalonians 4:13, Paul says, "Brothers and sisters, we do not want you to be uninformed *about those who sleep in death*, so that you do not grieve like the rest of mankind, who have no hope" (NIV). After saying this, Paul continues to explicate the second coming of the Lord and the future destiny of those who fall asleep. In 1 Thessalonians 5:1-2, Paul states, "Now, brothers and sisters, *about times and dates* we do not need to write to you, for you know very well that the day of the Lord will come like a thief in the night" (NIV). Again, after saying this, Paul keeps on giving instructions about why the parousia cannot surprise believers and how they should prepare themselves for the Lord's second coming.

The writer of Hebrews also employs a topical and thematic approach. In the first two chapters of Hebrews, the writer deals with the deity and supremacy of Jesus Christ, comparing him with angels. In Hebrews 4–8, the writer discusses the superiority of Jesus Christ as the high priest over the Old Testament human priests. Hebrews 9–10 delineates the superiority of Jesus Christ's atoning sacrifice over the old covenant sacrificial system. On the basis of these discussions, Hebrews 11 explicates the theme of faith, and Hebrews 12–13 expound the Christian life. In addition to these, we have numerous other examples of biblical writers' use of topical and thematic approaches in conveying divine revelation. Even if we recognize that there are various ways that truth might be presented, basing our approach on the way that the Bible presents divine truths provides the strongest foundation. Thus we can conclude that the topical approach is the most basic and fundamental manner of instruction of divine truths because it is deeply embedded in the entire Bible.

Patristic age. During the patristic age, church fathers also made the best use of a topical and thematic approach in their theological and apologetic endeavor. For example, Irenaeus of Lyons, who is regarded as the first theologian of the history of redemption/salvation (*Heilsgeschichte*), formulates his major theological writings—*Against Heresies* and *Proof of the Apostolic Preaching*—topically. Athanasius of Alexandria employs a topical approach as well. *Against the Heathen* and *Incarnation of the Word of God*, his two major theological works, show his employment of a topical approach that codifies and systematizes God's word to formulate doctrinal theses. In a similar vein, Augustine of Hippo also adopts a topical approach in his major theological writings.

Medieval age. Medieval theologians follow the topical and thematic approach to theology that the church fathers established. However, medieval scholastic theology—pioneered by Anselm of Canterbury, finding its climax in Thomas Aquinas, and consummated by Duns Scotus and William of Ockham—deviates in harmful ways from the tradition of formulating biblical doctrines through codifying God's Word by incorporating Aristotelian logic and other philosophical arguments, including neo-Platonism, into theological work. As a result, there was serious doctrinal confusion and distortion within the Roman Catholic Church in the late medieval age.

The Reformation. During the sixteenth-century European Reformation, Reformers such as Martin Luther (1484–1546), Philip Melanchthon (1497–1560), Ulrich Zwingli (1483–1531) and John Calvin (1509–1564) recovered the topical approach for doing theological work by returning to the principle of *sola Scriptura*. They scathingly criticized the doctrinal errors of medieval scholastic theology, reemphasizing the Bible as the only material source of the knowledge of God. More than anyone else, Melanchthon made an indelible impact on the restoration of the topical approach, which codifies and systematizes the Word of God in accordance with major doctrinal themes and subjects. His *Loci Communes* (Common Places or Common Topics) is an excellent example of the so-called *loci* approach, namely the topical approach, in Christian theology. John Calvin's *Institutes of the Christian Religion* is another superb example of a topical and thematic codification of God's Word. In the first edition of the *Institutes* (1536), Calvin discusses major doctrinal themes, including the law, faith, the sacraments, Christian freedom, ecclesiastical power and political administration. The first edition of the *Institutes* was expanded into the last edition (1559), which was almost five times larger than the first edition. The last edition also takes a biblically based topical approach that formulates biblical doctrines through codifying and systematizing the result of exegetical work on the Word of God. For this reason, Calvin's *Institutes* should be taken as a "systematic theology," methodically arranged in accordance with crucial topics of the Christian truth.

Post-Reformation Protestant dogmatics. From 1564 (the year of Calvin's death) to 1800, both Lutheran and Reformed theologians were engaged with confessional dogmatics, exemplified by Lutheran Johann Gerhard's *Loci Communes Theologici* and his Reformed counterpart Francis Turretin's *Institutes of Elenctic Theology.* Although they basically followed the theological method that the first-generation Reformers had established—the *loci* approach to theology—they pursued a new theological method, which was geared toward preserving the dogmas of the church (the official theology recognized by an organized church body). As a result, the confessions and creeds of organized ecclesial bodies, because they were reductionistic or tended to privilege particular theological traditions, began to have a disproportionate impact on Protestant dogmatics. In some extreme cases, the principle of *sola Scriptura* was eclipsed in the name of the preservation of the traditional dogmas of the church. Protestant dogmatic theology was accused of ossified and reified dogmatism without creative and dynamic reformulations of biblical doctrines on the basis of fresh results of exegetical work on the Scriptures.

Twentieth and twenty-first centuries. With the rise of neo-evangelicalism in the latter half of the twentieth century, the topical and thematic approach to theology began to be rediscovered and retrieved, with a renewed commitment to the principle of Scripture alone. Among the major evangelical theologians dedicated to the theological method of codifying and systematizing God's Word are Millard Erickson (1932–), Gordon R. Lewis (1932–), Bruce Demarest (1937–) and Wayne Grudem (1948–). On account of these evangelical systematic theologians' achievement, the topical and thematic approach remains the most popular and dominant method of theology within the circle of evangelical theology. I will discuss the contributions of these theologians below.

THE AIM OF THEOLOGY

What is the aim of theology from the perspective of evangelical theology that adopts the topical and thematic approach to formulating Bible doctrines by codifying God's Word? In other words, why do we engage in the theological task? I will answer these questions by presenting the primary and the secondary aim of theology. There is a fundamental consensus among evangelical systematic theologians that knowledge of God is the primary aim of theology.[2]

Definition of theology. In order to begin to understand the aim of theology from the perspective of evangelical theology, we have to first understand what theology is and why it is important to do theological work. First of all, in English, *theology* is composed of words referring to God and theological discourse. *Theology* derives from the Greek *theos* (God) and the Greek *logos* (study) to mean "the study of God" or "the science of God." Here *logos* can also mean "logic," "word," "reason" and "discourse." Theology is related to the word or discourse of God. It also means reasoning about God. Therefore theology has traditionally been seen as creating discourse about

---

[2]This claim does not deny that other Christian traditions share the same goal of theology but recognizes that the context for modern evangelicalism's emphasis on knowledge of God is its opposition to liberal theology. Theology describes human religious experience and not God as such, according to liberal theology. For example, see Friedrich Schleiermacher, *The Christian Faith*, ed. H. R. Mackintosh and J. S. Stewart (London: T&T Clark, 1999).

God. In the Chinese and Korean contexts, *theology* is referred to as 神學 (*shen xue* in Chinese and *shin hak* in Korean). Here the word 神 (shen) means "God" and 學 (xue) means "to learn." In an East Asian context, therefore, theology means learning about who God is, what God does and what kind of a relationship God has with human beings.

In the context of this discussion, we need to raise a crucial question. It is connected with the fact that we cannot find the word *theology* in the Bible. One should be able to find theological concepts, including the word *theology*, within the Bible if one's theology aims to be truly faithful to biblical revelation. However, it is not necessarily "unbiblical" for evangelical theologians to employ terms and concepts that are seemingly extrinsic to scriptural revelation. The key question is, "What is the nearest equivalent term for *theology* in the Bible?" It is important to appreciate in this context that, although the Bible does not employ the word *theology*, it is not difficult to find an equivalent idea for it in the Bible. It is "knowledge of God" or "knowing God." Throughout Scripture, the knowledge of God or knowing God is repeatedly and consistently emphasized. One of the best examples is 2 Peter 1:2-3: "Grace and peace be yours in abundance through the knowledge of God and of Jesus our Lord. His divine power has given us everything we need for a godly life through our knowledge of him who called us by his own glory and goodness" (NIV). This passage demonstrates that believers can receive abundant grace, amazing peace and everything we need for a godly life through knowledge of God. Our Lord Jesus Christ also said, "Now this is eternal life: that they know you, the only true God, and Jesus Christ, whom you have sent" (Jn 17:3 NIV). Amazingly, Jesus identified knowing God and Christ with eternal life!

We can find other good examples in the Old Testament. Exodus 6:7 reads, "I will take you as my own people, and I will be your God. Then you will *know that I am the LORD your God*, who brought you out from under the yoke of the Egyptians" (NIV). We have numerous similar verses in the Old Testament. Another good example is Deuteronomy 29:5-6, which reads, "Yet the LORD says, 'During the forty years that I led you through the wilderness, your clothes did not wear out, nor did the sandals on your feet. You ate no bread and drank no wine or other fermented drink. I did this so that you might *know that I am the LORD your God.*'" These passages indicate that God performed his mighty works so that the people of Israel might know him.

Thus knowledge of God or knowing God is the ultimate purpose and aim for God's redemptive engagement with Israel.

In this context, one may raise another critical question. When the Bible mentions the idea of knowledge of God or knowing God, does it signify merely cognitive, cerebral or informational knowledge of God? Absolutely not! *Yādaʿ*, the Hebrew term for "knowledge" or "knowing," never means merely head knowledge or cerebral knowledge but rather also experiential and relational knowledge. One meaning of *yādaʿ* is "having sexual intercourse" or "having a loving and intimate relationship." This implies that God wants us to know him personally, existentially and experientially. Thus the word *theology* cannot mean merely intellectual and academic pursuit of the information about God, but rather also personal commitment to have genuine relationship with God that results in mutual love between God and believers.

In addition, *ginōskō*, the Greek word for "knowledge" or "knowing," means knowledge by experience or through having an intimate relationship. In the New Testament the word *ginōskō* means interpersonal knowing within the context of the bride and bridegroom relationship.[3] Therefore the knowledge of God or knowing God in Scripture never means merely knowing about something but rather knowing someone intimately and, as a result, coming to love the one we know. Thus the Bible's emphasis on the knowledge of God is closely connected with God's ultimate ethical command, "Love the Lord your God with all your heart and with all your soul and with all your mind" (Mt 22:37 NIV; cf. Deut 6:5). Simply speaking, knowing God means loving God![4]

On the basis of this etymological and biblical definition of theology, we need to raise other important questions. Is theology a human task? In other words, is theology a science like biology or sociology? There is a consensus among evangelical theologians that theology is a human task because theologians and believers are the subjects and agents who are involved with studying, knowing and learning about God. However, theology is not

---

[3]See A. G. Patzia, "Knowledge," in *Dictionary of the Later New Testament and Its Developments*, ed. Ralph Martin and Peter H. Davids (Downers Grove, IL: InterVarsity Press, 1997), 638-40.

[4]One of the best books on the spiritual and theological significance of knowing God is James Packer's classic, *Knowing God* (Downers Grove, IL: InterVarsity Press, 1993).

merely a human task. It is also a divine task. This is because the Holy Spirit's illumination is absolutely essential and necessary for doing theology. Without God's empowering grace, one cannot understand divine truths and know God. In knowing and loving God, we totally depend on the Holy Spirit's sovereign and gracious work to provide us with supernatural light. So the apostle Paul prays for the Ephesian Christians, "I keep asking that the God of our Lord Jesus Christ, the glorious Father, may give you the Spirit of wisdom and revelation, so that you may know him better. I pray that the eyes of your heart may be enlightened in order that you may know the hope to which he has called you, the riches of his glorious inheritance in his holy people" (Eph 1:17-18). Therefore, doing theology is both a human and divine task from the perspective of evangelical theology.

Likewise, theology is a science like biology and sociology because theology has its own subject of knowledge, methodology of study, sources and community of theological engagement. But it is not merely a science. It is a mode of life to pursue, know and love the true and living God! Doing theology means engaging with God in a lifelong process of interpersonal relationship. It is like living and walking together with the triune God. In the process of doing theology, of course, we make use of and study the Bible, doctrines, church history and our religious experience. However, doing theology is not primarily about doing intellectual research but about walking and living with God on a daily basis.

Aims of theology. What, then, are the goals, purposes, aims and fruits of theology? Evangelical theologians believe that the primary aim and purpose of theology is growing in the knowledge of God. When we get to know God deeply, then we come to love him more passionately and faithfully. When we love God more, we come to obey and glorify God. In that sense, the ultimate aim and purpose of theology should be glorifying God by leading a life according to his holy will. Moreover, we obtain the wonderful byproducts or fruits of theology. The first fruit is that we come to know and deny ourselves. Our Lord Jesus says, "Whoever wants to be my disciple must deny themselves and take up their cross and follow me" (Mt 16:24). As John Calvin says, the more we know God's glory, majesty, love and grace, the more we know our finitude, sinfulness and weakness.[5] The better we know God, the more easily we can find our new identity in Christ and follow the Lord faithfully, denying our old ways of life. The second fruit of theology is that we come to better love and serve our neighbors. The more we know God and deny ourselves, the more we come to love our neighbors as ourselves, fulfilling the second aspect of the greatest commandment.

From the perspective of evangelical theology as defined here, the secondary aim of theology is to construct a system of Bible doctrines through the process of codifying God's Word in accordance with critical theological topics and themes. Here the word *secondary* is interchangeable with the word *subsidiary*. This means that the construction of a doctrinal system can never be the ultimate or even primary aim of theology. Rather, it is subsidiary in that a biblical system of doctrines can assist theologians and believers in knowing the triune God more deeply, personally and intimately. Therefore a biblical system of doctrines can never remain merely a system of cognitive and cerebral information but must apply biblical doctrines to practical aspects of the Christian life and spirituality.

In fact, from the perspective of evangelical theology, Christian theology embraces a variety of theological disciplines. First of all, biblical theology focuses on the truth that each book of the entire Bible conveys. For example, biblical theology includes the theology of the book of Romans, the theology of the book of Genesis and so on. Second, systematic theology concerns Christian doctrines formulated and arranged topically. For example, systematic theology includes the doctrines of sin, Jesus Christ, salvation, the last things and so on. Third, historical theology concentrates on the process of historical development of the church's theology. For example, historical theology includes the theology of the patristic fathers, of the Reformers, of the twentieth century and so on. Fourth and finally, practical theology focuses on practical aspects of the church's ministry and Christian life. It is important to appreciate the significant overlap between these four disciplines of theology; we should not overemphasize their division. Rather, we should see these four as an integrated whole. In other words, one unified Christian theology integrates the four subdisciplines into one system. This integrative perspective is crucial.

---

[5]John Calvin, *Institutes of the Christian Religion*, ed. John T. McNeill, trans. Ford Lewis Battles (Louisville: Westminster John Knox, 1960), I.1.2.

DESCRIPTION OF THE METHOD

Then what is the shape of the theological method of evangelical theology? In other words, what kind of theological procedure does an evangelical theologian go through? To help answer these questions, I describe the theological methods of several prominent theologians in the conservative evangelical camp. They are Millard Erickson, in his *Christian Theology*; Gordon Lewis and Bruce Demarest, in their *Integrative Theology*; and Wayne Grudem, in his *Systematic Theology*.[6]

Millard J. Erickson. Erickson discusses the method of theology and the process of doing theology in his *Christian Theology*.[7] According to Erickson, there are ten steps in the process of theological construction. The first is collecting the biblical materials from the whole of Scripture. Erickson states, "The first step in our theological method will be to gather all the relevant biblical passages on the doctrine being investigated. This step will also involve a thorough and consistent utilization of the very best and most appropriate tools and methods for getting at the meaning of these passages."[8] For this reason, exegesis of the biblical text is one of the most important tasks that the theologian is engaged with at this stage.

The second step is to unify the biblical materials. For Erickson, on the basis of the results of exegesis on the relevant biblical texts, the theologian "must next develop some unifying statements on the doctrinal theme being investigated. Rather than having simply the theology of Paul, Luke, or John on a particular doctrine, we must attempt to coalesce their various emphases into a coherent whole."[9] This task should be done on the assumption that in spite of the diversity of literary genres, historical backgrounds and cultural ethos of the relevant biblical texts, they convey unified, consistent and harmonious truths revealed by the triune God.

The third step is to analyze the meaning of biblical teachings. At this stage, according to Erickson, "once the doctrinal material has been synthesized into

---

[6]Millard J. Erickson, *Christian Theology*, 2nd ed. (Grand Rapids: Baker Academic, 1998); Gordon R. Lewis and Bruce A. Demarest, *Integrative Theology* (Grand Rapids: Zondervan, 1996); Wayne Grudem, *Systematic Theology: An Introduction to Biblical Doctrine* (Grand Rapids: Zondervan, 1994).

[7]Erickson, *Christian Theology*, 62-84.

[8]Ibid., 70.

[9]Ibid., 73.

a coherent whole," the theologian should ask, "What is *really* meant by this?"[10] In this step, the theologian should endeavor to expound the real meaning of biblical terms, ideas, notions and concepts.

The fourth step examines historical treatments of biblical teachings. Whereas the theologian is directly engaged with Scripture through exegesis, interpretation and exposition of the relevant biblical passage in the first three steps, in this step the theologian should pay attention to the historical development of the doctrine in question. In other words, in this step one integrates historical theology into systematic theology. Erickson argues, "Historical theology may be of direct value for constructing our own expressions of theology. By studying a period very similar to our own, we may find models that can be adapted for modern doctrinal formulations."[11]

The fifth step involves consulting other cultural perspectives. For Erickson, consultation with other cultural perspectives is closely connected with the theologian's global sensibilities:

> We noted earlier the phenomenon of globalization and the benefits of consulting other cultural perspectives. We may have been blinded to our own cultural perspective to the point where we identify it with the essence of the doctrine. . . . Interaction with other cultural perspectives will help us distinguish the essence of the biblical teaching from one cultural expression of it.[12]

I commend Erickson for affirming the necessity of engaging with global and multicultural theological perspectives.

The sixth step identifies the essence of the doctrine. In this step the theologian needs "to distinguish the permanent, unvarying content of the doctrine from the cultural vehicle in which it is expressed."[13] The seventh step looks for illumination from extrabiblical sources. The theologian should strive to integrate the truths mediated through general revelation into the process of doctrinal formulation. The eighth step is concerned with contemporary expression of the doctrine. Here the theologian needs to "give the essence of the doctrine a contemporary expression, to clothe the timeless

---

[10]Ibid.
[11]Ibid., 74.
[12]Ibid., 74-75.
[13]Ibid., 75.

truth in an appropriate form."[14] The ninth step develops a central interpretive motif: "each theologian must decide on a particular theme which, for her or him, is the most significant and helpful in approaching theology as a whole."[15] The tenth and final step involves arranging topics in order of significance. The theologian should engage with arranging "topics on the basis of their relative importance. This is, in effect, to say that we need to outline our theology, assigning a roman numeral to major topics, a capital letter to subtopics, and an arabic number to topics subordinate to the subtopics, and so on."[16]

Gordon Lewis and Bruce Demarest. Lewis and Demarest discuss theological method in their *Integrative Theology*. Although they uphold the value and relevance of systematic theology traditionally understood, they prefer to call their paradigm *integrative theology* rather than *systematic theology*. According to Lewis and Demarest, their methodology involves six distinct stages:

> (1) Defining and distinguishing one distinct topic or problem for inquiry; (2) learning alternative approaches to it from a survey of Spirit-led scholars in the history of the church; (3) discovering and formulating from both the Old and the New Testament a coherent summary of relevant biblical teaching by making use of sound principles of hermeneutics, worthy commentaries, and biblical theologies; (4) formulating on the basis of the relevant data a cohesive doctrine and relating it without contradiction to other biblically founded doctrines and other knowledge; (5) defending this formulation of revealed truth in interaction with contradictory options in theology, philosophy, science, religion, and cults; and (6) applying these convictions to Christian life and ministry in the present generation.[17]

On the one hand, we have some commonalities between Erickson's approach and Lewis and Demarest's approach. First, both perspectives adopt a topical and thematic approach. Second, they seek to formulate Bible doctrines on the basis of the result of exegesis and biblical-theological research. Third, both approaches seek to integrate historical-theological investigation into the formulation of Bible doctrines. Fourth, both approaches engage with other doctrines and knowledge to establish a system of Christian truth.

---

[14] Ibid., 76.
[15] Ibid., 80.
[16] Ibid., 82.
[17] Lewis and Demarest, *Integrative Theology*, 26.

Fifth, both approaches are conscious of the postmodern condition and take a more nuanced approach to epistemology. They abandon Scottish common-sense realism (associated with nineteenth-century Old Princeton theology) in favor of critical realism.[18]

On the other hand, Lewis and Demarest's approach goes beyond Erickson's approach in its more deliberate, robust and explicit apologetic endeavor to defend the system of biblical truth against all kinds of intellectual attacks and critiques. Lewis and Demarest also take more seriously than Erickson the importance and relevance of applying biblical and doctrinal "convictions to Christian life and ministry in the present generation."[19] They suggest as well that the theologian should use a verificational method rather than an inductive or deductive method. In spite of the differences in their emphasis and orientation, it is evident that the two approaches share many common interests and concerns in relation to the theological task.

Wayne Grudem. Grudem defines systematic theology as "any study that answers the question, 'What does the whole Bible teach us today?' about any given topic" before discussing theological methodology in his major work, *Systematic Theology.*[20] His definition of systematic theology is characterized by a topical and thematic approach to Christian truth. In addition, his approach to theology is primarily involved with codifying and systematizing the Word of God in order to formulate Bible doctrines on a given topic or theme. On the basis of these initial insights, Grudem raises a question about theological method, "How should Christians study systematic theology?" Grudem discusses an appropriate attitude that the Christian theologian should maintain in approaching systematic theology.

---

[18]Scottish common-sense realism was an empiricist movement that became a popular intellectual movement in the late eighteenth- and early nineteenth-century America. It affirmed that the senses perceive objects external to the mind in a straightforward and objective way—i.e., the correspondence theory of truth. Princeton theology was a style of theology developed at Princeton University (and later Princeton Theological Seminary) by Charles Hodge and later A. A. Hodge and B. B. Warfield. They assumed the fundamental principle of the correspondence theory of truth for theology and the interpretation of the Bible. Charles Hodge developed the topical and propositional method of theology that later became synonymous with evangelical theology. J. Gresham Machen, successor to B. B. Warfield at Princeton and the last of the Old Princetonians, was the bridge between Princeton theology and evangelical theology. Machen and the Princetonian method developed by Hodge became the foundation for the fundamentalists' and later neo-evangelical critique of liberal theology.

[19]Lewis and Demarest, *Integrative Theology*, 26.

[20]Grudem, *Systematic Theology*, 21.

First, Christians should study systematic theology with prayer.[21] This means we should acknowledge the absolute necessity of the help of the Holy Spirit, spiritual wisdom and insight for studying systematic theology. Second, the Christian should study systematic theology with humility and avoid an "attitude of pride or superiority toward others who have not made such a study."[22] Third, Grudem argues that the Christian should engage with systematic theology with rejoicing and praise because "the study of theology is not merely a theoretical exercise of the intellect. It is a study of the living God, and of the wonders of all his works in creation and redemption. We cannot study this subject dispassionately!"[23]

Grudem then tackles the task of theological method undertaken by the Christian systematic theologian: "We should study systematic theology by collecting and understanding all the relevant passages of Scripture on any topic."[24] Like Erickson, Lewis and Demarest, Grudem delineates several steps of doing theology from his perspective.

> (1) Find all the relevant verses. The best help in the step is a good concordance, which enables one to look up key words and find the verses in which the subject is treated. (2) The second step is to read, make notes on, and try to summarize the points made in the relevant verses. Sometimes a theme will be repeated often and the summary of the various verses will be relatively easy. At other times, there will be verses difficult to understand. . . . (3) Finally, the teachings of the various verses should be summarized into one or more points that the Bible affirms about the subject.[25]

Along with Erickson and Lewis and Demarest, Grudem seeks to integrate historical theology into systematic theology. He writes, "We need to be thankful that God has put teachers in the church. We should allow those with gifts of teaching to help us understand Scripture. This means that we should make use of systematic theologies and other books that have been written by some of the teachers that God has given to the church over the course of its history."[26]

---

[21]Ibid., 32-33.
[22]Ibid., 33.
[23]Ibid., 37.
[24]Ibid., 35.
[25]Ibid., 36.
[26]Ibid., 35.

Grudem also acknowledges the necessity and importance of using our reason in drawing conclusions and deductions from the statements of Scripture. He states, "We find in the New Testament that Jesus and the New Testament authors will often quote a verse of Scripture and then draw logical conclusions from it. It is therefore not wrong to use human understanding, human logic, and human reason to draw conclusions from the statement of Scripture."[27]

It is not difficult to notice substantial commonalities between Grudem, Erickson, Lewis and Demarest in terms of their basic approach to the theological task. It seems, however, that Grudem does not engage with epistemological issues emerging from the current postmodern condition. He seems to be committed to a more basic epistemology of common-sense realism. It is a rather conspicuous weakness of Grudem's discussion of theological method.

STRENGTHS AND WEAKNESSES

What are some major strengths and weaknesses of this approach? There are several conspicuous merits of the evangelical approach. First, this approach can enable theologians to fulfill the evangelical and Reformation ideal of *sola et tota Scriptura* (Scripture alone and in its entirety), because by employing this approach they can demonstrate their invincible commitment to the authority and veracity of the Word of God as the fundamental and final arbiter for the knowledge of God and the truth. In other words, this approach is consistent with the evangelical conviction that only the Bible is the completely trustworthy and sufficient source of divine truth. Although not exclusive, the Bible is the first and last source for evangelical theology. Second, this approach is consistent with the manner of communication of the truths that the Bible itself makes use of, which is the topical and thematic approach. As I have demonstrated above, many biblical writers employ the topical approach in conveying divine revelation—even if these topics are presented in various ways in the Bible itself. Third, this approach can materialize the ideal of an integrative system of the Christian truths by integrating other theological disciplines such as historical theology and

---

[27]Ibid., 34.

practical theology into the entire system of Bible doctrines or evangelical systematic theology.

In spite of these strengths, this approach also has several weaknesses as well. First, this approach can easily degenerate into a proof-text approach, if it is not accompanied by a serious, scholarly and responsible engagement with the text of the Bible. On account of inordinate passion for proving their truth claims by biblical evidence, theologians can easily distort the meaning of the relevant texts by ignoring their grammatical, historical, cultural and theological contexts. Many theologians who have adopted this approach have committed the error of *eisegesis*, imposing external and biased interpretive grids on the texts. Second, as Richard Lints has argued, this approach may not be able to explicate the whole truth of the Christian faith through an engagement with the entire structural shape of biblical revelation.[28] The topical and thematic approach seems to have an intrinsic weakness of dismissing some crucial aspects of the truth that are not properly dealt with in the process of prearranging topics. The agendas and presuppositions of the theologians can have a negative impact on the process of doing theology. Third, major works of systematic theology that take this approach have demonstrated the problem of excessive repetition. For example, the section on the doctrine of God or theology proper covers each person of the triune God. Major aspects of this discussion cannot help being repeated in the separate sections on Christology and pneumatology. In addition, some major aspects of soteriology should be reiterated inevitably in the discussion of pneumatology. For example, both pneumatology and soteriology should deal with the doctrine of sanctification as a crucial phase of salvation, which requires the Holy Spirit's personal and gracious involvement. Such repetitions can get in the way of a cogent, clear and concise formulation of Bible doctrines.

APPLICATION TO CHRISTOLOGICAL ISSUES

In this section, I apply the theological method of conservative evangelical theology to some christological issues to show how the topical approach of codifying God's Word might work in the context of doctrinal formulation.

---

[28]Richard Lints, *The Fabric of Theology: A Prolegomena to Evangelical Theology* (Grand Rapids: Eerdmans, 1993).

Among a variety of major christological issues, I will address the theme of the deity of Christ.

Identifying relevant texts. First of all, identify the relevant texts of the Bible that are connected with Christ's deity. The best examples must be those biblical texts that call Jesus "God" (*theos*). With the help of a credible concordance, it is relatively easy to identify those texts. They include John 1:1; 20:28; Romans 9:6; Titus 2:13; Hebrews 1:8-9; 2 Peter 1:1; and 1 John 5:20.

Additionally, identify other texts associated with Christ's deity. We can divide these texts into three categories. The first category is the divine names and titles attributed to Jesus Christ. For example, according to Isaiah 9:6, Jesus will be called "Wonderful Counselor, Mighty God, the Everlasting Father, Prince of Peace." Matthew 1:23 attributes the name "Immanuel" to Jesus. Jesus identifies himself with "the way and the truth and the life" (John 14:6 NIV). The second category is related to divine perfections attributed to Jesus Christ. For example, John 8:58 ("'Very truly I tell you,' Jesus answered, 'before Abraham was born, I am!'") demonstrates that Christ claimed eternity, a divine attribute. The third category is related to divine actions that Jesus performed, including forgiveness of sins, miracles (raising the dead, healing the sick, overruling natural forces and casting out demons), authoritative teaching, resurrection and ascension.

Exegesis: Grammatical/historical/cultural interpretation. After identifying relevant passages and texts of the Bible associated with the deity of Jesus Christ, the theologian must exegete them. The theologian's exegetical task begins with grammatical interpretation of the relevant texts, investigating the meaning of the words employed in their original Hebrew and Greek syntax and grammatical structure. It then proceeds to a careful consideration of the genre differences between the relevant texts. It is also crucial to consider the context of each passage. Through a process of grammatical interpretation, the theologian can construe the basic meaning of the relevant passages. An example can demonstrate why grammatical interpretation is crucial in grasping the basic meaning of the given text.

Titus 2:12-14 reads,

> It teaches us to say "No" to ungodliness and worldly passions, and to live self-controlled, upright and godly lives in this present age, while we wait for the blessed hope—the appearing of the glory of our great God and Savior, Jesus

Christ, who gave himself for us to redeem us from all wickedness and to purify for himself a people that are his very own, eager to do what is good. (NIV)

The NIV translation of this passage, especially Titus 2:13, indicates that Jesus Christ is identified with "our great God and Savior." It is important, however, to appreciate that other versions translate the Greek differently. For example, the KJV and ESV translate the Greek of Titus 2:13 as "Looking for that blessed hope, and the glorious appearing of the great God and our Saviour Jesus Christ" and "waiting for our blessed hope, the appearing of the glory of our great God and Savior Jesus Christ," respectively. Both translations do not overtly identify Jesus Christ with God. Scholarly debates are still going on over which translation best fits the Greek. At this stage the theologian can refer to grammatical analyses and studies of this passage. In particular, Murray J. Harris's book *Jesus as God* is a valuable resource for this issue.[29]

In addition, we should engage with historical and cultural interpretation of the given texts and passages. Without an appropriate consideration of the historical and cultural background of the texts, the theologian can easily distort and twist them. For example, it is difficult for contemporary Christians to understand that when Jesus identifies himself with the Son of God, he is claiming equality with God in the ancient Jewish context. In order to understand the historical and cultural background of the relevant passages, the theologian can refer to dictionaries of Bible background,[30] studies of historical and cultural background[31] and Bible commentaries.[32]

Biblical-theological study. After engaging with grammatical and historical/cultural interpretation, the theologian should proceed to theological interpretation of the given texts or biblical-theological study of the

---

[29]Murray J. Harris, *Jesus as God: The New Testament Use of Theos in Reference to Jesus* (1992; repr., Eugene, OR: Wipf & Stock, 2008).

[30]Cf. Craig A. Evans and Stanley E. Porter, eds., *Dictionary of New Testament Background* (Downers Grove, IL: InterVarsity Press, 2000), and T. Desmond Alexander and David Baker, eds., *Dictionary of the Old Testament: Pentateuch* (Downers Grove, IL: InterVarsity Press, 2003).

[31]Cf. Larry W. Hurtado, *How on Earth Did Jesus Become a God? Historical Questions About Earliest Devotion to Jesus* (Grand Rapids: Eerdmans, 2005).

[32]Cf. John H. Walton, Victor H. Matthews and Mark W. Chavalas, eds., *The IVP Bible Background Commentary: Old Testament* (Downers Grove, IL: InterVarsity Press, 2003); and Craig S. Keener, *The IVP Bible Background Commentary: New Testament* (Downers Grove, IL: InterVarsity Press, 1994).

relevant passages. At this stage the theologian should get help from the achievement of other scholars, including biblical theologians. One might, for example, consult the book *Jesus as God* for the relevant biblical and theological data for a correct and appropriate interpretation of those texts that call Jesus God. In addition, the theologian should make the best use of other biblical-theological studies that deal with New Testament Christology. For example, Richard Bauckham's *Jesus and the God of Israel* can provide the theologian with excellent resources for the identity of Jesus as the God of Israel.[33]

Integration of historical theology. At this stage, the theologian moves forward to integrate historical-theological research into the formulation of the doctrine of Christ's deity. In particular, the theologian should focus on the church fathers' christological engagement, researching doctrinal debates about the identity of Jesus Christ as God. For example, the theologian should pay attention to historic disputes over Christ's deity, including various early heresies denying the deity of Jesus Christ (adoptionism, Ebionism and so on), Arius's heretical arguments, Athanasius's rebuttals of Arianism, the Nicene Creed, and the notions of *homoousios* and *homoiousios*. Furthermore, the theologian should engage with controversies over the doctrine of the Trinity and the full equality of the Son with the Father and the Holy Spirit. Through this process of historical-theological engagement, the theologian can appropriate useful resources for formulating a solid doctrine of the deity of Jesus Christ.

Formulation of the doctrine. At this stage, the theologian embarks on the task of formulating the doctrine of the deity of Jesus Christ on the basis of the exegetical studies of the relevant texts (grammatical/historical interpretation), theological interpretation of the texts, biblical-theological research, and the integration of historical theology. When the theologian formulates the doctrine, he or she should employ crucial topics and themes relevant to the discussion of the deity of Jesus Christ. For example, the theologian can talk about Jesus Christ's divine attributes, including incommunicable and communicable attributes. Under the head of Christ's incommunicable attributes, the theologian can include such critical topics as Christ's aseity,

---

[33]Richard Bauckham, *Jesus and the God of Israel: God Crucified and Other Studies on the New Testament's Christology of Divine Identity* (Grand Rapids: Eerdmans, 2008).

self-sufficiency, eternity, immutability, omnipotence, omniscience, absolute sovereignty and so on. Under the head of Christ's communicable attributes, the theologian can include such important topics as Christ's love, grace, mercy, compassion, holiness, justice, righteousness and wrath. Moreover, the theologian can address Jesus Christ's divine works, including creation, providence, forgiveness of sins, supernatural performances, miraculous healings, authoritative teachings and so on. These divine works demonstrate the full deity of Jesus Christ.

Application of the doctrine to life, ministry and apologetics. After formulating the doctrine of Christ's deity, the theologian can apply the doctrine to the life, ministry and apologetic endeavor of the Christian. For example, the doctrine of Christ's deity can be applied to our prayer and worship. The Christian should not only revere but also worship and adore Jesus Christ because he is God! We give thanks to and sing praise to the Lord Jesus Christ. Furthermore, the Christian should enjoy his or her privilege to pray to Jesus Christ. Not only the Father but also the Son listens to our prayers and supplications. For this reason, we can approach the triune God with confidence and boldness. Furthermore, Christ's deity can be celebrated in the context of the Lord's Supper. At the table of the Eucharist, we not only remember the suffering and death of Jesus but also enjoy the presence of the resurrected Christ in and through the Holy Spirit, joyously anticipating his glorious return.[34] The doctrine of Christ's deity can also be applied to Christian apologetic endeavors. For example, a key issue in contemporary Christian thought and life related to Christology is religious pluralism. In the context of discussion of the uniqueness of Jesus Christ in relation to other religions, Christ's deity trumps founders and leaders of all other world religions. While Jesus Christ is the God who created such religious leaders as the Buddha, Confucius and Muhammad, these leaders are merely creatures and sinners before Christ, who will judge them righteously and justly. Applying the biblical doctrine of Christ to contemporary issues such as religious pluralism is a vital task of theology today.

---

[34]For an excellent discussion of the presence of Jesus Christ at the table of the Lord's Supper, see John Jefferson Davis, *Worship and the Reality of God: An Evangelical Theology of Real Presence* (Downers Grove, IL: InterVarsity Press, 2010).

CONCLUSION

The evangelical-theological method of codifying God's Word still has value, necessity and relevance for today. Formulating Bible doctrines according to critical topics and themes on the basis of appropriate exegetical work should be our first method of choice for doing theology. It will continue to make an indelible impact on the formation and sustenance of the identity of evangelical theology. However, the evangelical approach of codifying God's Word into Bible doctrines should avoid the proof-texting approach, eliminate the possibility of *eisegesis*, consider more seriously the structural shape of divine revelation, and prevent excessive repetition of arguments. Finally, the evangelical theologian should learn how to formulate Bible doctrines in the context of religious plurality and diversity. In the past, our conversation partners have been Western philosophers rather than other world religions. Biblical propositionalists should increasingly engage global and multicultural theological voices.

2

Missional Theology

LIVING GOD'S LOVE

JOHN R. FRANKE

In the highly influential volume *Missional Church: A Theological Vision for the Sending of the Church in North America*, the authors assert that mission must not be viewed as merely one of the many programs of the church. Instead, it is at the very core of the church's reason and purpose for being and must therefore shape all that the church is and does. Mission "defines the church as God's sent people. Either we are defined by mission, or we reduce the scope of the gospel and the mandate of the church. Thus our challenge today is to move from church with mission to missional church."[1] Since this volume's publication in 1998, the term *missional church* has become a commonplace in theological and praxis-oriented conversations about the nature of the church in a social climate that is decidedly and increasingly post-Christian. Indeed, the notion of the missional church has become ubiquitous, spawning numerous conversations, networks, programs and publications seeking to capture the dynamism inherent in the idea.[2]

The move from church with mission to missional church has significant implications for theology. Like the church, the impulses and assumptions that have shaped the discipline of theology in the West are those of Christendom

---

[1]Darrell L. Guder, ed., *Missional Church: A Theological Vision for the Sending of the Church in North America* (Grand Rapids: Eerdmans, 1998), 6. While Guder served as the project coordinator and editor of the volume, it was cowritten by a team of authors including, in addition to Guder, Lois Barrett, Inagrace T. Dieterrich, George R. Hunsberger, Alan J. Roxburgh and Craig Van Gelder.

[2]The breadth of the missional church conversation is surveyed and assessed in Craig Van Gelder and Dwight J. Zscheile, *The Missional Church in Perspective: Mapping Trends and Shaping the Conversation* (Grand Rapids: Baker Academic, 2011).

rather than the mission of God. If theology is to serve the life and witness of the church to the gospel, and if we assume that "the church can only exist as truly itself only when dedicated to the mission of God, a burning question ensues: How should one reinvent theology and theological education so that they flow naturally for an integral perspective on God's consistent will and activity in the world?"[3] Like the challenge facing the church in moving from church with mission to missional church, so the discipline of theology, if it is to serve the church and be faithful to its subject, must move from theology with a mission component to a truly missional conception of theology. Essential to missional theology is allowing the narrative of Scripture to shape the theological agenda rather than reading the Bible through the assumptions of culture. Missional theology, moreover, ends not in reflection but in living out the gospel in the church's particular cultural circumstances.

In what follows I offer a rationale, definition and method for missional theology and conclude with some remarks on the application of missional-theological method to Christology. In spite of this linear structure, it is important to realize that the practice of theology is always an interactive process and that convictions and commitments concerning Christology, as well as other matters, shape the definition and method of missional theology.

A RATIONALE FOR MISSIONAL THEOLOGY

A missional approach to theology arises from the conviction that the triune God is, by God's very nature, a missional God and that therefore the church of this God is missional by its very nature.[4] The idea of mission is at the heart of the biblical narratives concerning the work of God in human history.[5] Jesus' words recorded in the Gospel of John capture the missional call to the church: "As the Father has sent me, so I send you" (Jn 20:21 NRSV). As David Bosch observes, mission is derived from the very nature of God and must be situated in the context of the doctrine of the Trinity rather than ecclesiology or soteriology. In this context the logic of the classical doctrine of the *missio Dei*

---

[3]J. Andrew Kirk, *The Mission of Theology and Theology as Mission* (Harrisburg, PA: Trinity Press International, 1996), 2.

[4]See John G. Flett, *The Witness of God: The Trinity, Missio Dei, Karl Barth and the Nature of Christian Community* (Grand Rapids: Eerdmans, 2010).

[5]On the centrality of mission in Scripture, see Christopher J. H. Wright, *The Mission of God: Unlocking the Bible's Grand Narrative* (Downers Grove, IL: IVP Academic, 2006).

(mission of God), expressed as God the Father sending the Son, and the Father and the Son sending the Spirit, may be expanded to include another movement: "Father, Son, and Spirit sending the church into the world."[6] From this perspective, the church is seen as an instrument and witness of God's mission to the world, not its end. The various historical, cultural, global and contemporary embodiments of the church may be viewed as a series of local iterations of God's universal mission to all of creation.

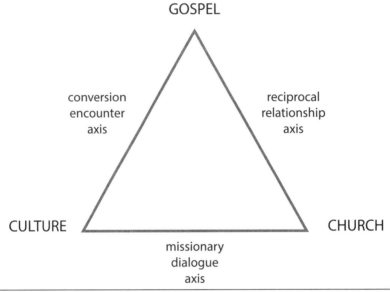

Figure 1. A triangular model of gospel-culture relationships
Source: Hunsberger, "Newbigin Gauntlet," 9.

The manifestation of God's universal mission to creation in local communities draws culture into the forefront of missional-theological conversation. Lesslie Newbigin provides an important interpretive framework for the development of missional theology.[7] Missiologist George Hunsberger has provided a helpful summary of Newbigin's work on the interactions

---

[6]David Bosch, *Transforming Mission: Paradigm Shifts in Theology of Mission*, 20th anniversary ed. (Maryknoll, NY: Orbis, 1991), 390.
[7]Among the many writings of Lesslie Newbigin on these interactions, see particularly *Foolishness to the Greeks: The Gospel and Western Culture* (Grand Rapids: Eerdmans, 1998); *The Gospel in a Pluralist Society* (Grand Rapids: Eerdmans, 1989); and *The Open Secret: An Introduction to the Theology of Mission*, rev. ed. (Grand Rapids: Eerdmans, 1995).

among gospel, church and culture. He speaks of three axes that form what he calls the Newbigin triad: the gospel-culture axis as the conversion encounter, the gospel-church axis as the reciprocal relationship, and the church-culture axis as the missionary encounter.[8]

The gospel-culture axis affirms that all articulations of the gospel are culture specific. According to Newbigin, we must acknowledge that there is no such thing as a pure gospel unencumbered by the trappings of a particular culture. "The gospel always comes as the testimony of a community which, if it is faithful, is trying to live out the meaning of the gospel in a certain style of life, certain ways of holding property, of maintaining law and order, of carrying on production and consumption, and so on. Every interpretation of the gospel is embodied in some cultural form," according to Newbigin.[9] He notes that even the simplest verbal statement of the gospel, such as Jesus is Lord, is dependent on the content that a particular culture gives to the word *Lord*. The gospel-church axis affirms that the understanding of the gospel of any particular community is shaped by the theological and ecclesial traditions of that community.

The church-culture axis affirms the plurality of the church as culturally distinct Christian communities embody varying conceptions of the gospel in the midst of their particular social and historical circumstances. The inexhaustible fullness of the gospel is made manifest in the cultural expansion of the church as communities emerge and interact with one another. The intercultural dialogue between these communities is vital to missional theology and provides resistance to an inflexible dogmatism that restricts the truth of the gospel and to the anything-goes relativism that eclipses it. This way of framing the interactions among gospel, church and culture helps communities to resist the danger of allowing the gospel message to be overly accommodated to culture on the one hand or viewed as being something entirely apart from culture on the other.

Having asserted the local character of all articulations of the gospel, I now turn my attention to the universal mission of God to which Christian

---

[8]George R. Hunsberger, "The Newbigin Gauntlet: Developing a Domestic Missiology for North America," in *The Church Between Gospel and Culture: The Emerging Mission in North America* (Grand Rapids: Eerdmans, 1996), 3-25. See also George R. Hunsberger, *Bearing the Witness of the Spirit: Lesslie Newbigin's Theology of Cultural Plurality* (Grand Rapids: Eerdmans, 1998).

[9]Newbigin, *Gospel in a Pluralist Society*, 144.

communities in all cultural settings are called to bear witness. I suggest that while the mission of God is complex and multifaceted, its central and compelling motivation is love. The biblical affirmation that "God is love" (1 Jn 4:8) points not simply to the love of God for the world but also to the eternal life of God lived in the ongoing relationship of love that constitutes God's being in and for Godself. This is the eternal trinitarian fellowship in which Father, Son and Holy Spirit participate together in the giving, receiving and sharing of love. From the beginning and throughout all of eternity the life of the triune God has been and continues to be characterized by love. This divine love is found in the reciprocal interdependence and self-dedication of the trinitarian members to one another. Indeed, there is no God other than the Father, Son and Spirit bound together in the active relations of love throughout eternity.

This love provides a profound conception of the reality of God as understood by the Christian tradition. Love expressed and received by the trinitarian persons among themselves provides a description of the inner life of God throughout eternity apart from any reference to creation. In addition to enjoying the support of the biblical witness and the tradition of the church, *love* is an especially fruitful term for comprehending the life of God since it is an inherently relational concept. Love requires both subject and object, and the life of God comprehends both love's subject and love's object. For this reason, when viewed theologically, the statement "God is love" refers primarily to the eternal, relational, intratrinitarian fellowship among Father, Son and Holy Spirit, who together are the one God.

The plurality-in-unity and unity-in-plurality that characterize the life of the triune God add an important dimension to this fellowship of divine love. It means that difference and otherness are part of the divine life. It is important to note in this context that the love of God is not an assimilating love. It does not seek to make that which is different the same; rather, God lives in harmonious fellowship with the other through the active relations of self-sacrificing, self-giving love. The Father, Son and Spirit are indeed one God, but this unity does not make them the same. They are one in the very midst of their difference. This love characterizes the mission of God from all eternity and is the compelling basis for the extension of the divine mission to the world.

From this perspective, creation itself can be understood as a missional act, a reflection of the expansive love of God, whereby the triune God brings into being another reality, that which is not God, and establishes a relationship of love, grace and blessing for the purpose of drawing that reality into participation in the divine fellowship of love. Jesus is sent into the world as a manifestation of the love of God for the world (Jn 3:16-17). In a similar fashion, the church is sent into the world as a continuing manifestation of the love of God (Jn 20:21).

To summarize: (1) the mission of God from all eternity is love; (2) creation is the result of the expansive nature of God's love, and God desires that all of creation come to participate in the fellowship of divine love; and (3) God calls forth a community to participate in the divine mission as an instrument and witness of the good news of God's love for the world by living God's love in the world for the sake of the world. In light of this, how should we understand theology so that it is consistent with the mission of God?

DEFINING MISSIONAL THEOLOGY

In spite of all the conversation about the missional church and missional theology, Benjamin Connor observes that while the usage of the term *missional* in conjunction with the church and theology has become ubiquitous, "there really is no shared notion about what missional theology is—to this point there has been no substantive crosscurrent of conversation about the parameters and shape of missional theology."[10] Drawing primarily from the work of Darrell Guder and George Hunsberger, he offers the following provisional definition:

> Missional theology is a kind of practical theology that explores in every aspect of the theological curriculum and praxis of the church the implications of the missionary nature of God with the purpose of forming congregations to better articulate the gospel and to live faithfully their vocation to participate in the ongoing redemptive mission of God in their particular context.[11]

What is particularly helpful here is the emphasis on the practical element of missional theology. Because the very purpose of missional theology is to

---

[10]Benjamin T. Connor, *Practicing Witness: A Missional Vision of Christian Practices* (Grand Rapids: Eerdmans, 2011), 11.

[11]Ibid., 39.

assist congregations to participate faithfully in the mission of God, it is inherently focused on life and practice rather than merely on an intellectual articulation and appreciation of the mission of God. This focus on the life of a community is a distinctive aspect of missional theology. Missional theology must be done in the context of a community committed to participation in the mission of God. While it certainly has an intellectual component, it is never simply an intellectual enterprise. On the basis of the considerations above, I suggest the following definition: missional theology is an ongoing, second-order, contextual discipline that engages in the task of critical and constructive reflection on the beliefs and practices of the Christian church for the purpose of assisting the community of Christ's followers in their missional vocation to live as the people of God in the particular social-historical context in which they are situated.[12]

This definition means that missional theology is contextual and dynamic. Theology always emerges from a particular set of circumstances and conditions that serve to give it a particular shape. From the cultural particularity of Galilee and Second Temple Judaism to the passage of Christian theology and tradition into numerous cultural settings, in every "missionary enterprise and conversion experience, people have met Christ mediated through cultures—both theirs and the culture of those who communicated the gospel to them."[13] Newbigin observes that the Bible itself "is a book which is very obviously in a specific cultural setting. Its language is Hebrew and Greek, not Chinese or Sanskrit. All the events it records, all the teachings it embodies, are shaped by specific human cultures."[14] Because the situation into which the church bears witness to the message of the gospel is constantly changing, the work of theology is an ongoing process: "The time is past when we can speak of one, right, unchanging theology, a *theologia perennis*. We can only speak about a theology that makes sense at a certain place and in a certain time. We can certainly learn from others (synchronically from other cultures and diachronically from history), but the theology of others can never be our own."[15]

---

[12]For a detailed exposition of this definition, see John R. Franke, *The Character of Theology: An Introduction to Its Nature, Task, and Purpose* (Grand Rapids: Baker Academic, 2005).

[13]Justo L. Gonzáles, *Out of Every Tribe and Nation: Christian Theology at the Ethnic Roundtable* (Nashville: Abingdon, 1992), 30.

[14]Newbigin, *Gospel in a Pluralist Society*, 144-45.

[15]Stephen B. Bevans, *Models of Contextual Theology*, rev. ed. (Maryknoll, NY: Orbis, 2002), 4-5.

The ongoing and contextual nature of theology suggests the companion notion of theology as a second-order discipline and highlights its character as an interpretive enterprise. As such, the doctrinal, theological and confessional formulations of theologians and particular communities are viewed as the products of human reflection on the primary stories, teachings, symbols and practices of the Christian church and therefore must be distinguished from these first-order commitments of the Christian faith. Theological constructions and doctrines are always subservient to the content of Scripture and therefore must be held more lightly.

Regarding the task of theology, Newbigin observes that while the ultimate commitment of the Christian community is to the biblical story, communities are also participants in a particular social setting whose whole way of thinking is shaped by the cultural model of that society in ways that are both conscious and unconscious. These cultural models cannot be absolutized without impairing the ability to properly discern the teachings and implications of the biblical narrative. Yet as participants in a particular culture we are not able to see many of the numerous ways in which we take for granted and absolutize our own socially constructed cultural model. Given this state of affairs, Newbigin maintains that the unending task of theology is to be wholly open to the biblical story. The result is that the narrative of Scripture shapes the church's view of the assumptions and aspirations of culture, rather than the church reading the Bible through the lens of culture. The task of theology is to express the biblical story in terms that make use of particular cultural models without being controlled by them. He concludes with the assertion that this can only be done if we are "continuously open to the witness of Christians in other cultures who are seeking to practice the same kind of theology."[16]

The particularity and, consequently, the limitation of each theological tradition suggest the need for both critical and constructive reflection on the beliefs and practices of the church. Critical reflection involves the ongoing examination and scrutiny of the beliefs and practices of the church in order to ensure that they are in keeping with the biblical narratives and not enslaved to cultural practices and patterns of thinking that are not consistent

---

[16]Lesslie Newbigin, "Theological Education in a World Perspective," *Churchman* 93 (1979): 114-15.

with the gospel and the mission of God. The critical aspect of the theological task implies the constructive. The task of theological reflection is not simply to find inconsistencies in the faith, life and practices of the community but also to provide insight into appropriate ways of assisting the church to live out its calling in particular settings. Constructive reflection involves the development and articulation of coherent models of Christian faith that are appropriate to the contemporary social-historical context.

The purpose of theology is to cooperate with the Spirit to form witnessing communities that participate in the divine mission by living God's love in the way of Jesus Christ for the sake of the world.[17] The shape of these communities is connected to the missional character of God's eternal life of love reflected in the biblical witness to God's love for the world. This is manifest in the sending of the Son and the Spirit for the purpose of reconciliation and redemption in order that the world might participate in the fellowship of love shared by Father, Son and Holy Spirit. The church is called to be a provisional demonstration of this fellowship of love in the present that anticipates the fulfillment of God's creative intention in the eschatological consummation of all things.

From this perspective, theology participates in this mission by working with the Spirit in the formation and development of a community of persons who believe in the gospel of Jesus Christ and live by it. Missional theology is an outworking of "the good news of God's love, incarnated in the witness of a community, for the sake of the world."[18] Therefore the practice of theology from a missional perspective has as its goal "not only greater knowledge of God and God's purposes but more reflective and intelligent participation in those purposes."[19] Of particular importance in the understanding and living out of God's purposes in the world is the call to love one another in response to the love of God: "Dear friends, since God so loved us, we also ought to love one another. No one has ever seen God; but if we love one another, God lives in us and his love is made complete in us" (1 Jn 4:11-12 NIV).

---

[17]On the work of the Spirit speaking in and through the Bible, see Stanley J. Grenz and John R. Franke, *Beyond Foundationalism: Shaping Theology in a Postmodern Context* (Louisville: Westminster John Knox, 2001), 57-92.

[18]Bosch, *Transforming Mission*, 532.

[19]Stephen B. Bevans and Roger P. Schroeder, *Constants in Context: A Theology of Mission for Today* (Maryknoll, NY: Orbis, 2004), 1.

DOING MISSIONAL THEOLOGY

Missional theology starts in the life and witness of a community that believes in the gospel and is prepared to live by it. As the community bears witness to the gospel in its particular social location—with all that this implies about the interaction of the community and its setting—it has missionary encounters and experiences that continually shape and challenge its conception of the gospel and Christian faith and their implications for witness in the world. These lived missionary encounters and experiences provide the starting point for cultural and theological reflection. This reflection begins with the formulation of questions to be wrestled with and responded to: What is going on in the culture? What needs, desires, concerns and challenges are reflected in these encounters and experiences? How are they addressed by the gospel? What insight into these situations is provided by Scripture? What contributions are made by Christian communities past and present to contemporary situations and challenges? How is God at work in the situation? What is the Spirit saying to the churches?

Because this reflection is the result of lived situations, it will result in missional action as the communities and individuals determine how they will respond to the particular situations and challenges they face. Determining a course of action will also raise important questions that require further theological reflection: What response constitutes faithfulness to the mission of God? What is the response of love? How might the community need to change? What sacrifices might be called for by individuals and the larger community? What are the implications of particular responses for the unity of the church? How will dissent be addressed? In this process of missional theological engagement, we can identify three sources: Scripture, culture and tradition.

First, Scripture is the principal means by which the Spirit guides the church, and hence the Bible is theology's norming norm. The Bible is, in the words of Newbigin, "that body of literature which—primarily but not only in narrative form—renders accessible to us the character and actions and purposes of God."[20] Through the pages of Scripture the Spirit communicates God's intentions for the world, equips the followers of Jesus for participation

---

[20]Newbigin, *Foolishness to the Greeks*, 59.

in those purposes in relation to their social setting, and connects the traditions of past communities with the contemporary proclamation of the gospel. This means that the work of exegesis is critical to the work of theology.

However, Guder observes that while virtually every Christian tradition affirms the centrality of Scripture for the church, it is possible "to be biblically centered, to expect and to experience biblical preaching, and not to be a church that acknowledges, much less practices, its missional calling."[21] He adds that this is precisely the crisis and the dilemma of much of the Western church in that it has appropriated the Scriptures in such a way that the central emphasis on the formation for mission has been missed. In this context it has become possible to hear the gospel as being primarily about what God's grace does for individuals: "It is possible to take the Bible seriously, persuaded that it is primarily about one's personal salvation. It is possible to preach the Bible in such a way that the needs of persons are met but the formation of the whole community for its witness in the world is not emphasized. It is, in short, possible to be Bible-centered and not wholeheartedly missional."[22] The problem is that Western Christendom reduced the gospel to individualism. The gospel transforms individuals, but it also redeems communities of faith.

In response to this situation, missional theology affirms that the texts of Scripture be read in community from an explicitly missional point of view as a means of forming communities for discipleship and participation in the mission of God. To accomplish this, the authors of *Missional Church* suggest that study of Scripture becomes missionally incisive by asking the following questions regarding the interpretation of biblical texts, particularly those of the New Testament:

> How did this text prepare the early church for its mission, and how does it prepare us for ours? What does this text tell us about the gospel? What makes it good news? What does this text tell us about ourselves and about our world? What does this text show us about the way the gospel is to be made known? How does this text challenge our organizational forms and functions? How should our organizational practices change in light of this text? How does this text challenge us to be converted?[23]

---

[21]Darrell L. Guder, "Biblical Formation and Discipleship," in *Treasure in Clay Jars: Patterns in Missional Faithfulness*, ed. Lois Y. Barrett (Grand Rapids: Eerdmans, 2004), 60.
[22]Ibid.
[23]Guder, *Missional Church*, 246.

Missional theology, therefore, works from the missional narrative of God's redemptive work in the Bible to the missional context of local communities of faith.

Second, questions such as those above used in the study and interpretation of Scripture will work with the Spirit to form missional communities, but this formation will always be shaped by the culture in which particular communities are situated. Evaluating church practices in light of Scripture helps the church allow the narrative of Scripture to shape its practice. While Scripture is theology's norming norm, the influence of culture is all-encompassing, extending to both the production and interpretation of the Bible. For some, the inclusion of culture as a source for theology is inappropriate and out of step with traditional notions of theology. However, as Stephen Bevans observes, in the history of theology the function of culture as a source for theology is really quite common, even if not explicitly acknowledged: "While we can say that the doing of theology by taking culture and social change in culture into account is a departure from the traditional or classical way of doing theology, a study of the history of theology will reveal that every authentic theology has been very much rooted in a particular context in some implicit or real way."[24]

Colin Gunton states the point succinctly: "We must acknowledge the fact that all theologies belong in a particular context, and so are, to a degree, limited by the constraints of that context. To that extent, the context is one of the authorities to which the theologian must listen."[25] The work of missional theology demands that theologians express the gospel through the language of the culture: the cognitive tools, concepts, images, symbols and thought forms through which contemporary people discover meaning, construct their worlds and form personal identity.

Viewed from this perspective, missional theology includes the attempt to understand and interpret the times in accordance with the purposes of God in order to assist the church to participate more faithfully in the mission of God. The task of listening to the culture entails being observant of the various venues and events that give expression to the ethos of one's time,

---

[24]Bevans, *Models of Contextual Theology*, 7.
[25]Colin Gunton, "Using and Being Used: Scripture and Systematic Theology," *Theology Today* 47, no. 3 (October 1990): 253.

such as literature, music, film, television programming, art, newspapers and magazines, as well as forms of institutional life. In this process theology seeks not only to respond to the cultural situation but also to learn from it. Not only does the theological interplay between gospel and culture serve to optimize our ability to address our context, but it can also enhance our theological constructions as well.[26] Indeed, whether occurring directly or, more likely, in an indirect manner, culture can be a means for gaining theological insight. In short, reading our culture can assist us in reading the biblical text, so as to hear more clearly the voice of the Spirit in our particular cultural circumstances. From this perspective, as provocative a claim as this may be, in addition to listening for the voice of the Spirit speaking through Scripture, theology must also be attentive to the voice of the Spirit speaking through culture.[27]

Third, the Christian tradition is then viewed as a series of local translations of the gospel and iterations of communal life based on the texts of Scripture in relationship to particular social, historical and cultural conditions.[28] Taking stock of this multifaceted tradition becomes an important element in the method of missional theology. While it is a vast ocean that is beyond full comprehension, the more we are aware of this history and all of its diversity, the more alert we can become to the voice of the Spirit at work in the witness of Christian communities and the "infinite translatability" of the gospel.[29] In this sense the Christian tradition serves as a source or a resource for theology, not as a final arbiter of theological issues or concerns but rather by providing a hermeneutical context or trajectory for the theological enterprise.[30]

---

[26]For further development of these interactions, see Clemens Sedmak, *Doing Local Theology: A Guide for Artisans of a New Humanity* (Maryknoll, NY: Orbis, 2002).

[27]For a fuller development of this theme, see John R. Franke, "'We Hear the Wonder of God in Our Own Languages': Exploring the Significance of the Spirit's Speaking Through Culture," *Cultural Encounters: A Journal for the Theology of Culture* 6, no. 1 (2010): 7-23.

[28]On this theme, see Lamin O. Sanneh, *Translating the Message: The Missionary Impact on Culture* (Maryknoll, NY: Orbis, 2008).

[29]Bevans and Schroeder, *Constants in Context*, 2.

[30]For a fuller discussion of the role of tradition in theology and its relationship to Scripture, see Stanley J. Grenz and John R. Franke, "Theological Heritage as Hermeneutical Trajectory: Toward a Nonfoundationalist Understanding of the Role of Tradition in Theology," in *Ancient & Postmodern Christianity: Paleo-Orthodoxy in the 21st Century*, ed. Kenneth Tanner and Christopher A. Hall (Downers Grove, IL: InterVarsity Press, 2002), 215-39.

This diverse and multicultural context is accessible in the history of mission, theology and worship, in past theological formulations and in the expansion and development of Christianity as a world movement.[31] The diversity and infinite translatability of the Christian tradition is a powerful reminder that it must not be viewed as a weapon to be employed against other communities with whom we may be at odds. As John Caputo remarks, a tradition should not be used as a weapon "to slam dissent and knock dissenters senseless, but a responsibility to read, to interpret, to sift and to select responsibly among many competing strands of tradition and interpretations of tradition. If you have a tradition, you have to take *responsibility* for it and its multiplicity. But that, of course, is the only way to conserve a tradition."[32]

As mentioned at the outset, the end of missional theology is not simply reflection but rather the action of bearing witness to God's love by living it out in the midst of the world for the sake of the world. From this perspective performance becomes a central metaphor for the work of theology. It is through the activity of performance that we actually "do" theology. The ultimate purpose of missional theology is not simply to establish right thinking or belief but rather to assist Christian communities in their missional vocations to live as the people of God in the particular social-historical contexts in which they are situated. The goal of theology is to facilitate participation in the mission of God by enabling authentic performance of the gospel by Christian communities.

N. T. Wright has proposed a performance-oriented model of biblical authority that moves along similar lines and is consistent with the missional approach to theology I am describing in this essay.[33] He uses the analogy of a five-act Shakespeare play in which the first four acts are extant but the fifth has been lost. In this model the performance of the fifth act would be facilitated not by the writing of a script that "would freeze the play into one form" but by the recruitment of "highly trained, sensitive, and experienced Shakespearean actors" who would immerse themselves in the first four acts

---

[31]Of particular importance here is Dale T. Irvin and Scott W. Sunquist, *History of the World Christian Movement*, 2 vols. (Maryknoll, NY: Orbis, 2001, 2012).

[32]John D. Caputo, *Deconstruction in a Nutshell: A Conversation with Jacques Derrida* (New York: Fordham University Press, 1997), 37.

[33]N. T. Wright, "How Can the Bible Be Authoritative?," *Vox Evangelica* 21 (1991): 7-32.

and then be told *"to work out a fifth act for themselves."*[34] The first four acts would serve as the authority for the play, but not in the sense of demanding that the actors should repeat the first parts of the play again and again. Instead their authority lies in their "forward movement," which calls forth an appropriate conclusion. It requires actors who are able to enter into the story in a way that is responsible to the earlier acts and developments as well as an understanding of how the earlier threads and themes "could appropriately be drawn together, and then to put that understanding into effect by speaking and acting with both *innovation* and *consistency.*"[35] This approach provides an affirmation of the authority of Scripture while allowing for an open and flexible approach to theology and mission that is consistent with the traditions of the church and alert to its particular cultural situation.

MISSIONAL CHRISTOLOGY

Christology is a vast topic with a rich history of reflection in the tradition of the church that has spawned numerous constructive proposals based on various elements in the witness of Scripture. From a missional perspective, two points are worth noting here with respect to the classical theological tradition as it relates to Christology.

The first is the relative lack of engagement with the mission of Jesus as it is narrated in the Gospels. The discussions have tended to focus on questions concerned with intratrinitarian relationships, the question of the relationship between the divine and human natures of the person of Christ, and the atonement. The shape of this conversation seems to suggest that the details of Jesus' life and ministry have little doctrinal significance for the major questions of Christology as they have been understood in the classical tradition. Commenting on this history Hendrikus Berkhof remarks, "As a rule, dogmatics has based itself on the proclamation structure of the epistles, not the story structure of the gospels."[36] This tendency has also had the effect of seeming to situate theological discussions in a more abstract context that often seems to be removed from the day-to-day life of the witnessing

---

[34]Ibid., 18 (emphasis original).
[35]Ibid., 19 (emphasis original).
[36]Hendrikus Berkhof, *Christian Faith: An Introduction to the Study of Faith* (Grand Rapids: Eerdmans, 1979), 293.

community. The consequence in traditional Christology has been twofold: favoring the so-called didactic epistles over the historical narratives of the Gospels, on the one hand, and abstract metaphysical formulas over the life and ministry of Jesus, on the other.

Second, the intuitions of the classical tradition have been formed and developed almost exclusively in the context of Christendom, a system of church-state partnership and cultural hegemony in which the Christian church maintained a unique, privileged and protected place in society. "Functional Christendom" is the continuing entailments of Christendom, even in the aftermath of its formal demise. Commenting on this history in the West, Newbigin remarks that much "of the substance of the Western Christian tradition—its liturgy, theology, and church order—was formed during the long period in which Western Christendom was an almost enclosed ghetto precluded from missionary advance."[37] In addition, the dominance of this tradition has impeded the reception and influence of the theological contributions of Christian communities from beyond the West. This tendency has left the impression among many students of theology that Western forms of Christology are more faithful to the interpretation of Scripture than are non-Western forms.

The method of missional Christology endeavors not only to formulate christological doctrines but to propose what it means for Christian communities to follow in the way of Christ, a way characterized by God's love revealed in the missional nature of Christ's life and ministry. To accomplish this task, missional Christology (1) develops a missional account of the life of Jesus based on Scripture, (2) brings this christological yield into conversation with the particular cultural context of the Christian community, and finally (3) resources historical traditions and contemporary approaches to Christology.

Missional Christology begins with the witness of Scripture. In John 20:21 Jesus tell his disciples, "As the Father has sent me, I am sending you." This classic missional text establishes the connection among the Trinity, Jesus, the church and mission. The sending of Jesus by the Father arises from the trinitarian relations shared by the Father and the Son, and the sending of disciples (and the church) by Jesus arises from the union of the church in

---

[37]Newbigin, *Open Secret*, 4.

Jesus and, therefore, in the Father as well. It is worth noting that Jesus' next action, recorded in John 20:22, is to breathe on the disciples and say, "Receive the Holy Spirit." Hence the disciples (and the church) are empowered for the continuation of the divine trinitarian mission through the work of the Spirit. Two elements of this text are central to missional Christology: the sending of Jesus by the Father, which calls our attention to the unique centrality of Jesus in the mission of God in the world; and the sending of the church by Jesus, who is the paradigm for our sentness into the world after the same pattern by which the Father sent him. The connection between these two elements implies that mission by the church is, by virtue of its union with Christ and empowerment by the Holy Spirit, mission done by Jesus, in union with the Father, through the Holy Spirit. This leads to a christocentric trinitarianism that is central for missional theology. The Gospel of John captures this unique centrality in Jesus' statement in John 14:6 that he is "the way and the truth and the life." Missional Christology, therefore, draws on Scripture to articulate the meaning of the missional nature of Christ for contemporary Christian communities in respect to their particular cultural and traditional contexts.

Consequently, Jesus Christ—his life, death and resurrection—is central for missional theology. The mission of Christ shapes the whole of human history and defines the meaning of the church and its calling in the world as an instrument and manifestation of God's mission in the world. It means that we should look to Jesus to discover how God acts in the world. As the divine incarnation of God's love and mission, Jesus lives out and exemplifies the way of God in the world. He is with God "in the beginning" and was sent into the world not only to tell us about God but to demonstrate how God wants us to live. And how does God want us to live? While this is obviously a complex question, the short answer is, as we have already seen, that God calls us to love. Of course, this is easily said, but the question is, what is love?

Many assume they know what love is. From the perspective of a disciple of Christ, our notions of love should not be determined primarily by our culture but rather by looking at Jesus, who is the living embodiment of God's gracious character as the one who loves. This love is not an abstract notion or a set of feelings but is rather characterized by the being-in-action of God in the person of Jesus Christ. Commitment to Jesus as the way, the truth and the life means that our understanding of true love, the love of God, is shaped by the particular way in which God loves in and through Jesus Christ. As the one sent by the Father, Jesus exemplifies the way of love in his mission to the world. Elements of this love and our participation in it can be gleaned from numerous texts of Scripture; here I will mention three.

The first is found in Luke's account of the opening of Jesus' public ministry on the sabbath at the synagogue in Nazareth: "The Spirit of the Lord is on me, because he has anointed me to preach good news to the poor. He has sent me to proclaim freedom for the prisoners and recovery of sight for the blind, to release the oppressed, to proclaim the year of the Lord's favor" (Lk 4:18-19). In calling disciples and creating a community of the Way, Jesus calls us to join him in his struggle for the liberation of human beings from all the forces of fear, oppression and marginalization. This aspect of the mission of God points to the value of liberationist and postcolonial theological perspectives in the work of missional theology.[38]

The second tells of Jesus and Zacchaeus the tax collector. When Zacchaeus, in response to Jesus, promises to give half of his possessions to the poor and pay back fourfold anyone he had cheated, Jesus says to him, "Today salvation has come to this house, because this man, too, is a son of Abraham. For the Son of Man came to seek and to save the lost" (Lk 19:9-10 NIV). The church has been sent into the world after the pattern of Jesus to seek the lost and to proclaim the good news of salvation in Christ. Hence evangelism is central to the liberating and reconciling mission of God to a lost and broken world.[39]

A third text stands at the heart of the gospel and shapes our participation in the way of Jesus:

> Who, being in very nature God,
>> did not consider equality with God something to be used to his own
>> advantage;

---

[38]For a recent discussion of mission in postcolonial perspective, see Marion Grau, *Rethinking Mission in the Postcolony: Salvation, Society and Subversion* (London: T&T Clark, 2011). For an evangelical appropriation of postcolonial thought, see Kay Higuera Smith, Jayachitra Lalitha and L. Daniel Hawk, eds., *Evangelical Postcolonial Conversations: Global Awakenings in Theology and Praxis* (Downers Grove, IL: IVP Academic, 2014).

[39]For a discussion of evangelism in missional perspective, see Bryan P. Stone, *Evangelism After Christendom: The Theology and Practice of Christian Witness* (Grand Rapids: Brazos, 2007).

rather, he made himself nothing
>by taking the very nature of a servant,
>being made in human likeness.

And being found in appearance as a human being,
>he humbled himself
>by becoming obedient to death—
>even death on a cross! (Phil 2:6–8 NIV)

The way of Jesus is not simply about the inwardly focused or otherworldly spirituality so common in our culture—or the social activism that is often viewed as its alternative. Rather, it is the way of the cross. Faithfulness to the way of Jesus means emulating his humility through the pursuit of a cruciform life lived for the sake of others. Such a life is an expression of discipleship in the way of Jesus and a witness to the love of God for the healing of the world.[40]

This affirmation also suggests that ultimate truth is not finally to be found in abstract notions or theories but rather in the person of Jesus Christ, the unique Son of God and the living embodiment of truth. From this perspective, knowing truth and participating in truth depend on being in proper relationship to this one person who is divine truth, a truth that is personal, active, relational and gracious. This affirmation that Jesus is the truth is a stark challenge to the abstract ideas of truth we commonly hold. In Jesus we discover that truth is not merely intellectual but personal and relational—truth for Christians is very much woven into the theme of love. This means that missional theology is not simply an intellectual pursuit but is a holistic approach that is concerned with personal, relational and spiritual formation as well.

In interpreting Scripture it is important to remember our cultural location as readers and the significance of this for the development of Christologies. These are shaped not simply by the words of the biblical texts but also by the situations and challenges we perceive with respect to our social situation. This helps us to make sense of the diversity of approaches to Christology in history. Of course, the pluriform character of Christology is the result of not simply the diversity of social settings into which the gospel

---

[40]For a development of this theme in Paul, see Michael J. Gorman, *Inhabiting the Cruciform God: Kenosis, Justification, and Theosis* (Grand Rapids: Eerdmans, 2009).

has been lived out and proclaimed but also the diversity of Scripture itself. The presence of Matthew, Mark, Luke and John, each with its own particular perspective on Jesus, alerts us to the plurality of christological reflection embedded in the pages of Scripture. This stands as an important reminder that the witness of the Christian community to Jesus Christ cannot be contained in a single universal account. Instead, it is always perspectival and characterized by a diversity of forms in keeping with the tradition of the biblical canon. This diversity of christological forms raises the question of the unity of the church in the face of its differing conceptions of Jesus. How can we conceive of the unity of the Christian community in the midst of a pluralist church that has been embodied throughout history and across cultures in such a dazzling array of forms and in which so much is debated and contested even about the Lord of the church? Put another way, how do the many confessions of Christology relate to the common confession that Jesus Christ is the one Lord of the church and the world?

A basic answer to this inquiry is that Christology is not the basis for the unity of the church. Rather, the unity of the church is found in the living presence of Jesus Christ in the Christian community. This presence is celebrated in the Eucharist, which is a symbol of the unity of the church in spite of the different ways in which it has been understood and practiced. The unity of the church is found ultimately in the living presence of Christ promised to his followers: "For where two or three gather in my name, there I am with them" (Mt 18:20 NIV). By the gift and witness of the Spirit, Jesus Christ is not only the example of Christian life and service but also a living presence in the midst of the Christian community.

Missional Christology does not seek a single, normative conception of the person and work of Christ. It acknowledges the importance of plurality in christological and theological construction while also affirming the centrality of the person of Jesus for all of life. It also resists an anything-goes approach that is characteristic of radical cultural relativism. It instead affirms a committed or "thick" plurality arising from convictions about the nature and character of God as a missionary, the unique role of Jesus in the mission of God, the witness of the Spirit to Jesus and the mission of God, and the trustworthiness of Scripture as the Word of God. Theologian Tom Oden captures this approach well, noting that "the circle of the

Christian tradition has an unusually wide circumference without ceasing to have a single, unifying center. It is Christ's living presence that unites a diverse tradition, yet that single presence is experienced in . . . spectacularly varied ways. But nothing else than the living Christ forms the center of this wide circumference."[41]

As a result, the diversity of contemporary ecclesial contexts and plurality of Christologies have two ready implications for the method of missional Christology. First, missional Christology plumbs the depths of the varied historic traditions and contemporary approaches to Christology. Second, missional Christology uses these historical and contemporary resources to illuminate the way particular communities of faith can participate in God's missional activity in ways appropriate to their context.

CONCLUSION

Missional Christology is always shaped by close engagement with Scripture; but because it is also rooted in the life of local communities and particular social and cultural settings, it will always be characterized by a thick plurality arising from missional Christian convictions. This christological plurality is the result of common Christian commitments and a deep engagement with the diverse particularity and missional unity of the biblical texts. As normative witness to the person and work of Jesus Christ, these texts themselves display christological, theological and missional plurality. As paradigmatic witnesses to the person and work of Jesus Christ as well as to the nature and task of the church sent into mission, they invite even greater plurality than that displayed in Scripture's pages.[42] In this way the church is invited into creative, communal participation in the mission of God in order that the good news of God's love, made known in Jesus Christ, might be extended to every tribe and nation and lived out in culturally appropriate idioms.

---

[41]Thomas C. Oden, *After Modernity . . . What? Agenda for Theology* (Grand Rapids: Zondervan, 1990), 176-77.

[42]For a detailed discussion of this missional plurality see John R. Franke, *Manifold Witness: The Plurality of Truth* (Nashville: Abingdon, 2009).

3

Interdisciplinary Theology

FRAMERS AND PAINTERS

TELFORD C. WORK

Theology is naturally interdisciplinary. How should we do theology in a consciously and responsibly interdisciplinary way?

Westmont College's motto is *Christus primatum tenens*: Christ holding preeminence in all things (Col 1:18).[1] He reigns in all our fields and church traditions, and his supremacy holds us together. Our life as a college—not just a collection, but a *collegium*, a true association of colleagues with a common calling—is an adventurous project of framing and painting our Father's world in his Son's light and Spirit's illumination. Here I argue that theology's unique role in that venture is to frame the painting, so to speak. I trace interdisciplinary theology's biblical basis and character, then explain how it can be done in a rigorous and disciplined way, then demonstrate Christology's interdisciplinary application to the complicated issue of homosexual practice among Christians.

SCRIPTURE AS A PRODUCT OF "EVANGELICAL METHOD"

Theology is like this because Christ, salvation, mission, the church and the Bible are like this. All we really have to do is follow in their footsteps. Consider how Scripture demonstrates and guides the interdisciplinary character of Christian life and thought.

The Old Testament reflects a people's ancient culture and is written in its ancient languages. Its writings display a range of influences from Israel's

---

[1]The motto comes from the KJV, and it inverts the order of the text.

surrounding Sumerian, Egyptian, Persian and Hellenistic cultures. Its collection of writings resists categorization. The "Torah," or instruction, is studded with songs, prayers and unforgettable characters. The Old Testament prophetic texts do not refuse the crosscultural exchange that proved so troublesome to Israel but instead foresee its redemption. The third section, entitled "writings," is a diverse collection of prayers, hymns, erotic poetry, observation, story and (in some arrangements) apocalyptic. In short, the Hebrew Scriptures are interdisciplinary.

The New Testament is, too. It is written in the old imperial language of foreign conquerors. Its "Torah," if you will, comes in the shape of four Greco-Roman *bioi*, or life stories, adapted to focus on Jesus of Nazareth's adventurous faithfulness to the Father and decisive confrontation with the world through its foreign and domestic agents. Its "writings" are mainly letters from the leaders, written in Hellenistic style, of the first few generations of Jesus' followers across the great distances of the Roman Empire. Its counterpart to the former prophets is Acts, which shows that fledgling church rapidly engaging the whole world with its good news, and its "latter prophet" is Revelation, whose crush of Old Testament tropes envisions the undoing and remaking of all creation and the earth's kings ultimately bringing their treasures into a new Jerusalem.

This occasional, contextualized, intercultural and interdisciplinary kind of canon could only have come from an intercultural community on a global mission. The church ended up with its Bible by remaining *apostolic*—faithful to its role in Jesus' mission to reclaim God's rebellious world. Any evangelical theological method—any disciplined approach to reflecting on God and God's gospel—must similarly reflect our mission to represent in all circumstances our Lord Jesus Christ to one another and to the ends of the earth. And that will tend to give it a similarly interdisciplinary character.

Apostolicity involves both something constant and something new, a historical center to conserve and a missional frontier to explore. When the church has abandoned its center and accommodated the gospel to the categories of its audiences, the result has been heresy. Arianism is a prominent example in the history of the church. But heresy has also resulted when the church has abandoned the frontier and sought merely to replicate the gospel as it was earlier understood—the New Testament's classic example being the circumcision party (Gal 1:6-7). Neither strategy could have yielded the Bible we have, because neither one respects God's consistent mission of salvation.

New generations in new situations have embarked on the same apostolic adventure that brought the gospel to them. Subsequent Christian tradition resembles all that we read about in the Bible. Church history features ever more inculturations of the faith, frequent crosscultural misunderstandings, betrayals and distortions (however well intended) of the good news that somehow still found fresh hearings, needed corrections and painful overcorrections, and unwieldy diversity alongside striking continuity.

FOLLOWING IN THE APOSTLES' FOOTSTEPS

Evangelical theological method in theology's wide-ranging contexts, then, involves a cultivated apostolic sensibility—not only realizing what Jesus' apostles were saying and doing but doing it along with them in new settings (Jn 20:21). This involves a spiritual training of our whole imaginations. Let the term *evangelical method* serve as shorthand for that apostolic tradition of forming us to articulate the gospel and its impact in various ways consistent with the canon and with resources from across disciplines.

At its core, the consistent tradition, which was in place long before anyone conceived of formal theological method, amounts to *investigating the gospel's implications for everything*—for every field of human endeavor relevant to Christ's kingdom. Christ holds preeminence everywhere, and (as Michael Polanyi and Alasdair MacIntyre show) all traditions of human learning, arts and sciences and humanities, including theology, share similar epistemic structures and intersecting claims. So Christian theology also involves the converse: *investigating the implications that all these other things hold for the gospel.*

Augustine is the West's most seminal interdisciplinary theologian. The tradition's apostolic sensibility of adventurous faithfulness is well and truly cultivated in him. His *De Doctrina Christiana*[2] famously commends classical reading and speaking strategies for strengthening the church's biblical practice. Yet it also stresses the obvious point that common areas of knowledge are essential to biblical interpretation. His call for preachers to know their flora and fauna, Hebrew and Greek grammar and symbolism,

---

[2]Augustine, *De Doctrina Christiana*, trans. D. W. Robertson Jr. (New York: Macmillan, 1958).

cultural arrangements, mathematics and musical instruments is conventional in most biblical studies or theology courses.[3] Once we admit the relevance of all this ordinary knowledge to understanding the mind of the church, we are already committed to a deeply interdisciplinary theology.

However, even as Augustine illustrates his commonplace observation, he hits a snag:

> Ignorance . . . renders figurative expressions obscure, as when we do not know the nature of the animals, or minerals, or plants, which are frequently referred to in Scripture by way of comparison. The fact so well known about the serpent, for example, that to protect its head it will present its whole body to its assailants—how much light it throws upon the meaning of our Lord's command, that we should be wise as serpents; that is to say, that for the sake of our head, which is Christ, we should willingly offer our body to the persecutors, lest the Christian faith should, as it were, be destroyed in us, if to save the body we deny our God![4]

Today's readers will applaud the first sentence but puzzle at the second. Does a snake keeper really understand Jesus' symbolism better than the reader who simply notices the allusion to that shrewd serpent from Genesis 3:1?

We can imagine poor Augustine puzzling over Jesus' approval of shrewdness, with its legacy of universal death. *No, it can't mean that! Then what does it mean?* Stumped, the bishop turns to his worldly learning. There he identifies a meaning that both smoothes the theological wrinkle and edifies the faithful.[5] *Snakes defend their most critical part! That must be Christ in us, made vulnerable by our fear of persecution!* His reasoning, so straightforward and clear to him, demonstrates a great peril and challenge facing interdisciplinary theology.

Augustine reads Matthew 10:16 in a brilliant and stunningly observant way that also honors the context of Matthew 10:17-22. But this clever suggestion is a classic instance of the overinterpretation of the overeducated. Human beings are pattern finders who naturally reason by making connections. The more one knows, the more connections one perceives—whether

---

[3]Ibid., 2.28.42.
[4]Ibid., 2.16.24.
[5]These considerations are precisely the "rule of faith" and "rule of charity" that he will commend later in the book.

or not they actually have a basis in reality. Interdisciplinary thinkers can see significance that isn't there.

In Augustine's own theology, the tendency to overinterpret often shows up as unwarranted allegories and spiritual interpretations that are informed more by his Late Antique Greco-Roman sensibilities than by the apostles' first-century Jewish ones. He should have paid closer attention to Matthew's immediate context. There Jesus warns his missionaries to flee persecution rather than throw their bodies at it (Mt 10:23). Jesus' mixed metaphor of sheep, wolves, serpents and doves calls his disciples to perceive the deeper meaning of the treatment they will receive (Mt 10:24-25) and to be ready for the demands it will make on their character (Mt 10:19). Zoology is not the key here; a little biblical literacy and close reading will do.

Augustine's approach helped create the elaborate medieval world that Europe's reformers dismantled. They were not against interdisciplinary theology as such; they employed classical, scholastic and Renaissance learning extensively. Their complaint was that Roman Catholicism had cluttered the pure gospel with temporal human traditions and adulterated it with "other gospels" fabricated by idolatrous human hearts. Whether or not their fears were well founded, they demonstrate a legitimate self-critical reaction to interdisciplinary excess. Syncretism is interdisciplinary theology gone bad—no longer disciplined by the gospel, either because it has become a generally undisciplined hodgepodge or a vassal of some other disciplinary lord than the apostolic faith.

How do we distinguish the good from the bad?

DISCIPLINING INTERDISCIPLINARY THEOLOGY

Theology is not just another discipline with a scope and tool set that transfers to any other academic field, even philosophy. The kingdom of God penetrates every other domain of human inquiry. In every one it manifests signs of Christ's present reign and identifies their connections with all others. This makes Christ known as Lord of lords. Its domain is intrinsically and uniquely comprehensive: God *and* creation, general revelation *and* special revelation, visible *and* invisible, old *and* new. Yet the nature of Christ's reign does not subsume other disciplines into theology. When theology's domain and specific character are truly appreciated,

Christian theology can be richly interdisciplinary, while other disciplines can be free to be their best selves.

One of the conflict narratives in the Gospels suggests such an interrelationship among the disciplines. Jesus points to the presence of "something greater than" both Solomon, the scientist of so-called general revelation, and Jonah, the prophet of "special revelation" (Mt 12:41-42). Solomon and Jonah personify two different forms of learning. Ordinary knowledge, in this case Solomon's natural learning, regards the world as an object for discovery, open in principle to all with the patience and perception to expose its nuances. Then there is the "apocalyptic" or revealed knowledge of Jonah, unveiling what is otherwise obscure so we can receive it in faith.[6] The contrast is not complete; they are complementary forms of wisdom that authorize any wise person to condemn Jesus' many unperceptive opponents.

What surpasses both the general and special revelation with which Jesus' audience was familiar is the kingdom of God. Its phenomena are "signs of the times" (Mt 16:1-3) that signal an eschatological fulfillment greater than the various natural *and* supernatural signs that anticipated it. This allows us to make distinctions besides general versus special revelation: The kingdom pertains to the new and eternal, not just the old and transient. The kingdom is mysterious to us and ever surprising, whereas both ordinary and prior revealed knowledge grow familiar (even Jonah's prophecy came as no surprise: Jon 4:2).

Christian theology thus explicates the kingdom's *framework* for old creation. This framework is doubly *obscure*: unveiled rather than ordinary, and eschatologically new rather than protologically old. *What* it frames is knowable through many and varied other disciplines, from natural and behavioral sciences to social sciences and humanities—even philosophy and religion. All these fields feature genuine knowledge and integrated bodies of wisdom.

Extending this metaphor of framing and painting articulates the integrity and interconnectivity of the disciplines. Just as a frame does not cover or dominate the painting it surrounds but presents and perfects it, so Christian theology cannot teach us everything and is not meant to.[7] An

---

[6]I expand on this observation in "What Have the Galapagos to Do with Jerusalem? Scientific Knowledge in Theological Context," in *Science and the Spirit*, ed. James K. A. Smith and Amos Yong (Bloomington: Indiana University Press, 2010), 15-33.

[7]If theology's role in this metaphor seems too modest, a bolder alternative is that of a body's skeleton and the differentiated and interrelating organs of flesh it frames from within (cf. Ezek 37:1-14).

artwork's mount board and frame hold its shape, protect it, interpret it and enhance it. Christian theologians perform the similar service of displaying the true shape and significance of all things in the kingdom's domain. The painters who profess other fields of learning refine our faculties for understanding creation and its goal, because it is in our old categories' midst that we perceive the presence of the new. This is why King Solomon and his student the Queen of Sheba are among the gospel's indispensable heralds and authoritative interpreters, along with Jonah the reluctant prophet and his unwelcome disciple, the city of Nineveh (Mt 12:41-42).

Theology and other learned traditions depend on one another. Christian theology specializes in the wisdom who is Jesus Christ, and many of us framers are dreadfully ignorant of Solomon's wisdom (and even Jonah's, now that Old Testament scholarship is in many ways its own discipline). We need to be careful not to lord it over our colleagues in other disciplines by warping, ruining or covering over their paintings—by dominating or neglecting fields whose insights complicate and contradict our streamlined and abstract visions.

Painters, whether specialists in the sciences or humanities, similarly overstep when they treat their fields or methods as frames for a comprehensive or totalizing account of reality. When one discipline subsumes a rival framework, it sets a created principality over the ascended Lord of all. Healthy interdisciplinary theology safeguards against intellectual imperialism. It recognizes that no one discipline provides a comprehensive account of life in this world. Not even theology, whose work would remain empty and irrelevant without the other disciplines in whose particular domains the kingdom manifests those signs of Christ's universal lordship.

Academic reductionism is widespread among framers and painters alike. When any discipline usurps the role of another, the significance of the whole is distorted.[8] Theology that is truly interdisciplinary retains the integrity and complementarity of both the framers' and the painters' disciplines. Solomon remains a philosopher and a scientist who studies creation in its own right rather than either reducing these to handmaidens of theology or

---

[8]In *De Doctrina Christiana* I.4 and II.20, Augustine describes it this way: the signs no longer point to the things they truly signify and no longer convey their realities, and we become trapped in a world of illusory idols.

magnifying them into a theory of everything. It is this very expertise that readies him to recognize genuine knowledge when he sees it, even if he must rely on the good news to appreciate its full significance.

HOMOSEXUALITY: AN INTERDISCIPLINARY CASE STUDY IN CHRISTOLOGY

Framing and painting do not follow an all-purpose formula for interdisciplinary theology, let alone a list of steps. They interact in dialogues that are shaped through specific occasions, particular church traditions (in my case a broadly evangelical-Pentecostal one), and the relevant disciplines. A successful project achieves *coherence, completeness, insight, elegance* or beauty and especially *fruitfulness.* The dialogue will not be easy; agreement will not just fall into place among disciplines developed in competition, conflict and isolation. A finding will suggest a new direction here or pose a problem there; editorial discretion will need to prioritize among endless possibilities.

A case study illustrates this dynamic and dialogical process in an application of Christology that quickly takes on an interdisciplinary character: the issue of homosexual practice among Christians. I am not choosing this issue to take a stand on gay marriage or some other item on America's contemporary social agenda. My purpose is to engage an obviously contextualized issue with a deep christological foundation whose discussion in academic evangelical circles quickly moves to hermeneutical, theological and interdisciplinary questions.

The "Foursquare Gospel" of the Pentecostal denomination by that name refers to Jesus as Savior, Baptizer with the Holy Spirit, Healer and Coming King. It does not confine Christology to doctrines such as incarnation and atonement. Foursquare Pentecostals ground their theological legitimacy in Hebrews 13:8: "Jesus Christ is the same yesterday and today and forever" (NIV). Evangelicalism is also christologically centered, in the good news of Jesus Christ. David Bebbington offers four common features of the evangelical movement that together distinguish it from other streams of Christianity.[9] They are: a special respect for the Bible as the Word of God,

---

[9]David W. Bebbington, *Evangelicalism in Modern Britain* (London: Routledge, 1989), 2-3.

a theology centered on the cross of Jesus as an atoning sacrifice, a conviction that lives need to be changed by the power of the good news, and a stress on expressing the good news in personal and ecclesial effort. These two sets of four do not coincide perfectly, but they provide correlated christological and evangelical-Pentecostal categories that inform a constructive and interdisciplinary treatment of homosexuality. As we shall see, in each one a different theological focus comes to the fore: the doctrines of Scripture, atonement, the last things and the church, respectively.

Biblical. The Foursquare Gospel frames Jesus as Spirit-baptizer with this verse: "You shall receive power when the Holy Spirit has come upon you; and you shall be witnesses to Me" (Acts 1:8 NKJV). The biblical writers' overriding concern is to support their communities' definitive identity in God's mission, promised to the patriarchs and fulfilled in Jesus Christ. Readers who treat the Word of God as nothing but a book of rules or source of inspiration, or even proclamation of unconditional pardon, are substituting foreign frameworks in which biblical passages no longer accomplish their intended redemptive purposes. Holy Scripture is a herald of the good news of God's kingdom, a record of its impacts, a medium of its saving grace and a disciplinarian of its disciples. It is bound inextricably with the Son who receives it as heir, obeys it as his Father's voice, speaks and interprets it with unparalleled authority, and authorizes it through his inspired witnesses.[10]

It is common enough to tie homosexuality either to Scripture or to alternative fields like biology. It is rare to do both at the same time, let alone treat them all in terms of Christology. When we do, what may have seemed simple and straightforward can become complicated and elusive.

In more than five years regularly attending a Pentecostal church, I never heard the topic of homosexual activity addressed. Biblical writers hardly ever mention it, making it in Richard Hays's words "a minor concern."[11] When they do, they place it alongside a number of other common human activities that are problematic for both old and new creation, unfaithful to Christ and incompatible with the good news. Hays observes that the few

---

[10]Telford Work, *Living and Active: Scripture in the Economy of Salvation* (Grand Rapids: Eerdmans, 2001).
[11]Richard B. Hays, *The Moral Vision of the New Testament* (San Francisco: Harper, 1996), 381.

biblical passages that speak to the practice all condemn it, viewing it over against the sexual norms of personal abstinence and marital chastity.[12]

Contemporary Christian traditions, nevertheless, have treated the scanty biblical material in ways that lead to diametrically opposite stances on homosexuality in the church.[13] While interdisciplinary theology must take into account relevant biblical material and interpret it accurately in context, what material counts as relevant is not self-evident. If the texts agree, how can they be taken in such different ways? Because framing and painting are matters of judgment.

We might extract abstract principles from Bible passages—for instance, "honor the structures of created human existence"—then use these principles to formulate rules of behavior. But what are those principles? If science supports the hypothesis that homosexuality is not a *perversion* of human nature but one *expression* of it, then the Torah's prohibitions and their New Testament appropriations might be reversed. A number of mainline Protestant theologians do just this, relocating homosexuality from under the doctrine of sin to under the doctrine of creation, as an original feature of human life that can be compatible with discipleship to our fully human incarnate Lord.[14]

Or, with liberation theologians, we might note that the Spirit's anointing on Jesus brings good news of deliverance and freedom for the oppressed (Is 61:1 in Lk 4:18) and abstract from the canon a principle of liberation—for instance, that God's mission is liberation from injustice. We might construe God's invitation of Gentiles into the church or Paul's gentle dismantling of the logic of Christian slavery in Philemon as an agenda of ever-expanding inclusion of humanity in all its diversity into the body of Christ. We might then envision other such revolutions. Social-scientific analysis then becomes

---

[12]Ibid., 391, 395. The texts situate homosexual activity in cultural contexts of ancient Near Eastern and then Greco-Roman cosmology as well as sexual practice, reflecting their senses of what is "against nature" but not merely conforming to those cultures' mores (387). They treat it along with other practices, freely chosen or not, as an outcome and symptom (along with self-righteousness, judgmentalism, and hypocrisy—1 Cor 6:7) of the deeper condition of "human fallenness," rather than being itself a root (386, 388).

[13]For one catalog of some influential approaches to biblical material in theology, see David Kelsey, *The Uses of Scripture in Modern Theology* (Philadelphia: Fortress, 1975).

[14]See Serene Jones and Clark M. Williamson, "What's Wrong with Us? Human Nature and Human Sin," in *Essentials of Christian Theology*, ed. William C. Placher (Louisville: Westminster John Knox, 2003), 133-81.

an appealing tool to identify further agenda items: sexism, class struggle, ethnic bigotry and racism—and perhaps "homophobia" and "heteronormativity." Like many who support women's ordination on liberationist lines, in similar fashion interpreters might set aside, along "biblical" lines, both the biblical prohibitions and nineteen centuries of tradition.[15]

Or we might abstract the principle that homosexual activity falls short of the kingdom of God. We might heed Jesus' endorsement and intensification of the Torah's moral law in the Sermon on the Mount and elsewhere, consider that the Spirit is at odds with the flesh and its desires (Gal 5:17-21), and reaffirm homosexual activity's traditional prohibition in the church, however empathetically. In that case, nontheological disciplines become relevant in very different ways. In staking out such a position, Hays draws on categories of sociology, communication and literary theory to sketch what he calls the New Testament's "symbolic world."[16]

All these approaches rely on Scripture for materially christological reasons. All follow Augustine's methodological playbook to tie human sexuality to Christ's character and mission. And their results quite obviously contradict. This method of shifting focus from the gospel's obscure framework to Christ's many domains and back is not some kind of formula that automatically obtains consistent results. It demands sound faculties of theological and hermeneutical judgment to guide interpretive instincts.[17]

Cross centered. The New Testament writers' interpretive judgment was formed especially through the cross. So an interdisciplinary theological project needs to determine the relevance of Jesus' death and resurrection to all concerned. In the case of homosexual activity, we have a clear biblical example of atonement's application.

Christ our Savior "was wounded for our transgressions" (Is 53:5 informs this element of the Foursquare Gospel). Both Pentecostalism and broader evangelicalism focus on the cross of Jesus Christ as an atoning sacrifice. "You

---

[15]If such a trajectory of liberation is imposed on the canon rather than truly discerning its course in the history of salvation, then a foreign logic, "another gospel," is doing the framing. This is a serious vulnerability in liberation theology. See William Webb, "A Redemptive-Movement Hermeneutic," *Journal of the Evangelical Theological Society* 48, no. 2 (June 2005): 331-49.

[16]Hays, *Moral Vision of the New Testament*, 396.

[17]David Yeago demonstrates this in "The Bible," in *Knowing the Triune God*, ed. James J. Buckley and David S. Yeago (Grand Rapids: Eerdmans, 2001), 49-93.

were bought at a price," Paul pleads twice in 1 Corinthians 6–7 (NIV). In paying for our sins, Jesus bought *us*. The many matters in 1 Corinthians, including sexual morality, are only a few of that purchase's limitless consequences.

The world roots identity in individual achievement, personal taste, ethnicity, profession, the family name, political party, alma mater, physical appearance, territory of origin, circle of friends, sheer imagination—and sexual orientation. Christians affirm *the* ultimate identifying community of Christ's body. Whether or not evangelicals embrace John Calvin's influential soteriology of penal-substitutionary atonement, and however much or little we borrow from other analyses of the cross, we agree with the broader ecumenical tradition that Christ's atoning work reforges his followers' identity. Our affiliations remain significant, but these designations no longer define us. Being bought by Christ subordinates every other identifier.

Our many social affiliations' continuing power makes even the honorable designations potentially problematic and the dishonorable ones dangerously contradictory. "You were bought at a price; do not become slaves of human beings" (1 Cor 7:23 NIV): litigious competition, ethnic striving through circumcision or its reversal, entering into slavery and even marriage can be tragic capitulations to lesser powers. "You were bought with a price. So glorify God in your body" (1 Cor 6:20 RSV): prostitution and all other sexual immoralities, including the homosexual varieties Paul mentions, betray our shared bodily relationship with Christ in the Holy Spirit.

The Corinthians are inclined to detach their lives from the kingdom's framework, or to reframe their lives according to some other paradigm. The results are community chaos and reassimilation into their old, doomed world. Paul labors to expose the far-reaching implications of being bought to every aspect of his readers' personal lives. He perceives spiritual significance in the Roman judicial system, which after all condemned its own Lord. He perceives spiritual significance in Christian partisanship and elitism. He sees that marriage is fraught with perilous spiritual power and that immorality of all kinds is spiritually destructive—particularly varieties that the church takes casually. His apostolic perception connects "private" behaviors with church-wide consequences of blessing or suffering. However the gospel *does* frame homosexual (and every other) behavior, it does not just "live and let live." Because we share the Corinthians' inclination to reframe our behaviors, we are in their position to heed Paul and frame as he does, discerning the relevance of Jesus' cross-centered story to every corner of our lives. Atonement's far-reaching implications beg our attention to the matter of conversion, the next element in both the Foursquare Gospel and Bebbington's evangelical profile.

Conversion minded. Paul's need to write chapter after chapter of occasional, interdisciplinary theology demonstrates that new identity in itself is not enough. He must remind his erring audiences that "you were washed, you were sanctified, you were justified" (1 Cor 6:11 NIV). Along with Matthew, Foursquare Pentecostals see "Jesus the Healer" taking our iniquities and bearing our diseases in healing the sick and casting out demons (Is 53:4 in Mt 8:14-17, cited in the Foursquare Gospel).

How does this apply to our topic? Christian attempts to treat homosexual orientation as an illness or even as demonic have largely failed and discredited the would-be healers. On the other hand, Hays testifies that "there are numerous homosexual Christians . . . whose lives show signs of the presence of God, whose work in ministry is genuine and effective."[18] Just what may a converted life look like? That is the topic of a lively debate. Lifelong struggle with incompatible desires, aided by the Word and sacraments and by discreet pastoral guidance? Victorious celibacy? Some—perhaps modest—change in orientation? Unions in the church? Gay marriage? Eligibility for special church offices, including leadership, regardless of sexual practice?

Such positions are always drawing on some vision or set of visions of "the good life." And these visions are always embedded—even, as we have seen, in the Bible itself—in specific cultures, in a particular eschatology that frames our lives with the kingdom's tasks and purposes, and in a particular anthropology that articulates what it means to be human in those temporal and eternal contexts. The interdisciplinary conversation is unavoidable. So is the hard work of theological framing and disciplinary painting.

With the rest of the New Testament, Paul's eschatology stresses able service in Christ's coming reign. This is a neglected frame of reference for Christian morality. Too many Christians reduce conversion and ethics to standards of guilt and assert prejudgments that violent criminals, idolaters, homosexuals

---

[18]Hays, *Moral Vision of the New Testament*, 398.

and other moral transgressors "are going to hell." Paul issues different warnings: "Do you not know that the saints will judge the world? . . . Do you not know that the wrongdoers will not inherit the kingdom of God?" (1 Cor 6:2, 9 NIV). Conversion's focus is not heaven or hell, but Christ's kingdom; not just entering but inheriting; not bliss or torment, but service or uselessness; not innocence or guilt, but readiness or unreadiness to reign with him. Like Jesus in the Gospels, Paul dwells on the present health of Christ's body and its readiness for Christ's future tasks. Christology frames issues of homosexuality in the healthiest possible way: *How are our bodies readied (or not) for the eschaton? In light of the biblical witness, is homosexual activity (perhaps in our context, perhaps in every context) problematic for present and future Christian service? If so, how? If not, why not?* Only specifically Christian theology is equipped to pose these framing questions.

Then, respecting eschatology's framing of the good life, how do we paint its details? One way to begin addressing issues of such complexity is drawing up an inventory of the most relevant topics and disciplines.

Healing's or conversion's relevance to homosexuality is so contentious that it may be best to set the topic aside temporarily and turn to *other* items on Paul's vice lists in 1 Corinthians 6:9-10 and 1 Timothy 1:9-10. There we find behaviors of great interest to the fields of psychology, sociology, politics, history and the arts. Idolatry, aggression, sexual passions, abuse of power, deception, contempt and substance abuse are an interdisciplinary cornucopia. So are the virtues that cry out nearby: love, sincerity, trust, peace, godliness, patience and all the rest of the world's purest longings and the church's prayers.

One of those items, aggression, is much more prominent in Paul's ethical teaching—perhaps in part because of his personal history of it. Here physiology, gender, genetics, development, environment, culture, circumstance and habituation all mingle in complicated ways. Neuroscience is casting new light on many of these. So both theology's framing work and insights from other disciplines are essential to grasping aggression's character and full significance. Violence's associations with drunkenness, culture and gender are visible in the Scriptures, but others are not. A major factor in the American violent crime rate's rise to its 1991 peak may have been lead poisoning.[19] Debates swirl over the role of other factors such as gaming, social media, employment, nutrition, availability of weapons and education. These do not make aggression any less relevant to Christ's sanctifying work than the factors already mentioned in Scripture. But they do inform it in possibly new ways. For instance, how should a church community treat aggressive members who may be victims of fetal alcohol syndrome or exposure to lead, or whose MAO-A-related genes might predispose them to such behavior? How is Jesus their healer and ours? Churches think pastorally through such matters all the time. We pay similar, if uneasy, attention to the various possible factors playing into homosexual orientation: genetics, gene expression, fraternal birth order, hormonal exposure *in utero*, developmental experiences such as childhood gender nonconformity and abuse, culture, and habituation, in much more elusive and probably combined ways.

The human trait of aggression is, so to speak, a double-edged sword. It is often biologically useful and regarded as appropriate in certain contexts in both Scripture and later Christian tradition, where it is sometimes extolled as a divine trait as well. In soldiers who lay down their lives for others, and above all in the Lamb (Rev 17:14), it coexists with altruism, patience and self-control. But human aggression goes powerfully wrong. Right after 1 Timothy 1's vice list we find Paul's confession that he is the worst of sinners. He does not rationalize or excuse his actions. He only pleads that Christ mercifully and patiently saved him.

In Philippians 3:6, Paul counts the zeal that led him to persecute the church as *an asset*. Zeal is a quality associated with aggression that Jesus can heal and use along with Paul's rabbinic training and fleshly standing as a Hebrew. Disordered zeal made Paul a murderer and an enemy of the cross; redemption made the murderer a cruciform apostle (Phil 3:10-11, 17) and a warrior against principalities rather than flesh (Eph 6:12).

Christ reigns over his body and is visible there, so we should expect similar transformation of lives characterized by any of the other activities on Paul's vice lists (1 Cor 12:5). Their perfecting is Christ in them (Col 1:27-28), so

---

[19]For statistics on US violent crime rates, see Uniform Crime Reporting Statistics, U.S. Department of Justice, Federal Bureau of Investigation, www.bjs.gov/ucrdata/Search/Crime/State/Stateby State.cfm (accessed April 12, 2016).

their stories are studies of Christ's saving work that disclose his mystery (Col 2:2-3).[20] Disciplines from literature to history to psychology study all kinds of admirable transformations of human qualities and train us to recognize them in the Lord's saints and saints-in-the-making. The Spirit's sanctification through Christ's reordering cross is the fixed point to which these disciplines can look to frame their painting properly. Whatever the good life is, it cannot just be the old life and it must proceed from his life.

The example of converted aggression suggests the existence of qualities that lie underneath *both* disordered and destructive behaviors and the reordered virtues. Paul's murderous zeal was remade, not annihilated. Might we look for sexual analogues? Even if homosexual practice is disordered, homosexual orientation scientifically correlates with qualities that are advantageous and responsible for at least some of the human race's success, such as female relatives' fertility[21] and even high intelligence.[22] Moreover, people with same-sex attraction are often admired for stereotypically associated qualities (such as artistic creativity), not in spite of them. Indeed, their goodness stands in such contrast with so many other types of people on Paul's vice lists (thieves?! murderers?! swindlers?!) that to a growing number of people homosexual practice simply does not belong on vice lists at all.

Of course, the same can be said for idolatry, another common item on those lists. Once considered detestable and still treated as dangerous (cf. 1 Cor 12:2), today it too sits awkwardly as a "vice" alongside others. American Christians tolerate idol worship outside the church in the broader culture and even forcefully defend its legality, and we condemn our own covetousness as idolatry (Col 3:5) far more consistently than we condemn outsiders' literal idol worship. After church, my family patronized a family doughnut shop with a Buddhist shrine tucked away in the back. We would munch away, free from anxiety about the owners' character or our food's purity. Might Paul have sat with us?

---

[20]Thus James William McClendon Jr. treats the stories of believers as source material for the doctrine of salvation in *Biography as Theology: How Life Stories Can Remake Today's Theology* (Nashville: Abingdon, 1974).

[21]Andrea Camperio-Ciani et al., "Evidence for Maternally Inherited Factors Favouring Male Homosexuality and Promoting Female Fecundity," *Proceedings of the Royal Society B* 271 (2004): 2217-21.

[22]Satoshi Kanazawa, "Intelligence and Homosexuality," *Journal of Biosocial Science* 44, no. 5 (2012): 595-623.

Some Christian patience with idolatry arises from our modern appreciation for hard-won civil freedoms of religion that we don't want to lose ourselves—a thesis worth engaging via history, political science and game theory. Then again, perhaps our reasons run deeper. Consider Paul's generous interpretation of idolatry in Athens, where he frames it as a commendable but uninformed, futile and unjust sign of religiosity that Christ will judge (Acts 17:31). Paul's patience honors the patience of Christ, who longs to turn idolaters into servants (1 Thess 1:9-10). If a Pharisee commissioned to apostleship can be that charitable toward people who systematically break the First Commandment, the same charity is warranted toward transgressors of less prominent rules while Jesus reaches and remakes them.

Active. With eschatology and charity we have already ventured into the last quadrant of the Foursquare Gospel, Christ the Coming King. It leads us to Bebbington's fourth evangelical hallmark: activism, the expression of the gospel in effort. The kingdom is a genuine order of new life breaking in amidst the old. As N. T. Wright puts it, Christian life actively *anticipates* the resurrection of the dead and the life of the age to come with faith, hope and love, through its Spirit-filled participation in Christ's mission.[23] Our deeds paint living Christologies as we come to know the one we follow. The framing and painting that is done here is a high-stakes affair. At stake is the health of a society, the clarity of the gospel message, and the reputation of the church and its soon-coming King.

American evangelicals were prominent in efforts to eliminate practices such as slavery, prostitution, alcoholism, substance abuse and abortion.[24] Whatever the wisdom or popularity of each cause, clearly abolitionists, prohibitionists and abortion protestors were activists for reasons rooted in the gospel. Implicit in their visions, if not explicit, are inherently interdisciplinary political theologies, contextualized to present occasions. When evangelicals regard homosexual practice as similarly destructive of both practitioners and others, their opposition to civil unions and gay marriage fits this classic pattern of activism. So do other evangelicals' efforts supporting gay marriage or nondiscrimination on other grounds.

---

[23]N. T. Wright, *After You Believe* (San Francisco: Harper, 2010), 66.

[24]Larry Whiteaker, *Seduction, Prostitution, and Moral Reform in New York, 1830–1860* (New York: Garland, 1987), shows that evangelicals took the then-unusual position that prostitutes were themselves victims of sexual immorality, not just perpetrators.

In our politicized and polarized environment, such efforts are the most public face of evangelical activism regarding homosexuality. However, Christians are involved in a host of other and quieter services for our King. All this may seem to stray from the theological topic of Christology, but Christ's identity is inseparable from his mission, work and lordship in every domain. Church fathers such as Athanasius did not hesitate to link the demise of pagan practices in the Christianizing Roman Empire to Christ's active reign.[25] The kingdom's *praxis* reflects the King's character, and vice versa.

If the framing doctrines of Scripture, atonement and eschatology are most prominent in Bebbington's other emphases, here ecclesiology stands out. A church is a Christology shared and literally fleshed out (1 Cor 2:16; 3:10-11)—"Do you not know that your bodies are members of Christ himself?" (1 Cor 6:15 NIV)—and a broken church implies a broken Christology (1 Cor 1:13).[26] So the fellowship of saints is naturally Paul's consistent missional concern in 1 Corinthians—"You yourselves wrong and defraud—and believers at that!" (1 Cor 6:8 NRSV)—as it is for the sexual ethics in 1 Timothy, Romans and Leviticus 18. Because this world's time is short, Paul wants us to practice "undivided devotion to the Lord" (1 Cor 7:35 NIV; cf. 1 Cor 7:29, 31). Only through our effortful devotion will we all come to know Jesus to be the world's Savior, Baptizer with the Holy Spirit, Healer and Coming King.

Christian theology's ecclesial focus is an essential corrective in a culture that emphasizes the state, the individual and voluntary associations. Secular self-understanding is not merely an unframed painting but a wall of clashing graffiti. Christ's royal, missional community is the indispensable practical *and* theoretical context for discerning the human flourishing that God is bringing to our conflicted world.

Where is Jesus when people are struggling? Whatever our stances on the morality of homosexual orientation or practice, Christians agree that it is not an easy burden and that same-sex-attracted people often need special support. Extending (and so exploring) Christ's *friendship* and *intercession* is prominent on most churches' official agendas for addressing issues of homosexuality and understanding its realities. Here, painting fields often

---

[25] Athanasius, *On the Incarnation of the Word* 8.55.
[26] Ephraim Radner, *A Brutal Unity: The Spiritual Politics of the Christian Church* (Waco, TX: Baylor University Press, 2012).

lead the way. The arts help people become effective communicators and skilled and empathetic listeners, and narrative is an irreplaceable resource for analyzing life's complexities. Theater, art, literature, music and history mediate essential interpersonal communications for a community's knowledge and welfare.

What does it mean for Christ's body to include sexual minorities (cf. Mt 19:9-12)? Cultural anthropology is skilled at perceiving life's cultural and intercultural dimensions and approaching them fairly. With the recent emergence of gay subcultures in societies where homosexuals had been isolated and closeted, homosexuality has taken on new cultural forms and, as we have seen, powerful social identities. Sociologists point out that cultures provide hermeneutical "scripts" by which members interpret their actions. A widespread American "gay script"[27] trains people to treat sexual orientation as a source of personal identity and adopts a civil-rights paradigm to respond to "antigay scripts" of oppression, shaming, self-loathing and dehumanization of sexual minorities. The gospel begets an alternative to both gay and antigay scripts by identifying a believer not with his or her sexual longings, either positively or negatively, but with Jesus Christ ("you were bought").

Activism in the face of these powerful opposing metanarratives involves the *praxis* of rejecting and fighting injustices perpetrated on sexual minorities, even by other sexual minorities. It sees whole people rather than a script's caricatures. It hesitates to accept a script's conventional terminology and assumptions. It refuses to single out the select sins of "outsiders," or to overlook or tolerate those of "insiders." It shows the same hospitality Christ showed to the zealots, tax collectors, centurions and Pharisees whose lives had been captured by their societies' scripts. Offering Christ's *healing resources* involves the so-called healing professions that cultivate skills in delving—not just listening to testimony, but evoking it and awakening insight that would otherwise remain unsaid and unknown—as well as skills of support. Grounded in both spiritual and psychological principles, the thriving recovery movement is an expression of the gospel's grace and accountability that cultivates its participants' insight into the nature of the kingdom and its King.

---

[27]Mark Yarhouse, *Homosexuality and the Christian* (Minneapolis: Bethany House, 2010).

CONCLUSION

Attending to Christ the soon-coming King of all kings draws this project to a close. He bought his people, reidentified us as his and remade us to serve him now and eternally. Interdisciplinary theology unpacks and demystifies abstract claims such as these by attending to their concrete shapes in specific ways of life, fields of inquiry and cultural settings. It does so through dialogical engagements between our churches' traditions of Christian teaching and the disciplines that are most directly relevant to these various aspects and provinces of the King's domain. It takes more than theology, but not less, to focus fruitfully on topics such as homosexuality—and everything else, because of the nature of the kingdom and its King of all kings—in the full light of the good news.

4

Contextual Theology

GOD IN HUMAN CONTEXT

VICTOR IFEANYI EZIGBO

The language we speak, the clothes we wear, the
way we interact with others are all taken for granted
until we find ourselves in another culture and
then it all stands out like a sore thumb.

LAURIE GREEN, *LET'S DO THEOLOGY:*
RESOURCES FOR CONTEXTUAL THEOLOGY

Each time the gospel crosses a cultural frontier,
a fresh set of intellectual materials is available for the task.
The theological workshop never shuts down;
its work is never complete.

ANDREW F. WALLS,
"THE RISE OF GLOBAL THEOLOGIES"

How should Christians express their understandings of God
and God's action in and through Jesus Christ from and for their own contexts? This is a question about theological method that can only be successfully answered in light of one's view of God, the goals and tasks of theology,
and the scope of theological sources. Questions about theological method

usually raise concerns about transgressions of boundaries,[1] the primacy of a given theological source over other sources, and the adequate use of theological sources.[2] Theological methods are complex in both definitions and applications because disentangling a theology's method from its content is an extremely difficult task since both are intricately intertwined. Also, many theologians borrow ideas from different theological methods. Yet a careful observer can identify an "overriding rationale" that "coordinates the various avenues of approach" a theologian has adopted in his or her theology.[3]

Five tasks will govern this essay. First, I will describe what it is to do theology contextually. Second, I will highlight some of the major turning points in the history of contextual theology. Third, I will discuss the issue of sources and resources in the construction of theology. The fourth section sets forth the rationale for drawing on the human context for contextual theology. Fifth, I will discuss and respond to some key concerns and myths about contextual theology. Finally, I will outline some helpful steps for doing contextual Christology.

WHAT IS CONTEXTUAL THEOLOGY?

Many people who reflect on what "contextual theology" is experience a dizzying frustration as they sift through the disparate, imprecise and competing ideas associated with it.[4] For many contextual theologians, the questions "Is contextual theology a sustainable theological field of study?" and "Is contextual theology a distinct form of theological inquiry?" have become unavoidable. The necessity of these questions stems from the contextuality of all theological claims and assertions. Every theology has a *human context*—an "accent" that reveals the experience, history, interest, bias, social location, culture and cosmological assumptions of the theologian or community that produces it. Every theology, therefore, is contextual!

---

[1]Craig Blomberg, "We Contextualize More Than We Realize," in *Local Theology for the Global Church: Principles for an Evangelical Approach to Contextualization*, ed. Matthew Cook et al. (Pasadena, CA: William Carey, 2010), 37-55.

[2]Stephen B. Bevans, *Models of Contextual Theology*, rev. ed. (Maryknoll, NY: Orbis, 2002), 3-27.

[3]John Macquarrie, *Principles of Christian Theology*, 2nd ed. (New York: Charles Scribner's Sons, 1977), 34.

[4]Some forms of what is today known as "contextual theology" have been variously described as "indigenized theology," "local theology" and "inculturation theology." For discussion on these terms see Robert J. Schreiter, *Constructing Local Theologies* (Maryknoll, NY: Orbis, 1985), 6-16.

But if all theology is by nature "contextual," is it not redundant to speak of "contextual theology" as a distinct form of theology?[5] The sustainability of contextual theology as a distinct way of doing theology lies in how theology's "contextuality" and "contextual theology" are construed. If by "contextual theology" we mean theologizing in a way that elevates human contexts to the status of an indispensable source or resource that shapes (and ought to shape) theology's structure and content, it follows that not all theologies are *really* contextual theologies. In other words, while human context is the component that makes all theologies inherently contextual, it is only when human context is used as one of the indispensable sources of theology (in genuine conjunction with Scripture and church traditions), and not merely as a lifeless stage on which theology is performed, that "contextual theology" is in effect done.

HISTORY OF CONTEXTUAL THEOLOGY: A SKETCH

While "contextuality"—the idea that theology is constructed from human contexts and should be applied to human contexts—is inherent to theology's nature, what is now known as "contextual theology" gathered momentum in the late twentieth century as some African, Asian and Latin American theologians began to question the relevance of Western missionaries' theologies for Christians in Africa, Asia and Latin America.[6] The missionaries were the products of cultures that were deeply conditioned by the Enlightenment, colonialism and imperialism. Some of the earliest Western missionaries failed to acknowledge that a transcultural missionary activity is itself a contextual process: a missionary conveys his or her understandings of the Christian message, which is colored by his or her contexts, to people of a different context. Many of the missionaries lacked the understanding, skills and/or willingness to empower the local Christian converts to do theology with the set of intellectual materials generated by their own

---

[5]Gustavo Gutiérrez has made this point vividly: "Every discourse on faith is born at a precise time and place and tries to respond to historical situations and questions amidst which Christians live and proclaim the gospel. For that reason it is tautological, strictly speaking, to say that a theology is contextual, for all theology is contextual in one way or another. Some theologies, however, take their context seriously and recognize it; others do not." See Gutiérrez, "The Option for the Poor Arises from Faith in Christ," trans. Robert Lassalle-Klein, James Nickoloff and Susan Sullivan, *Theological Studies* 70 (2009): 312.

[6]Schreiter, *Constructing Local Theologies*, 1-5.

contexts. Some missionaries construed Christian mission as an extension of the territorial boundaries of their nations and the theologies of their sending agencies.[7] Many missionaries operated with the derogatory views toward non-Western people that some Enlightenment thinkers promoted.[8] As postcolonial theologians remind us, contact with Western missionaries, colonialists and imperialists has shaped the theologies written by Africans, Asians and Latin Americans.[9]

In the 1800s and 1900s, some Africans such as Bishop Samuel Ajayi Crowther, Garrick Braide and Joseph Babalola confronted the missionaries with the inadequacies of Western theologies for African communities. For many of these African intellectuals, pastors and missionaries, the churches of Africa should be indigenous and self-propagating in their organization, leadership and theology.[10] Theological works that aimed to move beyond merely criticizing Western missionaries for foisting foreign theologies on African Christianity to constructive theologies that dialogued with the experience of Africans emerged in the 1950s and have flourished since then. In the 1960s and 1970s, some African theologians demanded the development of an "African theology whose scope must be sufficiently wide to comprehend the depths of the Christian faith and to interpret it to the people in terms of their understanding and needs."[11]

---

[7]The mission manifesto of Scottish missionary Thomas Pringle highlights this mindset. "Let us enter upon a new and nobler career of conquest. Let us subdue and salvage Africa by justice, by kindness, by talisman of Christian truth. Let us thus go forth, in the name and under the blessing of God, gradually to extend the moral influence . . . the territorial boundary also of our colony, until it shall become an Empire—embracing Southern Africa from the Keisi and Gareep to Mozambique and Cape Negro—and to which, per adventure, in after days, even the equator shall prove no ultimate limit." Quoted in Dorothy Hammond and Atla Jablow, *Myth of Africa* (New York: The Library of Social Science, 1977), 44.

[8]For discussion on the complex relationship between Western missionaries and the Enlightenment, see David J. Bosch, *Transforming Mission: Paradigm Shifts in Theology of Mission* (Maryknoll, NY: Orbis, 1991), 262-345; and Brian Stanley, ed., *Christian Missions and the Enlightenment* (Grand Rapids: Eerdmans, 2001).

[9]See Kwok Pui-lan, *Postcolonial Imagination and Feminist Theology* (Louisville: Westminster John Knox, 2005).

[10]See Lamin Sanneh, *Translating the Message: The Missionary Impact on Culture* (Maryknoll, NY: Orbis, 1989), 130-54.

[11]John Mbiti, "The Ways and Means of Communicating the Gospel," in *Christianity in Tropical Africa: Studies Presented and Discussed at the Seventh International African Seminar at the University of Ghana, April 1965*, ed. C. G. Baeta (Oxford: Oxford University Press, 1968), 332.

In Latin America, lively theological activities erupted in the 1960s as some Latin American theologians (both Protestants and especially Roman Catholics) began to explore new ways to explain the Christian message in a manner that exposed and undid the dehumanizing economic and political structures in Latin American countries. Some Roman Catholic theologians drew inspiration from the Vatican II Council's *Gaudium et spes*;[12] the Protestant evangelical theologians, like their Roman Catholic contemporaries, wrestled with the ideas of Karl Marx as they struggled to embody the life of Jesus Christ in the midst of poverty and dehumanization.[13]

Asian theologians were not left behind during these years of the flowering of theological activities that consciously critiqued Western theological hegemony in the late 1900s. In Asia, important theologians such as Shoki Coe and Choan-Seng Song were rethinking theology in light of their own contexts.[14] Coe, for example, was dissatisfied with the "indigenization" theological model because, for him, it implied "responding to the Gospel in terms of traditional culture" and consequently was in "danger of being past-oriented."[15] Coe preferred "contextualization" because unlike "indigenization," as he understood it, contextualization was "future-oriented."[16] Coe was, however, selective in his usage of "context" in theological construction. "To take context seriously," Coe argues, "does not necessarily mean . . . taking all contexts equally seriously because all are not equally strategic for the *Missio Dei* in the working out of [God's] purpose through history."[17] Despite limitations in articulating how these contexts might be identified, Coe raises a valid point that all contextual theology must address.

---

[12]Gustavo Gutiérrez, *A Theology of Liberation*, rev. ed. (Maryknoll, NY: Orbis, 1988), 7.

[13]Samuel Escobar, "Doing Theology on Christ's Road," in *Global Theology in Evangelical Perspective: Exploring the Contextual Nature of Theology and Mission*, ed. Jeffrey P. Greenman and Gene L. Green (Downers Grove, IL: InterVarsity Press, 2012), 67-85.

[14]Shoki Coe is credited by many as the first theologian to use the term *contextualization* to describe the theological reflections that use human context as a source of theology and not merely a recipient of theologies.

[15]Shoki Coe, "Contextualizing Theology," in *Mission Trends no. 3: Third World Theologies* (Grand Rapids: Eerdmans, 1976), 20.

[16]Coe writes, "So in using the word *contextualization*, we try to convey all that is implied in the familiar term *indigenization*, yet seek to press beyond for a more dynamic concept which is open to change and which is also future–oriented." Ibid., 21 (emphasis original).

[17]Ibid.

GOD, SOURCES OF THEOLOGY AND THE MAKING
OF CHRISTIAN THEOLOGY

God is the problem of theologians, as Jürgen Moltmann has reminded us in an intentionally provocative statement.[18] God is not a "being" or a "person" who can be subject to a scientific laboratory examination or inquiry. God's individual essence is different from the individual essence of human beings.[19] For example, God is self-existent; humans are creaturely beings. One of the major problems the ontological difference between God and human beings poses for theology is how human beings can say something reliable about God, whom they cannot physically examine. Many Christian theologians resolve this theological problem by proposing God's revelation as the basis of human reflection on God's identity and action.[20] This means that Christian theology is grounded not in an *unmediated* encounter between God and human beings but rather in a *mediated* encounter. Human beings, as Christianity teaches, encounter God through God's self-disclosure and action in the world, particularly in the life, experience and work of Jesus of Nazareth.[21]

Theologians should not assume, as Rowan Williams warns, that God's revelation is the "delivery of non-worldly truth to human beings in pretty well unambiguous terms."[22] Proposing Jesus as God's revelation does not provide a shortcut to the mystery of God. "Jesus is God's 'revelation' in a decisive sense not because he makes a dimly apprehended God clear to us," Williams argues, "but because he challenges and queries an unusually clear sense of God: not because he makes things plainer—on the 'veil-lifting' model of revelation—but because he makes things darker. . . . Jesus represents the *immediacy* of

---

[18]Jürgen Moltmann, *Experiences in Theology: Ways and Forms of Christian Theology* (London: SCM Press, 2000), 23.

[19]Thomas V. Morris, *Our Idea of God: An Introduction to Philosophical Theology* (Vancouver: Regent College Press, 2002), 163-65.

[20]There is no uniformity in Christian theologians' understandings of God's revelation. For an introductory discussion on different views of God's revelation, see Avery Dulles, *Models of Revelation* (Maryknoll, NY: Orbis, 1992).

[21]Kathryn Tanner has noted that "Jesus Christ is arguably the centerpiece of every Christian theology in so far as beliefs in and about him mark with special clarity the distinctiveness of a Christian religious perspective and have an impact, whether it is a matter for explicit theological notice or not, on an exceptionally wide range of other issues—for example, the Trinity, human nature and its problems, church, sacraments, God's relation to the world and the character of Christian responsibility." See Tanner, "Jesus Christ," in *The Cambridge Companion to Christian Doctrine*, ed. Colin E. Gunton (Cambridge: Cambridge University Press, 1997), 245.

[22]Rowan Williams, "Trinity and Revelation," *Modern Theology* 2, no. 3 (1986): 197.

divine presence and creativity in the world, and thus the overthrow of our conceptual idols."[23] What Christians *say* about God (theologizing) remains a *human construct*—human interpretations and appropriations of God's action, especially God's revelatory action in and through the life of Jesus Christ. Our theologies are only an approximation—we do not have the ability to explain and comprehend God's identity, action, modes of being and modes of operation exhaustively. All that we see are "only a reflection as in a mirror" (1 Cor 13:12). Given the finitude of human beings, Karl Barth's caution is appropriate: "As ministers we ought to speak of God. We are human, however, and so cannot speak of God. We ought therefore to recognize both our obligation and our inability and by that very recognition give God the glory. This is our perplexity."[24] Christian theologians should do theology with the expectation that their theologies can be fallible and also may never gain an exhaustive knowledge of God and God's action in the world.

There are four major sources (or resources) of theology, which are both asymmetrical and complementary in their functions and roles in theological construction.[25] These are Scripture, ecumenical ecclesial theological tradition, reason and human context. I do not intend to discuss all of these resources in detail because such a task falls outside the purview of this essay. I will only describe briefly what they are and how they ought to function in the construction of Christian theology.

Christian Scripture is the collection of "books" by the earliest Jewish and Christian communities that were written in different genres, from different sociopolitical, religious and economic contexts, and for different purposes. Christian communities regard these books as inspired by the Holy Spirit and also use them as authoritative texts for dealing with issues relating to Christian faith and practice.[26] Scripture functions as a raw material that can

---

[23]Ibid., 202-3.

[24]Karl Barth, *The Word of God and the Word of Man*, trans. Douglas Horton (New York: Harper & Row, 1957), 186.

[25]This means some of these resources can function in other capacities that are not their primary functions.

[26]Several biblical "canons" (the accepted list of books believed to be sacred, inspired and authoritative) exist today. As a Protestant theologian, I use the Protestant canon or Bible and give it a certain measure of normativity. I do not, however, disregard the theology of any theologian merely on the grounds that the theologian's Bible is different from the Protestant Bible, for example, the canon of Scripture accepted by the Roman Catholic Church.

be used to construct theology, a template of theological reflection and a test of Christian identity.[27] The second source, ecumenical ecclesial theological traditions, refers to the body of doctrines and beliefs, particularly those that were the products of the earliest ecumenical church councils, such as the Council of Nicaea (325 c.e.), the Council of Constantinople (381 c.e.) and the Council of Chalcedon (451 c.e.). Ecumenical ecclesial theological traditions function as a theological template. Also, when used properly, they can function as a test of Christian identity.[28] "Reason" as used here refers to the capacity of thought and the ability to think in an orderly and logical way.[29] Reason can function somewhat as a "processor" since it can be used to extract raw materials and also can be used to access, assess and assemble the materials. Reason can also function as a test of the cohesion and logicality of theologies. "Human context" is used broadly here to include cultures, experiences, social location, cosmological assumption, languages and thought forms. Human context functions as raw materials and also as the test of relevance. Table 1.1 is intended to illustrate the functions of these sources of theology.

HUMAN CONTEXT AS THEOLOGY'S INDISPENSABLE RESOURCE

I have proposed that using human contexts as an indispensable resource (or source) of theology is a major distinctive feature of contextual theology. Two interrelated questions may be asked when human context is proposed as one of theology's indispensable resources. First, on what grounds should human context function in such capacity? And second, *how* exactly should human

---

[27]The "understanding of the biblical authors developed gradually," and also "many statements in the Bible, especially those composed in the early stages, fall short of definitive truth." Avery Dulles, *Church and Society: The Laurence J. McGinley Lectures, 1988–2007* (New York: Fordham University Press, 2008), 71.

[28]As Robert Schreiter argues, "Any local theology that is Christian has to be engaged with the tradition, however a church might understand that tradition: the Scriptures, great conciliar and confessional statements, the magisterium. Without that engagement, there is no guarantee of being part of the Christian heritage." See *Constructing Local Theologies*, 95.

[29]Several factors (such as drunkenness, brain injury, sin—see 2 Cor 4:4) can temporarily or permanently impede the use of reason. On the impact of sin on human reason and intellect, Vatican II declares: "It can, with genuine certainty, reach to realities known only to the mind, even though, as a result of sin, its vision has been clouded and its powers weakened." See "The Pastoral Constitution on the Church in Modern World—The Dignity of the Human Person," in *Vatican Council II: The Conciliar and Post Conciliar Documents*, ed. Austin Flannery (Northport, NY: Costello, 1975), 915-16.

context function in such capacity? I will discuss the three functions of human contexts in the formation and construction of Christian theology, which I have highlighted in table 1.1, as a response to these questions.

Table 1.1

Resources	Scripture	Ecumenical Ecclesial Theological Traditions	Reason	Human Context
Raw Material	●			●
Theological Template (refined theological product)	●	●		
Tool (an instrument for processing raw materials)			●	●
Test of Christian Identity	●	●		
Test of Relevance (for contemporary societies)				●
Test of Cohesion			●	

First, human context is a *hermeneutical tool* for understanding, processing and refining "raw materials" for the construction of theology. Contextual theologians use human context to explain and appropriate the Christian gospel message in their communities. Our theologies mirror our cultures, history, experience, social location and agenda. Human contexts furnish and also condition the cognition and hermeneutical tools (such as language, thoughts, concepts and intellectual paradigms) theologians use to structure the content of their theologies. Human contexts, therefore, cannot be neatly separated from the cognitive structures that constrain and inform theological practice. Human contexts shape theological behaviors and practices.[30] Many theologians, including those who are unsympathetic to contextual theology, are becoming increasingly aware that their upbringings (which are shaped by their contexts) inform and shape their theologies. Two theologians might be asked to articulate the primary christological lenses they use to describe their understandings of Jesus' identity and significance. Their answers will most likely differ if they do not share the same historical context. Contextual

---

[30]Justin I. Barrett, "Theological Correctness: Cognitive Constraint and the Study of Religion," *Method and Theory in the Study of Religion* 11 (1999): 331-32.

theology is explicit about the influence and place of human context in the theological task. Context shapes all theology. Not all theologians and theologies, however, recognize the way that their context shapes them.

Consider two examples. A Peruvian theologian who experiences the daily deplorable living conditions of the poor may interpret Jesus primarily from the lens of a "preferential option for the poor."[31] An American evangelical theologian who is wary of the threats religious pluralism poses to Christianity's unique truth claims may be driven by a quest to discover "context-independent criteria" for identifying Christian universal theological truth claims.[32] The difference in these christological lenses does not mean the two theologians cannot share common christological or theological beliefs. Both might commit to the Christian claim that Jesus is God incarnate. The difference, however, highlights how human contexts deeply shape our theologies and what questions we attempt to address. When the Christian gospel crosses a cultural frontier it takes on new modes of expression and being, since it will encounter a "different climate of thought" and new theological questions, which are informed by different political, religious and socioeconomic milieus.[33] Theology mutates: it takes on new forms of expression when it encounters new cultures, cosmological assumptions, social locations and religious traditions. Theologians, like missionaries who cross cultural frontiers, should learn that "encountering the reality of God beyond the inherited terms of one's culture reduces reliance on that culture as a universal normative pattern."[34]

Second, human contexts can also function as *raw materials* theologians can harness, refine and use in developing their theologies, as well as providing the *workshop* for crafting their theologies. The doctrine of divine providence entails that God is at work in the world remaking what God has made. God's providential activity is displayed in the world, which directly or indirectly affects human contexts. "The laboratory space," writes Andrew Walls, "is not

---

[31]Jesus is construed as one who confronts material poverty by being in solidarity with the poor. See Gutiérrez, "Option for the Poor," 317-26.

[32]Harold Netland, *Encountering Religious Pluralism: The Challenge to Christian Faith and Mission* (Downers Grove, IL: InterVarsity Press, 2001), 289-97.

[33]Andrew F. Walls, "The Rise of Global Theologies," in Greenman and Green, *Global Theology in Evangelical Perspective*, 19-20.

[34]Sanneh, *Translating the Message*, 25.

in the study or the library. The major theological laboratory . . . lies in the life situation of believers or the church. Theological activity arises out of Christian mission and Christian living, from the need for Christians to make Christian choices and to think in a Christian way."[35] Human contexts have the capacity to generate raw materials in the form of fresh theological questions and needs. Contextual theologians also use human contexts as a workshop for theology. Particular contexts, therefore, provide both the raw materials and the space to craft theology. Many Dalit theologians, for example, develop their theologies to answer the questions generated by the pathos and sufferings of Dalits, which are the consequences of the theological and philosophical ideas of purity and pollution in ancient Hindu culture.[36] For many Dalit theologians, "Theological reflections . . . need to focus on the sociocultural as well as the economic realities of the life-situation of the oppressed sections in society."[37]

Third, human context is a *recipient* of theology: it is the "audience" for whom theology is performed. Human context, like an audience of a drama, will test whether a theology speaks meaningfully to the perennial needs of contemporary societies. Human context continually generates socioeconomic, religious, political and theological questions for Christian Scripture and commonly accepted theological confessions. Theology, like all fields of study that concern human beliefs and practices, cannot escape constantly shifting human experiences, cultures and social locations. If theology does not address these currents that constitute human contexts, it will become irrelevant to humanity. Christian theology is partly a product of human contexts because it engages the questions human life situations, hopes and experiences pose to the *Christian gospel*—God's vision for the world expressed in the life of Jesus Christ as witnessed by Scripture. The theologies that collapse as a result of the pressure coming from the theological questions generated by human contexts are in need of revision. The changing human context nudges theologians to be on their feet to construct theologies that speak meaningfully to human situations. Theology has a social consequence: it can improve or impoverish

---

[35] Walls, "Rise of Global Theologies," 19.
[36] M. E. Prabhakar, "Introduction," in *Towards a Dalit Theology*, ed. M. E. Prabhakar (New Delhi: Indian Society for Promoting Christian Knowledge, 1988), 2.
[37] Ibid., 3.

human conditions, worth, hope and aspiration. When our theologies are not addressing the theological questions and issues contemporary human contexts are generating, our theologies are in danger of being irrelevant even if they faithfully expound themes contained in the Bible.

Like other fields of study such as medicine, law, social work, anthropology, physics, etc., theology must demonstrate its relevance in language that identifies with the questions human beings are asking about their identity, their meaning and their place in the world, particularly their relationship to other living beings and nonliving objects, visible and invisible beings. While other fields of study are not the judge of theology's meaningfulness, theologians should recognize that developments in other fields of study—which can impoverish or improve human dignity, experience and knowledge of the world—affect theology. Theologians should not see other fields of study as rivals whose existence threatens their own. On the contrary, theologians (like experts in other fields) should become interdisciplinary in their search to improve the quality of the content of their theological answers to the questions people are asking about human dignity, justice, terrorism, health care, sexuality, forgiveness, racial prejudice, hopelessness, the meaning of life, ethical behaviors and other perennial questions about human existence. Theology cannot shy away from these issues because in many societies and cultures it has directly or indirectly inspired these social problems.[38] This is one of the reasons Christian theologians must develop theologies that confront and inspire people to engage constructively with these social problems. Achieving this task is one of the greatest tests of the relevance of Christian theology for our century.

CONCERNS AND MYTHS ABOUT CONTEXTUAL THEOLOGY

As with all fields of study, contextual theology suffers misconceptions in the hands of both its practitioners and unsympathetic critics. I have chosen not to adopt an "apologetic" route in responding to the major misconceptions about contextual theology that usually lead to an impasse. I have favored a dialogical route that highlights how contextual theologians can

---

[38]Only an incredibly careless observer can miss the religious and theological undercurrents in many of the terrorist acts and unjust oppressive structures (e.g., apartheid regimes, caste systems in India) in the world today.

negotiate contextual theology's identity in light of some popular concerns and misconceptions.

Contextual theology's relation to the issues of particularity and universality. Christian theology should attend to *particularity*—the unique history, memory, experience and aspiration of both the community that produces it and the community for which the theology is intended. Christian theology should also attend to *universality*—the commonly shared doctrines and beliefs of all Christian communities.[39] Christian theology, therefore, stands in relation to particularity and universality. But how is this dual relation to be construed? I suggest that the relationship should be dialogical—neither should theology subsume particularity into universality nor should it fail to be both critical and dependent on universally shared Christian beliefs and practices. On the one hand, the unique theological questions posed by a given local community, and the community's ways of appropriating the Christian message, should not be lost in the process of protecting a "universal" Christian theology. On the other hand, the desire to uphold the uniqueness of the theological identity and voice of a local Christian community should not obstruct meaningful conversations with other Christian communities that aim to enrich their commonly shared Christian theological identity.

To achieve this dialogical relation, Christian theologians are to discard unhelpful dichotomous mindsets. A dialogical mindset that is grounded in mutual respect, mutual exchange and mutual critique is a viable alternative to achieve the vision of "theological universals" that do not suppress "theological particularities." The primary goal of this process is not to attain metatheology or a "metatheological framework that enables" theologians to "understand, compare, and evaluate local theologies, the questions each is seeking to answer, and the sociocultural contexts in which each must define the gospel."[40] Rather, the goal should be to utilize the different theological voices coming from Christian communities around the globe to explore,

---

[39]I am aware of the difficulty in constructing beliefs and doctrines that all Christian communities will share. I am equally aware that for every commonly shared belief there is always a possibility of an exception or a dissenting position. Some of the commonly shared views that I have in mind in this context are the belief in God's existence and the belief that God has acted in the life and work of Jesus of Nazareth, the Christ.

[40]Paul G. Hiebert, "The Missionary as Mediator of Global Theologizing," in *Globalizing Theology: Belief and Practice in an Era of World Christianity*, ed. Craig Ott and Harold A. Netland (Grand Rapids: Baker, 2006), 302.

develop and express the magnitude of God's action in Jesus Christ. This was Paul's thoughtful admonition and prayer for Christians in Ephesus (Eph 3:18). While God and God's action in Jesus Christ will remain universally relevant to Christians, our understandings, expositions and appropriations of God and God's action in Jesus Christ may never enjoy such status.

Doing theology contextually can help theologians to see the uniqueness of their theologies, understand how their theologies differ from the theologies of other communities and also explore how they can learn from and teach theologians from other communities. "When local theologians are developing new, locally appropriate forms to communicate biblical meaning," Steve Strauss argues, "their insights will contribute to a richer, fuller understanding of biblical truth for the global church."[41] Many Western theology students, for example, who have not been introduced to South African "black liberation theology" may not know that many proponents of black liberation theologies in North America and Southern Africa share similar experiences and have learned from one another. Such students also may be quick to dismiss the impact of racism, sexism and classism on many forms of Christian theology. The students may also fail to probe the theological questions racism, sexism, classism, colonialism and other oppressive mindsets and structures generate for their communities.

Contextual theology, syncretism and relativism. Some theologians are uneasy with the notion of contextual theology because of what they perceive as contextual theology's syncretistic and relativistic tendencies. Shoki Coe warns that contextual theology should avoid the danger of "becoming chameleon theology, changing color according to the contexts."[42] People often ask me when I reveal that I am trained in both systematic theology and contextual theology, "How is contextual theology different from syncretism?" I was astonished the first time I was confronted with this question. One of the difficulties of the words *syncretism* and *relativism* is that they are not used in a neutral sense. If we define *syncretism* as an uncritical blending of opposing beliefs and practices, which results in the distortion of religious traditions, and

---

[41]Steve Strauss, "Creeds, Confessions, and Global Theologizing: A Case Study in Comparative Christologies," in Ott and Netland, *Globalizing Theology*, 152.

[42]For Coe, contextual theologians can avoid this danger by interpreting human contexts "in the light of *Missio Dei*," that is, "the missiological discernment of the signs of the times, seeing where God is at work and calling us to participate in it." See Coe, "Contextualizing Theology," 21.

view *relativism* as incredulity toward universally binding norms, both syncretism and relativism have no inherent connection with contextual theology. The vast majority of Christian contextual theologians see God's action in Jesus Christ, as witnessed by Scripture, as the universal norm for Christian theological reflections. Shoki Coe has noted that the "true and authentic catholicity [of the Christian gospel message about Jesus Christ] will become fully ours as we not only draw basic power from the same gospel, but as we are committed wholly to serve the same *Missio Dei* in diversified contexts."[43]

On the one hand, Christian contextual theology should not endorse and glorify every aspect of human contexts. On the other hand, Christian contextual theology cannot successfully escape non-Christian ideas and concepts when Christianity crosses a cultural frontier. Contextual theology should subject all human contexts to Jesus' critiquing and remolding works. Here suffice it to say that as the one who should define the identity of all Christian communities and consequently all Christian theological reflections, Jesus Christ can simultaneously critique and remold our contexts. Theology cannot be done in a contextual vacuum—theology is done by human beings, for all God's creatures and with materials that derive from human contexts. Contextual theologians borrow ideas from religious traditions (Christian and non-Christian), albeit not uncritically, to construct theologies that befit the immediate and *relative* needs of their local communities.

Contextual theology and scriptural authority. The dilemma of a theologian who believes that the Bible is God's emissary text and is the "final" authority for Christians in matters of faith and practice is to show how the Bible, which is written by different authors from different contexts, can perform such a function in Christian communities that do not share the biblical authors' historical contexts. Should the Bible at all times and in all situations be the primary source of theology, functioning as the final authority in all matters of faith and practice? Or should human contexts in some cases be the primary source, serving as a corrective to our theologies? Or should the Bible and human contexts enjoy equal status?[44] These questions are misleading because they fail to focus on the different functions and roles the Bible and human

---

[43]Ibid., 23.

[44]Contextual theologians do not share common answers to these questions. See Schreiter, *Constructing Local Theologies*, 25-36.

contexts play in the construction of Christian theology. Rather than defining the relationship of the Bible and human context in terms of precedence and subsequence, I suggest that the relationship be defined in terms of their actual roles in the formation of Christian theology.

Many theologians today are aware that the question, "Is your theology biblical?" is unhelpful in ascertaining the Christian identity of *a* theology when the question is not qualified. The issue is not so much about one's view of the nature of the Bible (for example, whether it is inspired and how to understand its inspiration). Rather, the issue is one's understanding of *how exactly Christian Scripture performs its task as an indispensable source of Christian theology.* When we come to the Bible with the intent to get clear answers to all our theological questions, we must be prepared to be disappointed, for in many cases the Bible confronts us with a quizzical face. The Bible is not a textbook containing an already-made theological answer to all theological questions of all times. Yet the Bible should perform the function and role of a chief test of the Christian identity of all theologies because, as many Christians believe, it is a collection of sacred writings inspired by the Holy Spirit (2 Tim 3:16).

What should theologians *look for* when they read the Bible with the expectation that it will function as a test of the Christian identity of their theology? Since the Bible is not a textbook with an already-made theological answer to all theological questions, theologians should not go to the Bible expecting clear theological answers or systematic dogmas. Also, as a collection of texts written by different people, from different times and for different purposes, the Bible contains disparate (although not unrelated) ideas and viewpoints.[45] Theologians should not use only the biblical texts that support their theological positions and ignore or force foreign views on the biblical texts that contradict their theologies. I propose we read the Bible with the intent to discover *Jesus' overarching vision of the ideal human being's relationship with God and their relationship with other creatures of God.* Some of the implications of this way of reading the Bible in the formation of Christian theology are noteworthy.

---

[45]For example, open theists cite biblical passages to support their claim that God does not know the future exhaustively (see Gen 6:6; 1 Sam 15:10, 35; 2 Pet 3:9), and classical theists also cite biblical passages to support their claim that God knows the future exhaustively (see Is 48:3-5; Acts 2:23).

But before discussing these implications, I will mention two broad, helpful guidelines theologians can use when they search the Bible for Jesus' overarching vision of these ideal relationships: (1) They should recognize that the New Testament does not present a uniform and systematic teaching on Jesus' understanding of such relationships. In many respects the New Testament can only serve as "raw materials" that theologians should excavate and use to reconstruct Jesus' vision of the ideal human's relationship with God and this human's relationship with other creatures of God. (2) The New Testament contains sufficiently clear concepts, thoughts and suggestions of Jesus that should be used as criteria to test Christians' understandings of Jesus' vision of the ideal relationship between God and his creation. The concepts, thoughts and suggestions include: (a) Jesus' critiquing and redirecting of ancient Jewish cultural, religious and theological traditions (Mt 5:17–6:24; Mk 3:1-6), (b) Jesus' teaching on God's providential care for God's creation (Mt 6:25-34; 7:7-12), (c) Jesus' teaching on human worth and dignity as God's image bearers (Mt 6:25-34), (d) Jesus' teaching on the liberation and empowerment of the oppressed and also on human social responsibility (Mt 7:1-6; Lk 4:16-21), (e) Jesus' teaching on the limitation of human beings' knowledge of God's modes of operation (Acts 1:6-8) and (f) Jesus' claim to enjoy a unique relationship with God (Lk 2:49; 4:43; Jn 10:30; 14:8-9).[46]

I will now return to discuss the implications of my proposal that we read the Bible with the intent to discover Jesus' vision of the ideal human's relationship with God and this human's relationship with other creatures of God. What are the steps that one might follow? First, it is a difficult task to excavate the Bible to identify Jesus' overarching vision of the ideal relationship between God and his creation and between human beings and other creatures. The following are a few factors that are responsible for this difficulty: (1) We do not come to the Bible as a *tabula rasa*; we come to the Bible with the "tools"—presuppositions, beliefs and experiences—that color and condition our exegesis. While it is not impossible, it is improbable, when we read Scripture, to hear something other than the voices that are deeply colored by our expectations, agenda and theological positions. Our contexts shape our

---

[46]There are other themes that I am unable to state here due to space constraints. I believe that the ones I have discussed are probably the most important, at least for this essay.

interpretations of a biblical text because we participate personally in the "life" of the text as we seek to understand its content and goals. (2) Scripture is a collection of books written in different genres and by different authors from different cultural, religious, social and political contexts.[47] Reading these collections of books as a "book"—the Bible—may undermine the unique claims and goals of each book in the collection. (3) Theologians who successfully identify a biblical text's locution, illocution and perlocution, to borrow the concepts of speech-act theory, should also demonstrate the continuing relevance of the biblical text for contemporary societies and cultures.[48] They should show that the text has the capacity to "make [people] wise for salvation through faith in Christ Jesus" and also show its capacity for "teaching, rebuking, correcting and training in righteousness" (2 Tim 3:15-16 NIV). (4) Some textual critics and biblical scholars have also doubted some of the words the Gospel writers ascribe to Jesus.[49] In spite of all these difficulties, I share the belief of many Christians who continue to view the Bible, taken as a whole, as a faithful witness to God's action in the world, particularly in and through the life of Jesus Christ of Nazareth (2 Cor 5:18-21).

The second implication of reading Scripture with the intent to discover Jesus' overarching vision of the ideal relationships among God, God's creation, human beings and other creatures of God is its *christological focus*. We learn from the apostle Paul that Christians should "have the same mindset as Christ Jesus" (Phil 2:5 NIV) and that they should also be people whose lives are governed by the "mind of Christ" (1 Cor 2:16). Jesus Christ creates and defines Christian identity. Rowan Williams rightly notes that "Christian identity is to

---

[47]Kevin J. Vanhoozer, *First Theology: God, Scripture and Hermeneutics* (Downers Grove, IL: InterVarsity Press, 2002), 157-58.

[48]Philosophers of language, such as John L. Austin and John Searle, and some theologians, such as Kevin Vanhoozer, have shown that human beings use "words" to perform three interconnected acts. The first is the *locutionary act*—the actual words or symbols uttered by a person (for example, "Jenna, run"). The second is the *illocutionary act*—the range of meanings of the words uttered (such as a request, an assertion, etc.). The third is the *perlocutionary act*—the resultant action that is conditioned by a person's understanding of the locutionary and illocutionary acts. For more discussions, see J. L. Austin, *How to Do Things with Words*, 2nd ed. (Cambridge, MA: Harvard University Press, 1975); John Searle, *Speech Acts: An Essay in the Philosophy of Language* (Cambridge: Cambridge University Press, 1969); Kevin J. Vanhoozer, *Is There a Meaning in This Text? The Bible, the Reader and the Morality of Literary Knowledge* (Leicester, UK: Apollos, 1998), 201-80.

[49]See Albert Schweitzer, *The Quest of the Historical Jesus*, ed. John Bowden (Minneapolis: Fortress, 2001); *The Five Gospels*, translated with commentary by Robert W. Funk, Roy W. Hoover et al. (New York: Macmillan, 1993), 5.

belong in a place that Jesus defines for us. By living in that place, we come in some degree to share his identity, to bear his name and to be in the same relationships he has with God and with the world."[50] The authors of the New Testament constructed their theologies in light of Jesus' teaching about God and the world.[51] Contemporary Christian communities should also adopt this christological approach to theology since Jesus ought to be the centerpiece of the lives of Christian communities. I should note that no single Christian community on its own can rule on what constitutes the ideal relationships between God and his creation and between human beings and other creatures of God that Jesus models. We need the voices of all Christian communities, and yes, even the competing voices, to accomplish this enormous task.

The third implication is that the Bible performs a *judicial-mentor function and role* in the formation and construction of Christian theology. Like a good mentor, the Bible provides a Christian theologian with an elastic parameter, marking out the lines that define Christian identity while inspiring the theologian to develop and use "nonbiblical" (that is, non-Hebraic and non-Greco-Roman concepts) to explain Jesus' teaching on the ideal human relationships with God and other creatures of God. As a good judge, the Bible rules on theologies that either compete with or remain faithful to Jesus' vision of the ideal human being's relationship with God and that human's relationship with other creatures of God. Theologies that compete with Jesus' vision as testified by the Bible, however true they may appear to be, will fail the test of Christian identity.

JESUS THE REVEALER: RETHINKING JESUS' VISION OF THE IDEAL RELATIONSHIP BETWEEN GOD AND HIS CREATION FOR NIGERIAN CHRISTIANITY

I want to summarize my discussion on contextual theology by applying it to Christology. The failure to do theology that answers contemporary questions generated by human contexts is a mark of a defective theology. And the failure to do theology that is informed and judged by the person and work of Jesus as witnessed by Scripture is a mark of defective Christian theology. Contextual Christian theology brings biblical Christology into conversation

---

[50]Rowan Williams, "Christian Identity and Religious Plurality," *The Ecumenical Review* 58, no. 1 (2006): 70.

[51]For example, see Paul's theologies of hope and resurrection in 1 Cor 15.

with the concrete circumstances of human life. But what is the procedure for doing so? In what follows, I describe three interrelated steps for doing contextual theology. I will use Nigerian Christianity to illustrate the application of contextual theology.

Step one: Diagnostic study of human contexts. Theology students should not only be trained in biblical hermeneutics (on how to interpret the Bible) and theological hermeneutics (on how to interpret theological traditions and positions). They should also be trained in "societal hermeneutics" (on how to interpret human societies). A contextual theologian studies a specific human context (or society) in order to identify issues that merit both theological reflection and response. Many theologians devote their time to answering theological questions their communities (or the intended recipients of their theologies) are not asking. Beginning with a diagnostic study of a specific community enables a theologian to avoid the error of superimposing irrelevant theologies on the community.

Visitors to Nigeria today will notice the conspicuousness of Christianity's presence in public buses, market places, billboards and innumerable church buildings. Unlike in the twentieth century, today Nigeria has become a major heartland of Christianity. A careful student of contemporary Nigerian Christianity will notice that many Christians devote themselves to Christian values but also use indigenous religious frameworks to explain or address existential issues such as illness, barrenness, poverty and diabolic forces (both structural and spiritual). The fieldwork I conducted in Nigeria in 2006 shows that many Christians are aware of this phenomenon. Some Christians see consulting oracles and priests of the local deities as an essential survival strategy. This dual religious allegiance has become somewhat of a *Christian habit!* Some Christians go to native doctors to acquire amulets for spiritual and physical protections, some pastors are believed to acquire spiritual powers from priests of local deities to perform miracles in churches, and some Christian herbalists consult the ancestors through oracles of indigenous deities for knowledge and inspiration.[52]

Step two: Harvesting and utilizing "theological materials" from human contexts, Scripture and ecumenical ecclesial theological tradition to construct theology. This step requires constructive theologizing. The goal should be to

---

[52]For extensive discussions on this issue, see Victor I. Ezigbo, *Re-imagining African Christologies: Conversing with the Interpretations and Appropriations of Jesus in Contemporary African Christianity* (Eugene, OR: Pickwick, 2010), chap. 3.

construct theologies that pass both *the test of Christian identity and the test of relevance.*[53] While most theologians have no difficulty harvesting theological materials from the Bible and theological traditions and using them to construct theology, few theologians care about overtly and consciously excavating and harvesting human contexts for theological materials. Such theologians construe human contexts either as a mere recipient of theology or as merely a stage on which theology is performed. Contextual theologians, however, intentionally and explicitly press human contexts, Scripture and theological traditions for theological questions and materials.

As a contextual theologian with interest in Christology, I approach many Nigerian Christians' dual allegiance to Christianity and the indigenous religions by asking: What sort of theological question or material does the dual allegiance generate for Christianity's teaching about Jesus Christ? In what way can theologians interpret and appropriate Jesus Christ befittingly to address the issue of dual allegiance? And does Jesus, as presented in Scripture, critique such dual allegiance? In *Re-imagining African Christologies*, I argue that the dual allegiance stems from three interrelated quests. They are: (1) the "quest to understand the blurry . . . interrelationship between the spiritual world and the world of human beings," (2) the quest to "maneuver and manipulate the spiritual world" to work in the favor of an individual or a community, and (3) the quest to identify a reliable "medium or person that can function as a lens" through whom one understands the events that happen, especially baffling, unpleasant events.[54] Teachings about the relationship between the spiritual and human worlds, found in both Christianity and Nigerian indigenous religions, are the source of these quests. I argue in the book that proposing Jesus Christ as a "revealer" of divinity and humanity is a helpful way to present Jesus as one who satisfies these quests by simultaneously critiquing and redirecting the actions they generate among Nigerian Christians.[55] I use the word *revealer* in this

---

[53]To pass the test of Christian identity, a theology should demonstrate faithfulness to Scripture, demonstrate affinity with Christian traditions and be Christ centered. To pass the test of relevance, a theology must engage constructively with the questions arising from the lives of the intended recipients of the theology. For more discussions on the tests of Christian identity and the test of relevance, see Victor I. Ezigbo, *Voices from Global Christian Communities*, vol. 1 of *Introducing Christian Theologies* (Eugene, OR: Cascade, 2013), 12-14.

[54]Ezigbo, *Re-imagining African Christologies*, 163-66.

[55]Ibid., 153-66.

context to describe Jesus as *one who embodies true divinity and humanity and conveys his vision of God and humanity by critiquing our preconceived notions of God, humanity and God's relationship with his creation.*

Step three: *Appropriating and applying theology to the studied human context.* A contextual theologian must show how his or her theology befits the context of the intended recipients of the theology. Returning to the issue of dual allegiance in Nigerian Christianity and my proposal of a revealer Christology, what are the advantages of proposing Jesus as a revealer? First, the word *revealer* captures the New Testament representations of Jesus' identity and work. I take my cue from Jesus' "You have heard ... but I tell you" sayings (Mt 5:21-48). These sayings show Jesus' readiness to recognize established traditions (the Torah and its traditional interpretations) and also his willingness to critique and redirect them in light of his vision of the ideal relationship between God and his creation. As a "revealer of divinity and humanity," Jesus "communicates and interprets divinity and humanity for the purpose of enacting a relationship between God and humanity."[56] Second, the revealer Christology model I present is in agreement with the christological confession of the ecclesiastical ecumenical conciliar confessions of Nicaea (325 C.E.), Constantinople (381 C.E.) and Chalcedon (451 C.E.). The councils are in agreement that Jesus is truly God and truly human. Third, contextual theology shows how Christian theology relates to the concrete circumstances of human life. In the example of Nigerian Christianity, presenting Jesus as the revealer of divinity and humanity also has advantages for Nigerian Christians: (1) It helps the theologian to avoid the mistake of disregarding the three quests that drive the dual alliance of Christianity and indigenous religions. (2) It helps the theologian to avoid the mistake of ridiculing the cosmological assumptions of Nigerian indigenous religions as mere superstition and also the mistake of discarding Nigerian indigenous religions as useless vehicles for expressing the Christian message about Jesus Christ. (3) It allows the theologian to acknowledge the three quests and at the same time satisfy them by empowering Nigerian Christians to rethink these quests and their expectations. Nigerian Christians who consult oracles and priests of local deities for

---

[56]Ibid., 153.

solutions can rely on Jesus to satisfy their quests. In this way Nigerian Christians can interpret and appropriate Jesus Christ from their own history and experience and at the same time invite Jesus Christ to critique and redirect their perceptions of God's responsibility to God's creation and their perceptions of the relationship between God and his creation.[57]

CONCLUSION

Theology does not *become* contextual. Theology *is* by its nature always contextual. Insofar as theology attends to human understandings of God's action in the world and also attends to human beliefs, behaviors and responsibilities in the world as God's creatures, it is conditioned by human contexts (historical background, language, experience, social location and culture). Some theologians contend that theology, however, can be done in *a*contextual or noncontextual ways. When theologians fail to attend to human contexts for theological materials and to use these materials to construct theologies, their theologies simply take on the context in which they do their work but are not genuinely acontextual or noncontextual, even if such claims are made. As I have shown in this essay, theology is in danger of being relegated to an esoteric sphere and to being perceived as an intellectual exercise with little or no relevance to human existential needs, if theologians fail to exegete human contexts, identify issues that merit theological reflection and response, and construct theologies that address the needs of the communities for which their theologies are intended. I have also shown that doing theology contextually keeps our theology fresh and relevant to the intellectual, social, religious and cultural issues in our communities. Contextual theologizing also awakens us to the need of listening to and engaging with voices from other theological communities.

---

[57]Ibid., 305.

5

Trinitarian Dogmatic Theology

CONFESSING THE FAITH

PAUL LOUIS METZGER

This chapter presents a confessional approach to theology framed from a particular trinitarian vantage point. The essay proceeds by way of a constructive reflection on the method of the theologian often hailed as the catalyst for a renaissance in trinitarian theology in Western theology, Karl Barth. It brings Barth into dialogue with other representatives of a confessional method, notably Dietrich Bonhoeffer and Colin Gunton, and it situates his work as a critical response to the liberal theological tradition often associated with Friedrich Schleiermacher. The first section sets forth the aim of confessional theology. The second section provides a description of the method in conversation with other practitioners of the method, accounting for strengths and weaknesses. My analysis includes an assessment of Barth's concern to safeguard against the objectification of revelation within the historical process. The third section applies the method to the issue of Christology, illustrating how a more comprehensive consideration of pneumatology strengthens Barth's christological and trinitarian confessional concerns.

THE AIM OF THEOLOGY: A TRINITARIAN METHOD

The story is told of a logician/mathematician at the university where Karl Barth once taught asking him to explain the intellectual basis for theology. Barth responded, "The resurrection of Jesus Christ from the dead."[1] Barth's

---

[1] See the account of this anecdote in Colin E. Gunton, *The Barth Lectures*, ed. P. H. Brazier (London: T&T Clark, 2007), 44.

response flew in the face of the reigning model of rational inquiry of the early to mid-twentieth century West—logical, scientific and historical positivism, which maintained that the presumed meaningfulness of all intellectual pursuits is judged by the canons of analytical philosophy, the natural sciences or history. Barth's response also broke with modern theology's assumption that external foundations serve as the intellectual basis for theological reflection. Early in the *Church Dogmatics*, Barth speaks critically of what he takes to be an overemphasis on method in theology hailing from Friedrich Schleiermacher.[2] Critical of liberal theological method, several items, nevertheless, provide the contours of a Barthian confessional theological method.[3]

To begin, for Barth, method must conform to the confession of faith grounded in God's revelation. Thus Barth's confessional orientation was central to his theological method. From Barth's vantage point, his response to the logician/mathematician suggests an adherence to the rightful subject matter of his own theological field of scientific inquiry—dogmatics grounded in the revelation event whereby *God reveals God by God.* The Father reveals the Son by the Spirit. Revelation is a trinitarian event wherein the Father (revealer) makes known the Son (revelation) through the Spirit (revealedness) in their oneness and threeness, threeness and oneness.[4] Fellow Reformed theologian Colin Gunton claims that Barth's theology was "an enquiry into the possibility of the knowledge of God on the strength of its actuality."[5] Following Anselm's lead, the method that Barth and Gunton each employ is "faith seeking understanding."[6]

---

[2]See Karl Barth, *The Doctrine of the Word of God*, vol. I/1 of *Church Dogmatics*, trans. G. W. Bromiley, ed. G. W. Bromiley and T. F. Torrance (Edinburgh: T&T Clark, 1975), 25-36. The reference to Schleiermacher comes at the conclusion of the critical reflection. See p. 36.

[3]Confessional or dogmatic theology is a general approach to theological method and not equivalent to Barthian theology, which is one particular kind of confessional theology. Barth, however, was the key modern figure who called theology back to its confessional roots. Many contemporary confessional theologians, moreover, work within and carry on the legacy of Barth's theology. This project works within the Reformed and Barthian dogmatic tradition of theology. Neither Barthian theology in particular nor Reformed theology in general, however, exhausts the scope of dogmatic theology. Dogmatic theology can be pursued within any confessional tradition of theology.

[4]See Karl Barth, *The Doctrine of the Word of God*, vol. I/2 of *Church Dogmatics*, trans. G. T. Thompson and H. Knight, ed. G. W. Bromiley and T. F. Torrance (Edinburgh: T&T Clark, 1956), 203.

[5]Colin E. Gunton, "The Truth . . . and the Spirit of Truth: The Trinitarian Shape of Christian Theology," in *Loving God with Our Minds: The Pastor as Theologian: Essays in Honor of Wallace M. Alston*, ed. Michael Welker and Cynthia Jarvis (Grand Rapids: Eerdmans, 2004), 343.

[6]See Karl Barth, *Anselm: Fides Quaerens Intellectum, Anselm's Proof of the Existence of God in the Context of His Theological Scheme*, The Library of Philosophy and Theology, ed. John McIntyre and Ian T. Ramsey (London: SCM Press, 1960).

Barth does not presuppose any prior foundation, not even a historical one, for the development of his theology. While no theologian wishes for theology to be mastered by other disciplines, Barth was especially concerned to make certain that the only foundation is God's revelation in Jesus Christ. Barth maintained that Protestant liberalism's engagement of modernity was insufficiently critical. Consequently, it had allowed certain Enlightenment procrustean presuppositions alien to the subject matter of God's revelation in Christ to straitjacket revelation and make it a predicate of history. In addition to his debate with Protestant liberalism, Barth is a dogmatic theologian operating in the Reformed tradition, which has been engaged in interconfessional dialogues and debates over the course of its history with Lutherans, Catholics and others. The historic confessions of these traditions serve as important foundation stones for theological discourse and argumentation in pursuit of greater understanding and resolution of theological problems and ecumenical tensions in contemporary theology.

As a result, *internal dogmatic considerations arising from theology's subject matter do matter and are critically important for solving all of theology's puzzles.* For example, there is a long-standing tension between Lutherans and Reformed over the relation of the two natures in the person of Christ.[7] The Lutherans have historically maintained that the natures relate directly to each other in the divine person, whereas the Reformed have maintained that the two natures relate indirectly. Barth goes further than many Reformed theologians in claiming that the second person of the Trinity wills "moment by moment" to take the human nature to himself. In this way, Barth further strengthened his Reformed conviction that while the divine "is capable of the human," the human is not capable of the divine. Barth, and to some extent his fellow Reformed theologian Gunton, presents a more indirect and mediated encounter between the divine subject and human subjects in history: contrary to the Lutherans, the divine nature is indirectly related to its human counterpart in the divine person. Barth's particular dialectical handling of the matter in view of Reformed theology emphasized God's

---

[7]It is worth noting that the Lutheran Robert Jenson references this debate as central to his theological discourse with the Reformed Gunton in the afterword to the volume dedicated to Colin Gunton's honor: Robert W. Jenson, "Afterword," in *Trinitarian Soundings in Systematic Theology*, ed. Paul Louis Metzger (London: T&T Clark, 2005), 219-20.

indirect relation to the world through the veil of Christ's creaturely flesh. This move made it possible for him to argue that God is revealed in history without becoming subsumed under history as a predicate that historians can objectify.[8] Although Barth would continue to nuance and develop his theology along incarnational lines as suggested here, he would never abandon this dialectical orientation that is bound up with his actualism. Barth's dialectical framework signifies that God is revealed in hiddenness and hidden in revelation. Barth's actualism means that God's being-in-act is made known moment by moment. Moment by moment God upholds the veiling and unveiling of his being-in-act realized in the incarnation. In so doing, God remains Lord in revelation. Barth's dialectical and actualistic incarnational thrust is central to his theological framework.[9]

How does this subject bear on theological method? Dogmatic theological method as represented by Barth endeavors to start and end with the confession of the faith, namely, faith in the revelation of God through the veiled mediation of Jesus Christ's humanity whereby the Father reveals the Son through the Spirit moment by moment. It moves from that confessional commitment to understanding the rest of life, including theology's relation to history, philosophy and other domains. Barth draws constructively and critically from the sources of Reformed theology in conversation with other Christian confessions—namely the Reformed understanding of the relation of the natures in the divine person and related notions—to develop his theology. In doing so, Barth develops his dogmatic theology in view of a dogmatic or confessional method rather than one conceived according to the canons of secular history, existentialist philosophy or some other framework.

As one can see from this discussion involving Reformed theology, Barth's confessional method entails not only consideration of revelation, which he

---

[8]See Bruce McCormack's discussion of the significance of the Reformed treatment of anhypostasis/enhypostasis for Barth's resolution to his long-standing tension concerning the relation of revelation to history. Bruce L. McCormack, *Karl Barth's Critically Realistic Dialectical Theology: Its Genesis and Development, 1909–1936* (Oxford: Clarendon Press, 1995), 21, 23. This move would set the stage for Barth's ongoing reflections on the relation of God's revelation to history in more constructive terms.

[9]Barth preferred the Reformed model, although he adjusted it to emphasize further the distinction between the divine and human natures. Barth held that the divine person chooses "moment by moment" to take up the human nature to himself. Thus Barth further emphasized the Reformed claim that while the divine "is capable of the human," the human is incapable of the divine. See McCormack, *Karl Barth's Critically Realistic Dialectical Theology*, 366.

understands to be Jesus Christ—the living Word. It also entails consideration of church proclamation or tradition in its witness to Christ through adherence to the biblical witness. In the opening volume of the *Church Dogmatics*, Barth maintains that *the Word of God is in threefold form*: Christ, the living Word, is revelation; Scripture, the written Word, is revelation's primary witness; the proclaimed word of the church is revelation's secondary witness.[10] Christian theology must account for this threefold content of the Word and in a manner that takes seriously the fact that God remains Lord in revelation.

The aim of theology according to this method signifies that theology's form must conform to its threefold content that discloses the trinitarian reality of God in a dialectical and actualistic manner. Given that Christian theology is a response to this dynamic revelation of God in Christ in the Spirit, theology as a discipline of rational inquiry must be true to the object of study at every turn. Every day the theologian must return anew to this threefold content, not simply reforming theology, but *to be reformed daily*[11] by this threefold Word as he or she takes up theological reflection on each and every doctrine of the faith. In keeping with what was stated earlier that God reveals God by God, the theologian realizes that revelation is in control of the encounter, not the theologian. Theology from this Barthian confessional vantage point must ever and always define its own canons of investigation in light of the God who has made himself known and continues to make himself known to us moment by moment in and through Jesus Christ's humanity through the Spirit. In this way, it proves to be in its own supernatural sphere a more natural scientific form of exploration.

True to form, the form of dogmatic theological method in Barth's theology matches the trinitarian content. Barth introduces the doctrine of the Trinity in *Church Dogmatics*, volume I/1. His rationale for giving "this doctrine a place of prominence" is that "its content [must] be decisive and controlling for the whole of dogmatics."[12] This starting point—the Trinity as revealed in the narrative of the Word made flesh—is very different from what Barth saw in the reigning liberal tradition: an ellipse with two foci,

---

[10]See Barth, *Church Dogmatics*, I/1, 111-12.
[11]Barth, *Church Dogmatics*, I/2, 682.
[12]Barth, *Church Dogmatics*, I/1, 303.

which tends to move toward a circle with one center, where the outcome endangers Christ's identity in favor of his exalted humanity.[13] In an effort to clarify this point, let us look elsewhere in Barth's corpus.

In the essay "The Humanity of God," Barth claims that Schleiermacher's theology (along with nineteenth-century theological immanentism as a whole) made humanity great at the expense of God.[14] The concept of God was in danger of being viewed as an infinite projection of human qualities onto the void, as Ludwig Feuerbach surmised. The solution is a dogmatic methodological one: Barth sees his theology from above enabling him to ward off the encroachment of Feuerbach's critique, namely theology as a human projection and the resultant secularization of the entirety of life. For Barth, Schleiermacher and his descendants, as well as Hegel and his tribe, were not able to safeguard against Feuerbach's assault.[15] For if theology begins from below in human consciousness or reason, Feuerbach's critique is compelling.[16] As Barth contends, "To repulse Feuerbach's attack effectively one must be certain that man's relation with God is in every respect, in principle, an irreversible relation."[17]

Schleiermacher conceived the theologian's task as showing that religion and Christian theology have a significant role within the dominant cultural worldview. Schleiermacher's *On Religion: Speeches to Its Cultured Despisers* is an apologetic for the Christian religion to those in German culture who despise the faith, claiming that it is the pinnacle of the very culture they esteem. In his introduction to Schleiermacher's work, E. Graham Waring writes, "Schleiermacher loved that in religion which was alive, and sought at once to show his 'despising' friends that it was not alien to their experience of culture, and to found it in human nature in such a way as to give it independent status."[18] Schleiermacher conceived of himself as participating in that "higher

---

[13]Karl Barth, "Schleiermacher," in *Theology and Church: Shorter Writings 1920–1928*, trans. Louise Pettibone Smith (New York: Harper & Row, 1962), 189.

[14]See Karl Barth, "The Humanity of God," in *The Humanity of God* (Atlanta: John Knox, 1960), 43.

[15]Karl Barth, "Ludwig Feuerbach," in *Theology and Church*, 227-28; Karl Barth, *Protestant Theology in the Nineteenth Century: Its Background & History* (London: SCM Press, 1972), 537. See Karl Barth, *The Epistle to the Romans*, 6th ed., trans. Edwyn C. Hoskyns (London: Oxford University Press, 1933), 236, for Barth's affirmation of Feuerbach's critique of religion.

[16]Barth, "Ludwig Feuerbach," 227-28.

[17]Ibid., 231.

[18]E. Graham Waring, introduction to *On Religion: Speeches to Its Cultured Despisers*, by Friedrich Schleiermacher (New York: Frederick Ungar, 1955), xii.

priesthood" that strives to awaken the slumbering germ of a better humanity, to kindle love for higher things, to change the common life into a nobler, to reconcile the children of earth with the heaven that hears them, and to counterbalance the deep attachment of the age to the baser side.[19]

This priesthood entails the conviction that those who are culturally adept should be truly religious. The flip side is also true. Schleiermacher held that religion, most truly the Christian religion, fulfills the aspiration of cultured humanity to be truly cultured, rather than as sharing in humanity's fundamental crisis and desperate need before God, as Barth maintained.

As a continuation of the predisposition within Schleiermacher to maintain that religion completes cultured humanity, neo-Protestantism focused attention on the pious human.[20] Following the anthropocentric turn in modern thought inaugurated by Descartes and honed and perfected by Kant, Schleiermacher as viewed through Protestant liberal eyes did not develop theology from the standpoint of God's revelation in Christ but from the framework of pious humanity—those who believe in God. Thus, from this vantage point, Christian theology is concerned finally with the individual who believes in God rather than with God in whom the individual believes.[21] Barth maintained that the first form of theology is Cartesian, with its emphasis on the human subject, whereas the second and favored theological framework is non-Cartesian, with its emphasis on the divine subject.[22]

In contrast to the school of thought hailing from Schleiermacher, Barth championed distinguishing doctrinal consideration of the singular identity of the Word, specifically Jesus Christ, from consideration of the believing individual or community in human culture. Still, he later nuanced his understanding and developed it in more incarnationally robust terms. For example, in his seminal and mature essay, "The Humanity of God," Barth

---

[19]Schleiermacher, *On Religion*, 8.

[20]Barth says that "Harnack was obviously speaking for Neo-Protestantism, whose proper object of faith is not God in His revelation, but man himself believing in the divine." Barth, *Church Dogmatics*, I/2, 367.

[21]See Karl Barth, "Concluding Unscientific Postscript on Schleiermacher," in *The Theology of Schleiermacher: Lectures at Göttingen, Winter Semester of 1923/24*, trans. George Hunsinger, ed. Dietrich Ritschl (Grand Rapids: Eerdmans, 1982), 278.

[22]Barth, *Church Dogmatics*, I/1, 190-227. For Barth, the Cartesian versus non-Cartesian divide transcends the traditional liberal-conservative division, since conservatives and liberals respectively often approach the content of faith based on a priori philosophical foundations.

goes so far as to admit that he was wrong where he was right: in safeguarding consideration of God's deity and Christ's identity in his early
years, he had failed to safeguard appropriate consideration of humanity and
God's constructive relations with his human creation.[23] He realizes that his
earlier overreaction might lead unwittingly to the fostering of autonomous
space for secularism to germinate and flourish.[24] In time Barth came to
speak of God's "sovereign togetherness with man"[25]—not a sovereignty over
against humanity (as with certain forms of classical theism) nor a divine
togetherness with humanity apart from God's sovereignty (as can be found
in forms of liberal immanentism). For Barth, "God's deity rightly understood includes his humanity."[26]

Barth sought to make space for the human and secular sphere while also
seeking to guard against promoting secularism and its encroachment on
God's revelation in Christ that constitutes the Christian faith. For Barth,
the actuality of God's revelation in Christ makes it possible for other domains and spheres to be present but never in such a way that revelation
claims are grounded in the secular.

In light of the foregoing conversation, could it not be the case that
many attempts to provide a *secular* basis for theology are actually based
in *insecurity*? As Barth wrote, theologians will actually gain more respect
among lawmakers and the like when we stick to the task before us,
"when we do not worry about what" they expect "of us but do what we
are charged to do."[27] Thus Barth did not seek to give a natural theological
basis for his theology determined by the scientific positivists, or one
founded in experience, as was true for many who saw themselves as
hailing from Schleiermacher.[28] Rather, Barth framed his theology in

---

[23]Barth, "Humanity of God," 44-45.

[24]Ibid., 45.

[25]Ibid.

[26]Ibid., 46.

[27]Barth, *Church Dogmatics*, I/1, xvi.

[28]The popular interpretation one finds in many textbooks contrasting Schleiermacher's "anthropo-
centric" theological method with Karl Barth's "christocentric" theological method has not gone
uncontested. Kevin Hector maintains that the general consensus that Schleiermacher's Christology is low (a "low" Christology thinks of Christ neither as fully divine nor as absolutely unique
as the Son of God incarnate) fails to account for "the crucial role that [God's revelational] actualism plays in [Schleiermacher's] theology." Kevin W. Hector, "Actualism and Incarnation: The High
Christology of Friedrich Schleiermacher," *International Journal of Systematic Theology* 8, no. 3

view of the revelation of the triune God in creation, reconciliation and the promised redemption.

Still, did Barth's approach account sufficiently for the fullness of revelation, which entails Christ's humanity? Barth claims that God gives himself to us without giving himself away or losing himself in the process: "God gives Himself, but He does not give Himself away. He does not give up being God in becoming a creature, in becoming man. He does not cease to be God. He does not come into conflict with Himself."[29] Here we find suggestions of Barth's robust defense of Chalcedonian Christology. Still, how is God's being mediated to the creaturely sphere? Does God engage the world thoroughly from within the historical process or with historical reservations? Given Barth's fear of historical positivism in which revelation becomes a predicate of history, does Barth fall prey to a form of revelational positivism in which secular history becomes at best a predicate of revelation and at worst irrelevant to revelation and/or where theology does not account sufficiently for God's hiddenness?[30] Moreover, are we ever dealing with the humanity of the

---

(2006): 307. The technical details of what this means need not detain us, except to say that in terms of method Schleiermacher does not necessarily build a picture of God and Christ on generalized notions of what it means to be a human believer. While acknowledging weaknesses like Schleiermacher's reluctant Sabellianism, Hector claims that there is nothing in Schleiermacher's Christology that requires the rejection of a robust form of trinitarianism, which also guides the shape of the rest of his theological system.

[29]Karl Barth, *The Doctrine of Reconciliation*, vol. IV/1 of *Church Dogmatics*, trans. A. T. Mackay et al., ed. G. W. Bromiley and T. F. Torrance (Edinburgh: T&T Clark, 1956), 185.

[30]Thus continuing discussions in Barth scholarship relate to wider principles of theological method in general: Did Barth give enough room for human reception of revelation and historical context, or did he merely assume God's revelation as a "given" that remains exterior to humanity? And what then are we to do in our own theologies? It is worth noting here criticisms of Barth related to revelational positivism as well as pneumatology for those interested in pursuing further work on Barth and theological method. Bonhoeffer critiqued Barth for arriving at a "positivism of revelation." Dietrich Bonhoeffer, *Letters and Papers from Prison*, ed. Eberhard Bethge, new ed. (New York: Simon & Schuster, 1997), 280-81. See also pages 328-29. Gunton dismisses the oft-leveled charge of revelational positivism as "foolish" in Gunton, "The Truth . . . and the Spirit of Truth," 343. However, Gunton does criticize Barth for what he believes is Barth's tendency to assimilate the Spirit's work to Christ's work, a point to which we will return. See also Colin E. Gunton, *Theology Through the Theologians* (London: T&T Clark, 1996), 105-6. See also page 115, where Gunton speaks of an overarching Western trajectory of devaluing Christ's humanity in view of a lack of appropriate attention being given to the Spirit, bearing even on the matter of how Christ's sinless human state is conceived. This is a debated subject in Barth studies. Philip J. Rosato argues that Barth is a theologian of the Spirit in *The Spirit as Lord: The Pneumatology of Karl Barth* (Edinburgh: T&T Clark, 1981). Bruce McCormack argues that Barth's earlier attempt at dogmatics—the *Göttingen Dogmatics*—is more trinitarian in scope than the *Church Dogmatics* and "is also more nearly 'pneumatocentric' in that the situation of

man, Jesus, or only the humanity of God, as Gunton sometimes remarked in reflecting on Barth's theology? Before we address possible correctives to Barth's theology involving consideration of Christology, we will need to discuss the broad parameters of the trinitarian method shared by Barth, Bonhoeffer and Gunton as Barth's fellow adherents and important interlocutors of confessional theology, accounting for strengths and weaknesses.

A DESCRIPTION OF THIS TRINITARIAN METHOD

Barth, Bonhoeffer and Gunton approach theology along confessional lines, more specifically from the vantage point of God's revelation in Christ declared by the church. They go so far as to maintain that theology must be done from the vantage point of *post*legomenon, not *pro*legomenon. *Prolegomenon* is defined as a "prior word." It is set forth at the outset of many systematic theologies to indicate what foundations are in place to govern the theological venture under way. *Postlegomenon* is a word offered in response to God's revelation, not one set forth in advance of God's revelation. Murray Rae writes, "A prolegomenon to Trinitarian theology . . . will not strictly be *pro*legomenon, a word in advance of God's speaking [which includes "substantive theological content"], but a *post*legomenon, a word in response to revelation that is enabled by God himself."[31]

In keeping with Rae's claim, for Barth, Bonhoeffer and Gunton, there is no philosophical foundation that precedes consideration of the revelation of God set forth in Jesus. The starting point and ending point is God revealed in him. This *confessional* methodological orientation shapes their theological claims and ethical stances. For example, Barth will not give consideration to God's unity apart from consideration of the particularity of God revealed in Jesus Christ. The christocentric revelation is distinctive of Barth's trinitarian framework. Whereas many instances of prolegomena shaped by natural theology will emphasize such themes as God's unity in light of Aristotelian metaphysics and then proceed to discuss God's triunity,

---

the human recipient of revelation stands very close to the heart of Barth's interests." Bruce McCormack, "What Has Basel to Do with Berlin? Continuities in the Theologies of Barth and Schleiermacher," in *Orthodox and Modern: Studies in the Theology of Karl Barth* (Grand Rapids: Baker Academic, 2008), 65.

[31]Murray Rae, "Prolegomena," in *Trinitarian Soundings in Systematic Theology*, ed. Paul Louis Metzger (London: T&T Clark International, 2005), 9-10.

Barth starts with God as one and three, three and one. All discussions of God's perfections or attributes begin and end with consideration of the Trinity. Barth's theological method is trinitarian throughout from the vantage point of God revealing God by God. The Father is the revealer. The Son is revelation. The Spirit is revealedness.[32]

A trinitarian postlegomenon also includes consideration of Scripture and church proclamation. Due to spatial limits, consideration will center on Christology and pneumatology proper in the development of a confessional trinitarian method. Mention was made earlier that Barth presents the Word of God in threefold form: Christ, the living Word, is revelation; Scripture, the written Word, is revelation's primary witness; the proclaimed word of the church is revelation's secondary witness. Donald Bloesch claims of Barth's view that "there is something like a perichoresis in these three forms of the Word in that the revealed Word never comes to us apart from the written Word and the proclaimed Word, and the latter two are never the living Word unless they are united with the revealed Word."[33] According to Barth, the theologian returns daily to the Word in this threefold form; theology is constituted and reformed constantly by this dynamic revelation event. Bound up with Barth's emphasis on the Word in this threefold form is his insistence that what we see in Jesus is what we get with God. There is no going around Jesus to get at God and his divine perfections or attributes. We see this for example in Barth's *Church Dogmatics*, Bonhoeffer's *Sanctorum Communio*, *Act and Being* and *Letters and Papers from Prison*, and Gunton's *Christian Faith* and *Act and Being*.

For one instance of many that could be offered, Gunton's trinitarian theology of revelation involving interpersonal mediation through the Son and Spirit led him to challenge the tradition modeled by Johannes Wollebius, who argued that "God is known in himself and in his works. He is known in himself absolutely in his essence, relatively in the persons."[34] To the contrary, Gunton

---

[32]Barth, *Church Dogmatics*, I/2, 203.

[33]Donald G. Bloesch, *A Theology of Word and Spirit: Authority and Method in Theology*, Christian Foundations 1 (Downers Grove, IL: InterVarsity Press, 1992), 190. Bloesch will later refer to Barth's connection of this threefold model of the Word of God to the unity within the Trinity involving the Father, Son and Spirit (314n10). See also Barth, *Church Dogmatics*, I/1, 120-24.

[34]Johannes Wollebius, in *Reformed Dogmatics: J. Wollebius, G. Voetius and F. Turretin*, ed. John W. Beardslee III (Grand Rapids: Baker, 1977), 37, quoted in Colin E. Gunton, *Act and Being: Towards a Theology of the Divine Attributes* (London: SCM Press, 2002), 88-89.

maintains, "The three persons are the being of God, and if we know the Father through the Son and in the Spirit we know the being of God."[35] The latter approach involves a dynamic accounting of the divine perfections or attributes developed in view of God's trinitarian acts in history rather than by the modalistic and agnostic treatment of the perfections present in much of Western theology.[36] While Barth, Bonhoeffer and Gunton approach consideration of the Godhead and its relation to the church and world differently, they share this fundamental conviction that dogmatics as part and parcel of the life of Christian community must be grounded in God's revelation in Christ. In other words, Jesus does not simply illustrate God. He explicates deity, as made clear from such passages as the following: John 1:1-3, 14, 18; 14:6-7; Hebrews 1:1-3.

So, how do they approach differently consideration of God's relation to the church and world? Bonhoeffer and Gunton criticize Barth for what they take to be a lack of proper regard for the human sphere. For Bonhoeffer, Jesus does not appear truly graspable, this-worldly, and concretely given; for Gunton, in Barth's thought, we are never truly dealing with the humanity of the man Jesus, only the humanity of God.

It is important to pause at this point to make clear the rationale for how this discussion fits within the outline for the essay set forth at its outset. Given how central Christology is to each of these figures' theological method, we cannot limit consideration of this doctrine to the third section, which will focus on the application of this method to the issue of Christology. There we will analyze how consideration of pneumatology bears on the subject of Christology proper and Christ's work in the world, and how the church participates in God through Christ and the Spirit. How we frame Christology in this section—which focuses on a description of Barth's trinitarian method in critical conversation with diverse practitioners—will bear on the last segment of this presentation.

Further to an earlier claim, Barth's critique of Protestant liberalism, which in his estimation failed to account for divine transcendence, included

---

[35]Gunton, *Act and Being*, 112.

[36]While Barth prefers the term *Seinsweise* (mode of being) to the word for "person" in analyzing the three distinct hypostases of the triune God, he rejects modalism. His word choice reflects his effort to guard against an individualistic understanding of *person* in the modern context. See for example Barth, *Church Dogmatics*, I/1, 348-68, for his introduction and rationale for his use of the language "three distinctive modes of being."

Barth's concern for the liberal tradition's denial of Jesus' divine identity. Barth sought to safeguard against the reduction of Christ to an object of inquiry through the canons of presumed scientific analysis, which subsumes revelation under the historical process (i.e., historical positivism) and leaves us with nothing more than the vapor of Jesus' breath. The result of such a narrow historical line of inquiry is a failure to attend to revelation's rightful subject matter—Jesus' divine identity.[37]

Barth's *Romans* commentary is often noted as an example of his rigorous rebuttal of Protestant liberalism. In that work, he writes in a fashion reminiscent of Kierkegaardian existentialism of the infinite, qualitative difference between God and humanity, time and eternity. Only later will he come to analyze the relation of God and humanity in a more constructive manner that safeguards against historical positivism, involving Chalcedonian-like categories of distinct though integral or inseparable relations: revelation occurs in history without being objectified in it. For Barth, the eternal Word makes himself known by becoming incarnate in history in an indirect manner through the otherness or difference of creatureliness. The subject of revelation is not a person that comes into existence as a result of the union of the divine and human natures; rather, the subject of revelation is the divine person of the eternal Word who takes to himself a concrete human nature in becoming incarnate as Jesus Christ.[38]

Bonhoeffer does not focus his energies in the same way as Barth does on safeguarding or preserving God in Christ's distinction from the world in his self-giving. Bonhoeffer frames divine transcendence in view of Jesus' concrete engagement of us—his being for others. As Bonhoeffer claims in *Letters and Papers from Prison*, Jesus' concrete givenness for others in history is what grounds or establishes his transcendence and his infinite capacities of omnipresence, omniscience and omnipotence.[39] While they do share a distinctively and refreshingly christological emphasis and a concern for addressing

---

[37]As Barth says, God, not "the historical fact of Jesus of Nazareth, ... alone is the content of revelation." Karl Barth, *The Göttingen Dogmatics: Instruction in the Christian Religion*, trans. Geoffrey W. Bromiley (Grand Rapids: Eerdmans, 1990), 1:91.

[38]See McCormack's seminal work concerning this christological development involving the dialectical appropriation of the Protestant scholastic twin motifs of anhypostasis and enhypostasis: *Karl Barth's Critically Realistic Dialectical Theology*, especially 21, 23, 362, 367, 435.

[39]Bonhoeffer, *Letters and Papers from Prison*, 381.

the secular age in which they lived in constructive terms,[40] Bonhoeffer appears to be much more concerned with the concrete way in which God's self-giving in Christ occurs. While acknowledging and emphasizing the centrality and supremacy of Christ,[41] Bonhoeffer also goes to great lengths to highlight that Christ is indeed "graspable." For Barth, the focus is on God's grasping of us in Christ, not our grasping of Christ as such. In Barth's thought, God freely gives himself to us as he takes us to himself rather than freely places himself at our disposal, as for Bonhoeffer.[42] Whether or not Bonhoeffer intended such a connection, there is a seeming parallel with Lutheranism, which claims that the two natures relate directly to each other in the divine person. For his part, the Lutheran Bonhoeffer claims that there is a direct connection between God and the world. The focus is on the union or connection that involves distinction, not the distinction in the union as such, as Barth often tends to emphasize.[43] The following comment in Bonhoeffer's *Act and Being* is instructive:

> In revelation it is not so much a question of the freedom of God—eternally remaining with the divine self, aseity—on the other side of revelation, as it is of God's coming out of God's own self in revelation. It is a matter of God's *given* Word, the covenant in which God is bound by God's own action. It is a question of the freedom of God, which finds its strongest evidence precisely in that God freely chose to be bound to historical human beings and to be placed at the disposal of human beings. God is free not from human beings but for them. Christ is the word of God's freedom. God is present, that is, not in eternal non-objectivity but—to put it quite provisionally for now— "haveable," graspable in the Word within the church. Here the formal understanding of God's freedom is countered by a substantial one.[44]

---

[40]See for example my work on Barth: *The Word of Christ and the World of Culture: Sacred and Secular Through the Theology of Karl Barth* (Grand Rapids: Eerdmans, 2003).

[41]One source where this is very apparent is Bonhoeffer's *Life Together: The Classic Exploration of Christian Community* (New York: Harper & Row, 1954); see for example his discussion of community "In and Through Jesus Christ" on 21-26, where he speaks of the centrality and supremacy of Christ in the Christian community.

[42]John D. Godsey, "Barth and Bonhoeffer: The Basic Difference," *Quarterly Review: A Scholarly Journal for Reflection on Ministry* 7, no. 1 (Spring 1987): 9-27; Andreas Pangritz, *Karl Barth in the Theology of Dietrich Bonhoeffer* (Grand Rapids: Eerdmans, 2000).

[43]See for example the discussion of this theme on 144n88 of my study on Barth: *Word of Christ and the World of Culture*.

[44]Dietrich Bonhoeffer, *Act and Being*, vol. 2 of *Dietrich Bonhoeffer Works*, ed. Wayne Whitson Floyd Jr. (Minneapolis: Augsburg Fortress, 1996), 90-91 (emphasis original).

It is worth noting at this point that Gunton as well as the later Barth (after the time period in which Bonhoeffer's *Act and Being* is written) speak of God's relation to the world as centered in Christ in similar terms. While they may not share Bonhoeffer's use of the terms "placed at the disposal of human beings" or "graspable" given their more Reformed notions of the indirect mediation of the divine nature to the human nature through the divine person, still they guard against viewing aseity as a matter of divine independence involving distance and detachment; rather, it is God's completely sovereign and gracious self-giving to the world in and through the person of Jesus.[45]

Bonhoeffer's concern has merit, although his particular criticism of Barth bears at best limited credence in that Barth's thought evolved as reflected in the "Humanity of God" essay. Moreover, Gunton's criticism that Barth subsumed pneumatology under Christology may apply to Bonhoeffer's work as well. It has been argued that Bonhoeffer does not give sufficient consideration to pneumatology either and that Gunton's pneumatological emphasis might preserve better the distinctive identity of Christ in relation to the church. According to David Höhne, Bonhoeffer's effort to bring together or unite Christ's presence with the collective person of the church, most notably in the sacraments, does not sufficiently safeguard the particular identity of Jesus Christ as the God-Man.[46] In Höhne's estimation, Bonhoeffer does not adequately differentiate the distinctive work of Christ and the Spirit in shaping or constituting the church, which in turn does not safeguard his theology in this sphere from the threat of modalism. Gunton goes beyond Bonhoeffer at this point by underscoring the claim that it is through the Spirit that Christ is identified with the ecclesial community.[47] For Höhne, this move safeguards the particularity of Jesus as the God-Man as well as protects theology from monism's advance.[48] As Don Schweitzer maintains, the Spirit of God, on this view, "opens" up to others the new reality present in the person of Jesus Christ. At the same time, this view

---

[45]See Gunton, *Act and Being*, 20; see Karl Barth, *The Doctrine of God*, vol. II/1 of *Church Dogmatics*, trans. and ed. G. W. Bromiley and T. F. Torrance (Edinburgh: T&T Clark, 1957), 303.

[46]David Höhne, *Spirit and Sonship: Colin Gunton's Theology of Particularity and the Holy Spirit* (Surrey, UK: Ashgate, 2010), 152.

[47]Ibid., 155, 161.

[48]Ibid., 161.

serves to preserve the distinctive and unique identity of Jesus' person.[49] What is important to note in this discussion is how dogmatic considerations such as the relation of one doctrine to another (such as Christology and pneumatology) are employed to solve theological puzzles. Dogmatic method of this kind proceeds by way of internal dogmatic considerations. So, what might a sustained consideration of pneumatology make possible for christological reflection? In what follows, energies will be focused elsewhere in attending to pneumatology's bearing on Christology proper and its significance for christological reflection in a secular context.

AN APPLICATION OF THIS METHOD IN OUTLINE FORM

Dogmatic theology develops its method confessionally. What are the primary questions of dogmatic theology? In keeping with what has been argued throughout this essay, key questions at least for Barthian dogmatic theological method include: Given the trinitarian framework that God reveals God (specifically the Word of God) by God, how does one develop a method that conforms to the content of revelation rather than controls it? Another way of putting it is, given that God remains Lord in revelation, how does one develop a method that remains open to the dynamic unveiling of God (contrary to historical positivism)? Last, given the trinitarian content of revelation, how does one develop a method that accounts centrally for intratrinitarian confessional themes for solving theological puzzles (such as proper attention to the humanity of Christ)? The doctrines of the church's confessional standards frame the method, as with Barth. More specifically, the doctrine of the Trinity grounds the method for Barth, since this doctrine is foundational to all theology. All other doctrines rise and fall in relation to it. So, in good Reformed form, Barth keeps returning to the ground of theology, being formed and reformed by the Word through the Spirit daily. Given spatial limits, we will concentrate attention on the confessional theme of pneumatology's relationship to Christology and pose the methodological questions in more specific terms, as employed here.

In what follows, dogmatic theology uses pneumatology to resolve concerns pertaining to the revelation of Christ and Christology. What makes

---

[49]Don Schweitzer, review of *Spirit and Sonship: Colin Gunton's Theology of Particularity and the Holy Spirit*, by David Höhne, *Toronto Journal of Theology* 27, no. 1 (Spring 2011): 128.

it dogmatic? It works within a trajectory of dogmatic theology (in this case, Reformed theology as critically conceived by Barth), addresses one of its central theological categories, and seeks to resolve a theological problem within that theological category. What makes this methodological approach trinitarian? It works from the presupposition that God is triune and draws on the activity of the Holy Spirit in the life of Christ to resolve two theological problems in Barthian Christology.

The approach to pneumatology's shaping of Christology will center on two questions. The questions are: How does one guard against what Barth feared as the reduction of God's revelation in Christ to the state of human piety and projection and what I refer to as historical positivism? From another angle, how does one promote a more humane theology that accounts more fully for Christ's humanity, humanity come of age and the church as a participant in revelation in a secular world? The responses will account for Gunton's charge that in Barth's thought (for our purposes, the era of the *Church Dogmatics*) pneumatology is subsumed under Christology and not given enough robust consideration. The answers to these questions will also assist in the pursuit of a postlegomenon of Word *and* Spirit that accounts for Barth's own musing in his late reappraisal of Schleiermacher: one might be able to write "a theology of the third article" (the Holy Spirit) where knowledge of the first two articles of the faith (the Father and the Son) is "shown and illuminated in its foundations through God the Holy Spirit."[50] Such accounting hones, develops and clarifies the dogmatic tradition represented by Barth by attending to internal dogmatic considerations to solve theological puzzles, including the needs noted in this section of the essay: the construction of theological safeguards against human projection and historical positivism on the one hand and the construction of a framework for a more humane theology on the other hand. Ongoing work in Barth studies includes exploration and development of Barth's suggestion that this approach could prove beneficial in bridging the divide between Schleiermacher and himself.[51]

Here are the three reflections that seek to account for Barth's suggestion and that concentrate on pneumatology's import for Christology: greater

---

[50]Barth, "Concluding Unscientific Postscript on Schleiermacher," 278.
[51]See again ibid.

attention to Jesus' consciousness of the Spirit helps us address more adequately historical questions about Jesus; greater attention to the Spirit's formation of Jesus helps us address more adequately Jesus' humanity in a secular world come of age; and last, greater attention to the Spirit's work of uniting the church to Jesus helps us bring Jesus' work into the present without exhausting his identity in the church. The first reflection accounts for the initial question set forth above in this paragraph, and the second and third reflections account for the ensuing question.

Jesus' consciousness of the Spirit. Taking seriously the presence of the Spirit in Jesus—including Jesus' Spirit consciousness—helps us guard against historical positivism and affirm Christ's uniqueness while attending fully to historical research.[52] Further to Barth's dialectical and actualistic moves, attentiveness to Jesus' consciousness of the Spirit also helps safeguard against human projection and historical positivism. As Jesus is recorded as saying in John's Gospel, one cannot determine the movements of the Spirit (Jn 3:1-8). The work of the Spirit is not of the flesh; thus revelation never falls prey to human projection or becomes a predicate of historical analysis whereby it is subject to human control. However, the Spirit's constitution of revelation takes place in human history; thus revelation is accessible, though in indirect, mediated form.

Furthermore, given that dogmatic theology, according at least to Barth, takes seriously Scripture as revelation's primary witness, it is important that consideration be given to New Testament studies and its contemporary engagement of the historical Jesus debate. Here we turn to N. T. Wright's discussion of Jesus' consciousness or awareness of God as his "Abba" Father's "deeply personal presence and purpose, strength and guidance" in his life and

---

[52]Further consideration on the Holy Spirit's relation to Jesus could advance a possible rapprochement between Barth and Schleiermacher in keeping with Hector's claim in an earlier footnote, namely, that Schleiermacher's theology does not necessarily exclude a robust trinitarian understanding of Christ and the church. The point here about Jesus' consciousness of the Spirit complements an actualist Christology facilitated by God-consciousness, as it indicates God-consciousness is not an in-built anthropological foundation but remains dependent on the gratuitous, moment-by-moment gift of God's revelation by the Holy Spirit. Barth's own actualism would also need to be accounted for in any further discussion of this possible rapprochement for the sake of theological method that furthers this conversation. See also George Hunsinger's discussions of actualism in Barth's theology in *How to Read Karl Barth: The Shape of His Theology* (Oxford: Oxford University Press, 1991).

what that understanding entails for his identity and mission.[53] Wright is one of the foremost figures in the debate over the historical Jesus. In his work with leading Jesus Seminar scholar Marcus Borg, he discusses Jesus' identity. Wright argues for a construction of Jesus' identity from below—from history—rather than from above—theology proper. From his own historical reconstruction, Wright comes to the conclusion that he who announced the kingdom also saw himself as the coming king. Wright states, "To suppose that because the early Christians regarded Jesus as messiah, any suggestion that Jesus himself shared this belief *must* be a retrojection from later Christian theology is to let the hermeneutic of suspicion play dog-in-the-manger to actual historical reconstruction."[54]

In response to Borg's preferred language and claim that Jesus was a "Jewish mystic" and Spirit person, Wright argues that not only did those who recognize Jesus as such view him as the Messiah, but Jesus did as well. While one cannot from the historical vantage point prove that Jesus was the Messiah, one can make a rigorous case that Jesus saw himself as such in an age ripe with messianic speculation and messianic hopefuls. For Wright, historical reconstruction that accounts not simply for all the historical tools at our disposal today but also for the first-century life situation from which Jesus emerged[55] leads him to conclude: "Jesus . . . believed himself to be Israel's messiah, the focal point of its long history, the one through whom Israel's God would at last deal with its exile and sin and bring about its longed-for redemption."[56]

Wright's historical reconstruction of Jesus' "veiled"[57] claim to be Messiah does not lead us directly to Chalcedon, but it does not present a roadblock either that would lead to the historical positivist's charge that Jesus is only human. Jesus' messianic consciousness was no doubt bound up with his consciousness of the Spirit of God's unique presence in his life, as such texts as Luke 4:1, 14, 18-21 convey. Jesus is no mere human. This point, along with Wright's historical reconstruction, provides a complement to Barth's emphasis

---

[53]N. T. Wright, "The Mission and Message of Jesus," in *The Meaning of Jesus: Two Visions*, by Marcus J. Borg and N. T. Wright (San Francisco: HarperSanFrancisco, 1999), 35.
[54]Ibid., 47 (emphasis original).
[55]Ibid., 50.
[56]Ibid., 49.
[57]Ibid.

on dogma and addresses in part Carl Braaten's historical concern involving Barth for a full-orbed treatment of Jesus in our day.[58] In the end, a Barthian approach to confessional theology taken here does not necessitate a rejection of historical concerns, even while guarding against historicism; rather, historical concerns can serve to support and nuance dogmatic theological method and confession pertaining to Christology and pneumatology.

Jesus' constitution by the Spirit. Mention has already been made of Gunton's remark that insufficient consideration of the Spirit's mediatory work in the life of Jesus made it impossible for Barth to speak satisfactorily of Jesus' humanity as reflected in his essay "The Humanity of God." For his part, Gunton spoke of the humanity of the man, while remaining ever vigilant to guard against Nestorianism. Accounting more fully for the Spirit's constitution of Jesus makes possible a more realistic treatment of Jesus whereby he can truly give himself to us as fully "graspable," that is, concretely given in history, as Bonhoeffer wishes, without fear of compromise. This move is illustrative of a dogmatic theological method along Barthian lines in that one must account for intraconfessional, in this case, trinitarian considerations: pneumatology plays a role in framing a Christology that more adequately attends to Jesus' humanity as truly human.

Concerning pneumatology, God's transcendent powers are displayed in human weakness without separation or erosion, as the Spirit of God makes possible the union of the two natures in Jesus' person and preserves Jesus' humanity from being overshadowed by the divine nature. The Spirit on whom we also depend makes Jesus' weakness the vehicle for the power of God. There is no coercive taking back the world to God, but rather God's transformation of the world through Christ's cruciform life. As Bonhoeffer writes, it is only as the God-forsaken God who suffers that God is with us and helps us.[59] Among other things, this move provides the groundwork for developing further a theological method that is not based in secularism but that nonetheless engages a post-Christendom and secular age.

---

[58]Carl Braaten argues that Barth did not attend sufficiently to a historical account of the Christian faith, focusing primarily on dogma and *kerygma* (i.e., proclamation). All three components—dogma, *kerygma* and history—are vital. Carl Braaten, "The Gospel for a Pagan Culture," in *Either/Or: The Gospel or Neopaganism*, ed. Carl E. Braaten and Robert W. Jenson (Grand Rapids: Eerdmans, 1995), 8-15.

[59]Bonhoeffer, *Letters and Papers from Prison*, 360.

What is the methodological move here? As in the case of Barth, this approach starts with the dogmatic category of Christology and the revelation of God in Christ rather than another source such as universal religious experience, science or even biblical propositions detached from God's revelation of Jesus' identity and actions. It moves from that confessional commitment and weds it to other theological categories, such as pneumatology. The aim is to develop the dogmatic tradition by drawing on resources within that tradition, thereby safeguarding against the subversion of the confessional starting point of the dogmatic method. Jesus really is as God the man for others who gives himself to humanity come of age and the creation as a whole without manipulation, without reservation and as concretely given since the transcendent Spirit of the Lord upholds him.[60] Safeguarding the confessional approach to method in the case of intraconfessional considerations involving the Spirit also safeguards against the sabotaging of human freedom and progress.

The Spirit does not invade human history in constituting Jesus' life. While unique and distinctive, the Spirit's work in Jesus' incarnation, crucifixion and resurrection is bound up with the Spirit's constitutive, perfecting work in the entire creation. Thus, attention to the Spirit helps to account for Bonhoeffer's concern about a divine intrusion in the world;[61] God in Christ does not appear as a *deus ex machina*, but as God who is truly with us throughout history in all its creatureliness and secularity.[62]

God is with us in creation and history through what Gunton, under the influence of Irenaeus of Lyons, calls God's "two hands"—the Son and Spirit. In his *Christian Faith*, Gunton argues that the fundamental difference between his and Schleiermacher's theology represented in his own *Christian Faith* pertains to mediation. According to Gunton, Schleiermacher conceives

---

[60]Gunton speaks of the transcendent work of the Spirit in making possible Jesus' immanent work in history. See the quotation from the unpublished manuscript of Gunton's first volume of his multivolume systematics, and ensuing discussion on the Spirit's work in relation to the Son in this regard, in Paul Cumin, "The Taste of Cake: Relation and Otherness with Colin Gunton and the Strong Second Hand of God," in *The Theology of Colin Gunton*, ed. Lincoln Harvey (London: T&T Clark, 2010), 67.

[61]Bonhoeffer speaks of God's engagement of the world in Jesus as opposed to a *deus ex machina* perspective. See 281, 341 and 361 of *Letters and Papers from Prison*.

[62]See Gunton's insight in this regard concerning the doctrine of the Holy Spirit in guarding against a *deus ex machina* model of God's engagement of the world in Gunton, *Theology Through the Theologians*, 118.

God as mediated through our experience in a threefold manner. In contrast, Gunton claims that we experience God through the mediation of the Son and Spirit. Gunton claims that the implications for the Christian life and broader culture are significant. For Gunton, in Schleiermacher's Sabellian account of the Trinity, God may be very different from what our experience of God would suggest, undermining our trust in the gospel, "the structures of our world" and "the course of our history. Only if God is unconditionally the Lord of the world, life and history are we able to engage in the day to day tasks of life in the confidence that they are worthwhile."[63] Through his trinitarian account of creation, Gunton addresses what he takes to be the fundamental crisis of our culture: "a crisis of belief in the reality of creation."[64] Far from imposing a theology on creation, theology as framed in light of the Son and Spirit allows nature to be addressed on its own terms in all its creaturely otherness.

Through the Son and Spirit, God works in history to transform and perfect the creation from the inside out. Through the Spirit, the Son is clothed in "the tired and soiled matter" of the world[65] to start the transformative work that through the Spirit will reach its intended climax in the recapitulation of all things. Though not framed as an "apology" for the Christian faith like Schleiermacher's volume *On Religion*, Gunton's pursuit of bearing witness to the Trinity not as a *deus ex machina* but as the transcendent God transforming the historical process from within history in the cruciform Savior through the Spirit serves as speeches to the Christian faith's "cultured despisers" in our day.

Jesus can give himself fully and concretely to the world as the incarnate and cruciform Messiah to transform and perfect the creation since the Spirit constitutes and upholds him. The Spirit makes it possible for Jesus to relinquish power by empowering him. Jesus' quickening and constitution by the Spirit make it possible for Jesus to go lower than any one of us would go and beyond where we could ever imagine him going. Jesus' kenosis (Phil 2:6-8) is accompanied by what P. T. Forsyth and Hugh Ross Mackintosh would call *plerosis* (fullness), which is "the work of the Holy Spirit in the self-fulfillment

---

[63]Gunton, *Christian Faith*, 179.
[64]Ibid., x.
[65]Ibid., 32.

of Christ."[66] Mackintosh refers to it in the following way: "This *plerosis* or development and culmination of the Redeemer's person, is an event or fact which answers spiritually to the great *kenosis* from which it had begun."[67]

The Spirit who was active in creation prior to Christ is active in creation today in a variety of ways, most notably through Jesus' church. The church participates in Christ's cruciform life and does not suppress but bears witness to creation and culture's ultimate redemption and transformation from the inside out in history.

Connection and continuation through the Spirit. Further to Bonhoeffer's concern for making revelation graspable or tangible in history, Jesus is truly present to the world in an ongoing manner in his church and through the Spirit. The Spirit connects Christ and the world, most notably through the church. Thus Jesus does not hover above the world but is tangibly present through the Spirit in the life of the church who makes it possible for the church to participate in revelation. Once again, intraconfessional considerations are key methodologically: pneumatology and with it ecclesiology play a key role in the doing of theology. Jesus is the man for others (as Bonhoeffer said), and the church is a church for others through the Spirit, who opens the divine circle to include the world in its grasp, upholding and preserving and perfecting Jesus' humanity in giving him over to the world for its transformation. Such transformation does not take place as a *deus ex machina*, that is, as an imposition and eradication of the world. Rather, this movement occurs from within the world order and creaturely process in which the church participates as the communal body of Jesus' incarnate life through the Spirit.

Jesus is the sole incarnation of God. The church is not a second incarnation alongside him. Thus we must guard against speaking of Christians and the church as incarnations and should be very cautious about using language like "being Jesus" to those in our midst. Still, we should take seriously the exceedingly great mystery that we are Christ's body and that Jesus as the incarnate Word acts through his people by the personal agency and power of God's Spirit. As Jesus' body, we participate in his life. He continues

---

[66]Robert R. Redman Jr., *Reformulating Reformed Theology: Jesus Christ in the Theology of Hugh Ross Mackintosh* (New York: University Press of America, 1997), 134.

[67]Hugh Ross Mackintosh, *The Doctrine of the Person of Jesus Christ* (Edinburgh: T&T Clark, 1912), 494. For works by Forsyth that include this framework, see *The Person and Place of Christ* (London: Independent Press, 1909); and *The Work of Christ* (London: Independent Press, 1910).

to minister in and through his ecclesial body, as the book of Acts makes clear. Luke begins the book of Acts (Acts 1:1) by claiming that he had earlier written about what Jesus "began to do and teach." Thus he claims that Jesus continues to act and teach. Jesus now works through the Christian community in his ascended reign through the Spirit (Acts 1:8-11; 2:1-47; see also Jn 14:15-31; 15:26-27; 16:1-15). Although distinct, the church does not exist or experience God apart from the incarnate Jesus. While not to be confused, Jesus ministers chiefly through his church. Jesus continues to minister incarnationally through his ecclesial body. The church is Jesus' body (1 Cor 12:27; Eph 5:23 also indicates that the church is Jesus' body; Col 1:18 refers to Christ as the head and the church as his body). While the church does not extend or continue the incarnation, Christ continues his incarnate life and work through his body, the church.

The Spirit is responsible for distinguishing and connecting the church as body to Jesus, its head. As a result, the church does not replace Jesus, its risen and ascended Lord. And yet, there is a vital—not virtual—connection between Jesus and us. Too great an emphasis on the connection between Jesus and the church may undermine the distinction between them. Alternatively, a lack of emphasis on the profound connection between Jesus and the church can lead to the opposite extreme. The mediation of the Spirit safeguards against these excesses.

Greater attention to pneumatology complements Christology in furthering the trinitarian renaissance in theology as developed by Barth and his interlocutors. Postlegomenon along these lines takes seriously Jesus as the first and final Word as mediated by the Spirit and to whom Scripture and the church bear witness. Confessional theology that is vital and life-giving will take seriously the basis for the church's confession—God's revelation in Christ in the power of the Spirit—no matter the spirit of the age.

PART TWO

RESPONSES

6

A Bible Doctrines/ Conservative Theology Response

SUNG WOOK CHUNG

FRANKE'S MISSIONAL THEOLOGY

In this chapter, I will respond to the other four views on evangelical theological method. First of all, I thoroughly enjoyed John Franke's essay on missional theology. Franke's essay has many compelling points with which I resonate deeply. First, I totally agree with Franke that the move from church with mission to missional church is legitimate and relevant in the contemporary context and has important implications for theology. I am definitely in agreement with Franke and other missional theologians that the church is and should be ontologically missional or mission oriented. This paradigm-shift, Franke contends, should make an impact on the reformulation of the identity and character of theology. I agree with his contention.

Second, in terms of the rationale for missional theology, Franke argues that missional theology is grounded on a new vision of the missional God, namely, the triune God that the entire Scripture reveals and depicts from the first chapter of Genesis to the last chapter of Revelation. The missional God who is triune has been on a mission and engaged with the redemption of humanity and the whole creation from the point of the fall of humanity up to the consummation of the mission of God. This affirmation is closely connected with the identity of the church as a *sent* community by the triune God who exists in the *koinonia*/fellowship of sending and being sent; the Father sends the Son, the Father and the Son send the Holy Spirit, and the triune God sends the church to the world. In this context of the mission of the triune God, the church is not the end of God's missional work but the witness to and the instrument for it. I definitely agree with Franke on this point as well.

On the basis of these initial insights, Franke summarizes his arguments in terms of the rationale for missional theology. For Franke:

> (1) the mission of God from all eternity is love; (2) creation is the result of the expansive nature of God's love, and God desires that all of creation come to participate in the fellowship of divine love; and (3) God calls forth a community to participate in the divine mission as an instrument and witness of the good news of God's love for the world by living God's love in the world for the sake of the world.[1]

Franke's presentation of the rationale for missional theology is so pertinent and persuasive that I have no reservations about agreeing with him that future evangelical theology should feature a missional perspective.

Third, in terms of defining missional theology, Franke makes several significant points. He argues that missional theology is by nature practical because it aims to help Christians to participate faithfully in the mission of God. Therefore, missional theology is not primarily about intellectual exploration of doctrinal themes and truths revealed in the Bible, including such themes as God's nature and Christ's person, but about critically reflecting on the Christian church's beliefs and practices in relation to the triune God's mission. At this juncture, I cannot help expressing my concerns about his arguments. In other words, Franke seems to argue that missional theology is the only option available and acceptable for evangelical theology. If this is what he wants to contend, I cannot agree with him.

As I have contended in my essay, I believe that theology's primary task is to explore intellectually what the Bible teaches about central doctrinal themes such as God, humanity, Christ, the Holy Spirit, salvation, the church and the last things, by codifying biblical truths on the basis of faithful exegesis of the scriptural text. Of course, theology must be practical in that it should continuously expound ways to apply scriptural doctrines to particular contexts of specific individuals and communities. Nevertheless, Franke's missional theology seems to undermine or deemphasize the intellectual dimension of theology, which is intrinsic to its character.

---

[1] See p. 57 in this volume.

Furthermore, for Franke, missional theology is always contextual and dynamic, emerging from a particular and specific cultural setting. Therefore, theology is not primarily about pursuing permanent and universal truths about God and his relationship to humanity and the world but about constructing theologies that are applicable to specific times and spaces. Of course, it is undeniable that every theological construction inevitably reflects or is conditioned by its own cultural circumstances and social backgrounds. However, it never implies that we cannot glean eternal and unchanging truths from the Scripture. God has given us his word to teach doctrines about himself and his relationship to us (2 Tim 3:15-17).

In terms of doing missional theology, Franke also makes good points. For him, Scripture is the primary means by which the Spirit leads the church, and hence the Bible is theology's norming norm. He also believes that the work of exegesis is crucial to the work of theology. I have no reservation about this point. Undoubtedly, theology should be grounded on rigorous and faithful exegetical endeavor. Otherwise, theology can easily fall down to whimsical or subjective projection of theologians' personal aspirations and wishful imaginations without any objective credibility.

I also believe that conservative evangelical theologians should consider seriously Franke's suggestion that when we do theological work, we should pay more attention to cultural interpretations because culture should be taken as one of the sources of theology. Conservative evangelical theologians should be reminded that every theological endeavor cannot help being colored or conditioned by its own cultural norms, values and ethos.

My conclusion in relation to Franke's essay is that conservative evangelical theologians should make every effort to integrate the merits of missional theology as Franke has proposed into their own theological work, putting aside what they see as its demerits and weaknesses. In other words, they can appropriate Franke's insights in the context of codifying God's word and formulating biblical doctrines.

WORK'S INTERDISCIPLINARY THEOLOGY

Telford Work argues that theology is interdisciplinary by nature and theologians should do their theology in a more consciously and responsibly interdisciplinary way. I totally agree with this point. I definitely believe that theology must be interdisciplinary, even though Scripture should be taken as the primary source and norm, which makes theology's interdisciplinary character alive and well.

Work goes on to argue that the Old and New Testaments are interdisciplinary, which means the entire Scripture reflects multifaceted literary genres and personal/national experiences. It is not difficult to agree with his contention because evangelical theologians have always believed that Scripture has both unity and diversity. On the one hand, it has complete unity in terms of fundamental ideas of who God is, what God does, and what God requires of human beings. On the other hand, it contains colorful plurality in that it employs a variety of cultural stories and historical genres.

Work believes that the apostles set a normative paradigm for interdisciplinary theology, which is geared toward examining the gospel's implications for everything, that is, every area and aspect of human life in relation to the kingdom of God. Interdisciplinary theology should follow faithfully the footsteps of the apostles. In addition, Work is convinced that interdisciplinary theology should do the reverse as well, that is, examine the implications of all other things for the gospel. I would like to welcome this point wholeheartedly. As I have indicated in my essay, Gordon R. Lewis and Bruce A. Demarest endeavored to construct an interdisciplinary theology by integrating all the different sources, including arts, sciences and humanities, into their theological work without compromising the essential character of theology, which is codifying God's Word in accordance with prominent and permanent themes and topics that Scripture intends to teach us.

What, then, are major characteristics of interdisciplinary theology as a discipline? Work argues that Christian theology as interdisciplinary theology does not swallow up distinctive identities and roles of other disciplines but rather makes them free to be themselves. It is like Jesus saying to people, "Then you will know the truth, and the truth will set you free" (Jn 8:32 NIV). For Work, as the kingdom of God penetrates every other area of human life and its domain is intrinsically and uniquely comprehensive, so interdisciplinary theology should be penetrating other disciplines and comprehensive enough to provide frames for their paintings. I deeply resonate with Work's excellent insights and appreciate his groundbreaking contribution in relation to how to connect theology tightly and meaningfully with other disciplines. This will be a superb antidote to theology's perennial tendencies to hide in its own closed ghetto without genuinely and redemptively engaging with other disciplines.

Work continues to explore the metaphor of framing and painting in terms of the relationship between interdisciplinary theology and other disciplines. He contends:

> Just as a frame does not cover or dominate the painting it surrounds but presents and perfects it, so Christian theology cannot teach us everything and is not meant to. An artwork's mount board and frame hold its shape, protect it, interpret it and enhance it. Christian theologians perform the similar service of displaying the true shape and significance of all things in the kingdom's domain.[2]

I think that Work's metaphor is pertinent and sustainable, but it is too modest, as he acknowledges. As an alternative, he proposes a metaphor of a body's skeleton and the differentiated and interrelating organs of flesh it frames from within.

This is definitely a bolder metaphor than the one of framing and painting. Nevertheless, I think he should have gone further. I believe we should take a more organic metaphor, which means that theology should be understood to be like a force that gives life to other disciplines. In other words, theology should be viewed as a pumping heart that provides life-giving blood to all the other organs of the human body. Even though a human heart gives life to all other organs of human flesh, it never warps, ruins, dominates, or neglects the distinctive roles and contributions of other organs to human health. In a similar vein, theology gives life and meaning to other disciplines without usurping the distinctive visions and insights of each different field of knowledge.

If I am allowed to push the metaphor a bit further, I can agree with Work's argument that theology and other learned disciplines are interdependent. The health of all other organs of a human body is absolutely dependent on the health of its heart. Conversely, the health of all other organs of a human body can make a decisive impact on the health of its heart. They depend on each other for their health and life. Likewise, in the context of the pursuit of

---

[2]See pp. 78-79 in this volume.

kingdom truth, the health of theology depends on that of other disciplines, and the quality of other disciplines relies on that of theology.

By acknowledging such a mutual and interdependent relationship, theology can avoid its temptation to usurp the unique roles and functions of other disciplines, listening to their distinctive voices and integrating their truth claims into its own domain. Furthermore, no individual discipline can attempt to impose its reductionistic agenda on other disciplines in an imperialistic manner. Mutuality and complementarity should be promoted among these disciplines, even in the relationship between theology and other disciplines.

Again, my final concern about Work's proposal for interdisciplinary theology is that we should not compromise theology's primary task, namely, formulating biblical doctrines by codifying God's Word and applying them to our concrete life situations. Without compromising its principal character, I am convinced, we can integrate the interdisciplinary method that Work has suggested here into our theological enterprise.

EZIGBO'S CONTEXTUAL THEOLOGY

Based on the fundamental insight that every theology is contextual, Victor Ezigbo defines contextual theology in a refreshing way to be "theologizing in a way that elevates human contexts to the status of an indispensable source or resource that shapes (and ought to shape) theology's structure and content."[3] In addition, his short sketch of the history of contextual theology contains penetrating insights into why contextual theology is necessary and essential to the health of future Christian theology. As an Asian/Asian American theologian, I resonate deeply with his plea for contextual theology.

Addressing God as a theological problem, Ezigbo argues that Christian theology is about reflection on God's being and action on the basis of a mediated encounter with God in and through God's self-revelation focused on the life, experience and work of Jesus of Nazareth. I tend to agree with him that God's self-disclosure is centered on the person and work of Jesus Christ. However, it seems that Ezigbo deemphasizes Scripture as a propositional and objective divine revelation per se, and I have a concern about that.

---

[3]See p. 95 in this volume.

Ezigbo does a good job in arguing that Christian theology remains a *human construct* with human limitations and fallacies. Therefore, human theological constructions are permanently approximations, not exhaustions of the divine truth. I wholeheartedly agree with his point. However, we must not forget, as I have argued in my essay, that by codifying God's Word in accordance with major doctrinal themes and topics, we can gain the best approximation of the divine truth as God intends to reveal to and teach us. In this sense, I cannot emphasize too much that a theologian's view of Scripture makes an indelible impact on his or her practice of theology.

Ezigbo identifies four major sources of theology: Scripture, human context, ecclesial theological tradition, and reason. He acknowledges that Christian Scripture is inspired by the Holy Spirit and is the authoritative text for dealing with issues relating to Christian faith and practice. For him, Scripture is a raw material for the construction of theology, a template of theological reflection and a test of Christian identity. I do not have any issues with what he affirms in relation to Scripture. I do have, however, reservations about what he does not affirm in terms of Scripture. He does not use the revelatory phrase "the Word of God" in relation to Scripture. For me, his view of Scripture is not thick enough to sustain evangelical theological convictions.

One of Ezigbo's intriguing points is that human context includes cultures, experiences, social location, cosmological assumptions, languages and thought forms and can be both raw materials and the test of relevance for theological construction. His idea of human context goes beyond the idea of experience, which has been traditionally identified as one of the *quadriga*, four sources of theology including Scripture, experience, reason and tradition. I think this is a helpful move in that the idea of human context is expanded to include not only human personal experience but also collective cultures and other varied constituencies of cultures.

Ezigbo continues to discuss why human context is the indispensable source of contextual theology. With regard to this issue, he makes three points. First, "human context is a *hermeneutical tool* for understanding, processing and refining 'raw materials' for the construction of theology."[4] His exposition of this point is persuasive and pertinent. In particular, I appreciate that he acknowledges that

---

[4]See p. 101 in this volume.

theologians with different human contexts can share common christological and theological beliefs even though their different contexts will shape their hermeneutical approaches in a significantly different manner.

Second, for Ezigbo, "human contexts can also function as *raw materials* theologians can harness, refine and use in developing their theologies, as well as providing the *workshop* for crafting their theologies."[5] Even though I tend to agree with what he contends here, I need to point out that only Scripture as the Word of God can provide answers for the questions and needs generated by human contexts.

Third, Ezigbo contends that "human context is a *recipient* of theology: it is the 'audience' for whom theology is performed."[6] I think his point is correct. All theologies including contextual theology must be relevant to the social conditions and cultural situations where their audiences are located. In this context, Ezigbo argues that contextual theology must be interdisciplinary, recognizing that advancements in other disciplines inevitably influence theology. Here Ezigbo demonstrates his fundamental agreement with Work's vision of interdisciplinary theology.

After the discussion of the definition and sources of contextual theology, Ezigbo addresses concerns and myths about contextual theology. The first concern is connected with contextual theology's relation to the issue of particularity and universality. With regard to this concern, Ezigbo suggests that without compromising the permanent relevance and significance of Christian universal beliefs, Christian theologies should address specific questions and needs of particular communities. Thus theological particularity and universality should not be in a dichotomous but dialogical relationship. I believe Ezigbo's suggestion to be wise and practical.

The second myth is related to contextual theology's syncretistic and relativistic tendencies. In terms of this concern, Ezigbo points out that there is no inherent and intrinsic connection between contextual theology and syncretistic relativism. Rather, Christian contextual theology should and can avoid all kinds of syncretism and relativism by allowing Jesus Christ to critique and remold all of human contexts including other religious traditions. I believe that Ezigbo's suggestion is powerful and persuasive.

---

[5]See p. 102 in this volume.
[6]See p. 103 in this volume.

The third and final concern is associated with contextual theology's tendencies to undermine scriptural authority. Ezigbo argues that the Bible is not a textbook that can provide an already-made theological answer or systematic dogmas for all theological questions of all times. Rather, for Ezigbo, the Bible confronts us with a quizzical face in many cases. He continues to argue that the New Testament does not provide a uniform and systematic teaching on Jesus' understanding of the ideal human being's relationship with God and humans' relationship with other creatures of God. Rather, he believes that the New Testament contains clear concepts, thoughts and suggestions of Jesus that theologians can employ as criteria to test Christians' understanding of Jesus' vision of the ideal relationship between God and his creation. Furthermore, he suggests that the Bible performs a *judicial-mentor function and role* in Christian theology. Even though I do understand why he makes such an argument in terms of Scripture's function in theology, I cannot help disagreeing with his arguments. As I have demonstrated in my essay, we can glean scriptural and universally relevant answers to the questions of what we should believe and how we should act in relation to God, other human beings and other creatures by codifying God's word and formulating Bible doctrines on the basis of faithful and responsible exegetical engagement, because Scripture is living and is the unified Word of God that is "useful for teaching, rebuking, correcting and training in righteousness, so that the servant of God may be thoroughly equipped for every good work" (2 Tim 3:16 NIV).

METZGER'S TRINITARIAN DOGMATIC THEOLOGY

In his fine essay, Paul Metzger presents a trinitarian theological method for dogmatic and confessional theology in line with Karl Barth. He attempts to depict major features of a Barthian confessional theological method. First, for Barth, theological method must conform to the church's confession of faith grounded in God's revelation. And God's revelation for Barth is a trinitarian event: the Father (revealer) makes known the Son (revelation) through the Spirit (revealedness). Borrowing help from the Reformed tradition, Barth criticized liberal theology that presupposed a historical foundation apart from God's revelation in Christ.

Second, for Barth, internal dogmatic considerations arising from the subject matter of theology are critical for resolving all theological puzzles.

This means that theology must remain *theological* and confessional without being subsumed by the canons of secular history, existential philosophy or any other human thought forms and frameworks. As a corollary, for Barth, theology should address the question of church proclamation or tradition in its witness to Christ, consistent with biblical witness to Christ. As a result, Barth formulated the doctrine of the threefold form of the Word of God: Christ, Scripture and proclamation. Therefore, for Barth, the form of theology must correspond to its threefold content focused on the revelation of the trinitarian reality of God in a dialectical and actualistic manner.

Thus the form of Barth's dogmatic theological method is consistent with the trinitarian content of divine revelation. For Barth, the doctrine of the Trinity must have primacy over all other doctrines, and the content of the doctrine of the Trinity must be decisive and controlling for the whole of dogmatics. This trinitarian orientation distinguishes Barth's dogmatics from all other liberal theological formulations, including Schleiermacher's anthropocentric theology. Schleiermacher's liberal theology was not concerned with theology from the vantage point of God's trinitarian revelation but with the religiosity of pious humanity.

On the basis of these insights into Barth's theological methodology, Metzger describes the nature and character of the trinitarian method. First of all, as Barth, Bonhoeffer and Gunton have emphasized, trinitarian theology must be done from the vantage point of *post*legomenon, not *pro*legomenon. This means that theology should be a response of witness and confession to God's trinitarian revelation centered on Christ, a word posterior to God's speaking. Therefore, there is no philosophical foundation that precedes the Christ-centered revelation of the triune God. This confessional standpoint frames the whole of dogmatics.

Second, a trinitarian postlegomenon embraces consideration of Scripture and church proclamation as well. Scripture is the primary witness to the living Word, Jesus Christ, and church proclamation is the secondary witness to it. As a conservative evangelical theologian, I have reservations about Barth's view of Scripture. I believe that Scripture is not merely a witness to revelation but God's propositional revelation. In spite of these reservations, I believe that conservative evangelical theologians should learn from Barth's trinitarian approach to dogmatics. Traditional evangelical theology has not been trinitarian enough. It is high time that evangelical theologians develop a robustly and thoroughly trinitarian theology, which is consistent with codifying God's word and formulating biblical doctrines according to major theological themes and topics. The Trinity should not comprise merely a specific section of systematic theology but rather penetrate into all the other areas of biblical doctrines, which means evangelical systematic theology must be embedded in trinitarian theology. In other words, there must be a *perichoretic* relationship between the doctrine of the Trinity and all other areas of biblical doctrines.

Third, the trinitarian method engages with consideration of God's relation to the church and world. As Barth, Bonhoeffer and Gunton have set a good example of, God's relation to the church and world must be centered on Jesus Christ, the second person of the Trinity and the mediator between God and humanity. I have no serious reservation about this feature of the trinitarian method. Christ's relationship to his own humanity can provide for us an excellent vantage point from which to approach God's relationship to the church and world.

CONCLUSION

In the final analysis, I believe that conservative evangelical method centered on codifying God's Word and formulating biblical doctrine according to major themes and topics on the basis of faithful and rigorous exegetical engagement is not necessarily contradictory to and exclusive of other methodological proposals. Rather, I am convinced that conservative evangelical theology can incorporate the merits and strengths of all of the other methodological points of view presented in this volume into its own theological enterprise.

In fact, Millard Erickson's *Christian Theology* and Gordon R. Lewis and Bruce A. Demarest's *Integrative Theology* powerfully demonstrate that they have already incorporated the legitimate insights of interdisciplinary theology and contextual theology into their theological work. Of course, it is undeniable that conservative systematic theology has many things to be desired in terms of its robustly missional and trinitarian character. I hope that future evangelical systematic theology will be more intentional and active in integrating the valid insights of missional theology and trinitarian dogmatic theology into its own theological work.

7

A Missional Theology Response

JOHN R. FRANKE

In 1993 evangelical theologian Richard Lints was able to write with justification that the evangelical tradition had "not been nurtured to think methodologically."[1] While evangelical theologians produced numerous works concerned with the content and exposition of theology, they had given little attention to methodological concerns and did not generally apply themselves to the careful examination and explication of their philosophical and theological presuppositions. Instead, they tended to bypass questions of method and moved directly to the task of making theological assertions and constructing theological systems, as though the process of moving from the ancient biblical text to the contemporary affirmation of doctrine and theology were largely self-evident. The essays in this volume provide ample evidence that this situation has changed considerably and that evangelical theologians have started to engage constructively with the task of taking methodological questions more seriously.

The result of this methodological engagement is an increasing variety of perspectives with regard to the contexts, assumptions, starting points and procedures that shape evangelical theology. The contributors to this volume represent a significant cross-section of the diversity of methodological perspectives that characterize contemporary evangelical thought, but they do not exhaust it. Additional chapters might have included particular methodologies arising from

---

[1]Richard Lints, *The Fabric of Theology: A Prolegomenon to Evangelical Theology* (Grand Rapids: Eerdmans, 1993), 259.

different confessional traditions or from traditionally underrepresented constituencies and perspectives in the evangelical community. While some of these have been addressed in a general way in a few of the chapters, the contextual specificity of these perspectives could have easily justified the inclusion of chapters on Reformed, Lutheran, Wesleyan or Pentecostal methods, as well as those on evangelical feminist, womanist, black, Hispanic and Asian approaches among others. Of course, this would have required a much longer book. The point is that once methodological questions and their implications are seriously acknowledged and engaged, increasing theological diversity inevitably follows. Indeed, one of the most basic conclusions of the theological methods on display in this volume is that the Bible can be read in a multiplicity of ways, leading to a variety of theological outcomes and conclusions.

Sung Wook Chung's articulation of conservative theology is an admirable description of what was for many years a standard form of evangelical theology. This codification or concordance approach to theology is characterized by a commitment to the Bible as the source book of information for systematic theology. As such, it seems to be viewed as a rather loose and relatively disorganized collection of factual, propositional statements that are in need of systematic organization. The task of theology then becomes that of collecting and arranging these varied statements in such a way as to bring their underlying unity into relief and reveal the system of timeless truths to which they point. In the North American context this approach looks back to Charles Hodge and the Old Princeton tradition as continuing to provide a basic and reliable paradigm for the task of doing theology in the contemporary setting. Hodge maintained that the task of theology "is to systematize the facts of the Bible, and ascertain the principles or general truths which those facts involve."[2] Hodge's own understanding of theology is generally derived from the scholasticism characteristic of post-Reformation Protestant orthodoxy and its emphasis on a rationally ordered system of doctrine based on the contents of the Bible.[3] Many evangelical theologians followed this approach through much of the twentieth century and regularly looked back to the influence of late nineteenth- and early twentieth-century

---

[2]Charles Hodge, *Systematic Theology* (New York: Scribner, Armstrong, 1872), 1:18.
[3]For a detailed discussion of theological method in the Reformed scholastic tradition, see Richard A. Muller, *Post-Reformation Reformed Dogmatics*, 4 vols. (Grand Rapids: Baker, 1987–2003).

Princeton theologians such as Hodge, B. B. Warfield and J. Gresham Machen in the construction of theology.[4] This general approach to theology has been, and continues to be, a standard bearer at numerous evangelical institutions and among the members of the Evangelical Theological Society.

In the latter half of the twentieth century, this approach was developed and detailed by Carl F. H. Henry, perhaps the leading voice of conservative evangelical theology during this time and a chief architect of the theological culture that continues to hold sway at many leading evangelical institutions. Henry asserts that the sole foundation of theology rests on the presupposition that the Bible, as the self-disclosure of God, is entirely truthful in all that it teaches and that the truth of God that it contains is presented in propositional form.[5] From this perspective Henry asserts that the Bible is the sole foundation for theology and, therefore, the task of theology is simply "to exhibit the content of biblical revelation as an orderly whole."[6] It would be hard to overstate the influence of Henry on the development of this approach to evangelical theology, and it is somewhat surprising that he is not mentioned in Chung's essay given his significance for the works of Millard J. Erickson, Gordon R. Lewis, Bruce A. Demarest and Wayne Grudem.

While each of these authors acknowledges the significance of tradition to some extent in the exposition of theology and an awareness of cultural issues, their tendency to limit normative theological reflection to the exposition of the biblical text means that they have often been able to sidestep the thorny issues surrounding epistemology and cultural setting that have shaped contemporary discussions of theology. It is worth pointing out that this relative lack of engagement with these issues has not been because of the lack of an approach to theological method but rather due to a particular understanding of method that has generally been taken for granted in conservative evangelical circles.

One of the principal shortcomings of this approach is the assumption that the various texts found in canonical Scripture can be assumed to share

---

[4]For an assessment of the influence of the Old Princeton tradition on American evangelicalism, see George Marsden, *Fundamentalism and American Culture: The Shaping of Twentieth-Century Evangelicalism, 1870–1925* (New York: Oxford University Press, 1980).

[5]For Henry's exposition of the thesis that the Bible is the sole foundation for theology, see Carl F. H. Henry, *God, Revelation and Authority* (Waco, TX: Word, 1976), 1:181-409.

[6]Ibid., 1:244.

conceptual consistency such that they can be abstracted from their original contexts and genres and woven into a systemic whole. While those who practice this approach are quick to point out and defend the notion that none of the parts of Scripture contradicts another, they often seem to assume that a lack of contradiction implies coherence. However, as evangelical theologian Kevin J. Vanhoozer asserts,

> strictly speaking, the diverse canonical parts neither contradict nor cohere with one another, for both these notions presuppose either the presence or absence of conceptual consistency. But this is to assume that the various books of the canon are playing the same language game. They are not. Two notions that occupy different conceptual systems are nevertheless *compatible* if neither negates the other.[7]

The lack of conceptual consistency that is the result of the numerous and varied language games that make up the texts of canonical Scripture would seem to raise a challenge to the very notion that the content of the Bible can be codified in the ways suggested by Chung and the evangelical theologians he cites.

This helps us to understand the diversity of theological conclusions that result when this method is followed. Because of the contextual and diverse nature of Scripture, the Bible can be read in different ways. Conceptual clarity and consistency is in the eye of the beholder rather than in the text itself, and this produces alternative and competing conclusions that are more reflective of the convictions of various interpreters than the biblical texts themselves. Chung himself points that one of the weaknesses of this approach is the danger that "inordinate passion" for proving truth claims based on "biblical evidence" can lead to the distortion of texts in an effort to make them conform to a particular system of thought or doctrine.[8]

A final concern regarding this approach is related to its relative lack of engagement with the situatedness of both interpreters and the texts themselves. In this approach, the challenges of contextuality are generally viewed from the perspective of translating and communicating secure theological truths into other cultural settings rather than understanding that all theologies,

---

[7]Kevin J. Vanhoozer, *The Drama of Doctrine: A Canonical-Linguistic Approach to Christian Theology* (Louisville, KY: Westminster John Knox, 2005), 275.
[8]See p. 46 in this volume.

including our own, are the products of particular social and historical circumstances. The tendency in the codification approach to view contextualization largely as an activity to be performed rather than a fact of all interpretive work easily leads to assumptions of cultural universality regarding particular theological systems and conclusions.

Telford Work's essay explores theology as an interdisciplinary exercise that is inherently dynamic and dialogical. This approach to theological method leads to an open-endedness regarding theological and practical matters that is reflective of alternative critical judgments and to an awareness that no single discipline "provides a comprehensive account of life in this world."[9] In his discussion of homosexual practice among Christians as a case study for interdisciplinary theology, he explores the ways in which contemporary Christian traditions have treated the biblical material in ways that lead to diametrically opposed stances on homosexuality in the church. What I particularly appreciate about Work's essay is its affirmation of interdisciplinary theology as an interpretive exercise that is inherently contextual and open to a variety of conclusions within the framework of a confession of the Lordship of Christ and the authority of Scripture.

Work's essay demonstrates the nature of theology as a continual process that is resistant to the sort of absolute conclusions that many in the church seem to crave. Because the work of theology in assisting the church in the formulation and application of its faith commitments in the varied and shifting context of human life and thought is an interdisciplinary enterprise, it is subject to new thought patterns. In the same way that our historical and cultural context shapes our understanding and perceptions of reality, so they influence our understandings of God and the expression of our faith. Whatever the conclusions that different communities arrive at regarding homosexuality in the church, no one would dispute that recent thinking about genetics and shifting cultural patterns and assumptions has produced a new set of circumstances that require fresh attention.

The nature and development of interdisciplinary discourse reminds us that culture is not a preexisting social-ordering force that is transmitted externally to members of a cultural group who in turn passively internalize it. Such a

---

[9]See p. 79 in this volume.

view is mistaken in that it isolates culture from the ongoing social processes that produce and continually alter it. Culture is not an entity standing above or beyond human products and learned mental structures. Recent thinking regarding culture and the interdisciplinary forces that shape it has triggered a heightened awareness of the role of persons in culture formation. Rather than exercising determinative power over people, culture is conceived as the outcome and product of social interaction. Clifford Geertz provided the impetus for this direction through his description of cultures as comprising "webs of significance" that people spin and in which they are then suspended.[10] This understanding of culture leads to the conclusion that its primary concern lies in understanding the creation of cultural meaning as connected to world construction and identity formation.

At the center of the process of creating cultural meaning is the development of a shared order of our variegated experiences. Society mediates to us the tools necessary for the development of this interpretive framework. While this interpretive outlook gives the semblance of being a given, universal and objective reality, it is in fact constantly undergoing revision and restructuring as generation after generation seeks to reimagine communal identity. This process includes the symbols that provide the shared meanings by which we understand ourselves and pinpoint our deepest aspirations and longings. In this way we express and communicate these central aspects of life to each other, while struggling together to determine the meaning of the very symbols we employ in this process.

In describing theology as an interdisciplinary exercise, Work invites us to enter into this ever-shifting milieu as followers of Christ entrusted with the gospel and called to continually grapple with its message in the midst of changing circumstances. Therefore, no matter how persuasive, beautiful or successful past theologies or confessions of faith may have been, we are always faced with the task of confessing the faith in the context of the particular circumstances and challenges in which we are situated. The interpretive character that is fundamental to interdisciplinary theology means, in the words of Garrett Green, that theology, like all interpretive activity, will "be historically and culturally grounded, not

---

[10]Clifford Geertz, *The Interpretation of Cultures* (New York: Basic Books, 1973), 5.

speaking from some neutral vantage point but in and for its human context. One corollary is that the theological task will never be completed this side of the Eschaton, since human beings are by nature historical and changing."[11] From my perspective, one of the conclusions of Work's interdisciplinary approach to theology is that, in one sense, all theology is local in that all attempts at doing theology will be influenced by the particular interdisciplinary thought forms and practices that shape the social context from which it emerges.

Victor Ezigbo's essay focuses directly on the contextual character of theology. He makes the important point, clearly implied and affirmed by other essays but perhaps not so directly stated, that theology "does not *become* contextual" but "*is* by its nature always contextual."[12] In my experience such an assertion is often distressing to evangelicals who think that it somehow compromises the ability of the church to bear witness to the truth of the gospel. If we are immersed and embedded in our languages and cultural settings of our own making, how can we speak of truth beyond our linguistic contexts? One of the common suggestions for overcoming this embeddedness is the notion that in divine revelation God breaks through our linguistic limitations in order to provide access to ultimate reality.

In response to this claim, I would maintain that God does not break through language and situatedness but rather enters into the linguistic setting and uses language in the act of revelation as a means of accommodation to the situation and situatedness of human beings. In support of this claim, I would point to the distinction between finite human knowledge and divine knowledge. Even revelation does not provide human beings with a knowledge that exactly corresponds to that of God. The infinite qualitative distinction between God and human beings suggests the accommodated character of all human knowledge of God. For John Calvin, this means that in the process of revelation God "adjusts" and "descends" to the capacities of human beings in order to reveal the infinite mysteries of divine reality, which by their very nature are beyond the capabilities of

---

[11]Garrett Green, *Imagining God: Theology and the Religious Imagination* (San Francisco: Harper & Row, 1989), 186.

[12]See p. 115 in this volume.

human creatures to grasp due to the limitations that arise from their finite character.[13] Calvin's approach is consistent with the biblical, theological and philosophical idea that the finite cannot comprehend the infinite. In other words, revelation itself is contextual as a divine accommodation to human finitude and situatedness.

The contextual character of divine revelation, in which God makes use of situated language and perception to establish relations with finite human beings, points also to the contextual character of the Bible. One of the implications of this is the plurality of Scripture, an inspired yet diverse collection of witnesses to divine revelation. From this perspective the Bible is not so much a single book as it is a collection of authorized texts written from different settings and perspectives. Each of the voices represented in the canonical collection maintains a distinct point of view that emerges from a particular time and place. In other words, the Bible is polyphonic, made up of many voices. Hence, we should not be surprised by the theological, methodological, ecclesial and hermeneutical diversity of the Christian tradition.

This raises a point of concern, perhaps slight, but one that I will mention because of its potential significance and certainly one that, from my perspective, deserves further conversation. Ezigbo mentions that while Christian theology must attend to the particularity of its contextual forms, it must also attend to universality. Now in one sense, I agree with this, and when he speaks of the concern that particularity should not obstruct meaningful conversation with other Christian communities in order to enrich a shared Christian identity, I am in full agreement. But when he speaks of universality as "the commonly shared doctrines and beliefs of all Christian communities,"[14] I find that I want to put the matter differently. Now to be fair, he qualifies this in a footnote that mentions only two items of this universal commonality, belief in God's existence and that God has acted in Jesus of Nazareth. I suspect he would name some other beliefs as well, but how does he understand the category of doctrine? While Christian communities may share common beliefs, their understandings (or doctrines)

---

[13]On Calvin's understanding of the accommodated character of all human knowledge of God, see Edward A. Dowey Jr., *The Knowledge of God in Calvin's Theology*, 3rd ed. (Grand Rapids: Eerdmans, 1994), 3-24.

[14]See p. 105 in this volume.

concerning these beliefs often differ widely, so much so that some will say of others that they are not really Christian because of their divergent conceptions regarding God, Jesus, salvation and the like.

Rather than identifying universality in terms of commonly shared doctrines and beliefs, I prefer the framing of Stephen Bevans and Roger Schroeder, who speak of constants in context.[15] While they identify certain constants that have been shared by Christian communities, they also point out that the particular content of these constants is not the same among various communities for a variety of contextual factors. It is the commonality of shared beliefs and the questions they generate that constitute the unity of the faith. While the answers to questions about God, Jesus, humanity, salvation and the future have varied and even been at odds through the two millennia of Christian history, the issues they raise are perennial in the church as it lives out its missionary calling in various settings. "As *questions*, however, they remain ever present and ever urgent, because how they are answered is how Christianity finds its concrete identity as it constitutes itself in fidelity to Jesus' mission."[16] Viewing the matter in this way maintains a role for universality, but not in the sense of understanding it in terms of commonly shared doctrines or theological positions.

Paul Metzger's essay develops a confessional or dogmatic form of theological method following the contours of Karl Barth's approach in conversation with other thinkers and in particular is a response to the liberal theological tradition associated with Friedrich Schleiermacher. I am particularly appreciative of Barth's thought in its development of an open-ended approach to theology that resists notions of systematic theology and dogmatic certainty in the framework of a truly confessional theology. Barth achieves this by means of a dialectical theological method in response to the divine actualism described by Metzger. In my own thinking on Barth's theological method, I have concluded that one of the most important aspects of the dialectical approach to theology is that it resists any comprehensive views or final conclusions. These are not the accents I find in Metzger's essay, and I wonder how he would respond to my conclusions. I will briefly summarize

---

[15]Stephen B. Bevans and Roger P. Schroeder, *Constants in Context: A Theology of Mission for Today* (Maryknoll, NY: Orbis, 2004).
[16]Ibid., 34.

them here and invite readers to a longer explanation if they are interested in a more detailed account.[17]

However, while a dialectical method is preferable, this is not because it is more successful than other ways of speaking of God. Barth maintained that as Christian theologians "we ought to speak of God. We are human, however, and so cannot speak of God. We ought therefore to recognize both our obligation and our inability and by that very recognition give God the glory."[18] Hence, the fundamental assertion remains for Barth that as finite creatures we cannot speak authoritatively of God. From the standpoint of human beings, theology is impossible. It becomes possible only where God speaks when God is spoken of. Since human beings have no control over this self-revelatory speech, they are always dependent on God in the task of theology. Given the reality of this state of affairs, what humans are able to do is bear witness to their creaturely inadequacy by the continual negation of theological assertions by the affirmation of alternative and opposing assertions. This ongoing practice of setting statement against statement constitutes the shape of Barth's dialectical theological method.

But this dialectical method *is not* the means by which humans are able to speak of God. It is rather an emergency measure adopted as the only possible way to bear witness to the impossibility of human speech about God in light of their obligation to bear witness. The dialectical method serves as the means of bearing formal witness to the inadequacy of human beings for the task of theology and their dependence on God. This does not mean that dogmatics is utterly impossible; it simply means that where it is possible, it is only so as a divine possibility. Only by the grace of God in which God takes up human words and uses them for the purposes of self-revelation does dogmatics become possible by the will of God. For Barth, this means that from the human standpoint theology is a nonfoundational enterprise that must be provisional and open-ended. Theological methods function as heuristic conceptions that enable complex issues and questions to be opened up for reflection and critical scrutiny but do not lead to secure

---

[17]John R. Franke, "No Comprehensive Views, No Final Conclusions: Karl Barth, Open-Ended Dogmatics, and the Emerging Church," in *Karl Barth and American Evangelicalism*, ed. Bruce L. McCormack and Clifford B. Anderson (Grand Rapids: Eerdmans, 2011), 300-322.

[18]Karl Barth, *The Word of God and the Word of Man*, trans. Douglas Horton (New York: Harper, 1957), 186.

theological conclusions that are uncontestable. That this is the case is derived from the very character of the Word of God itself as the material principle of dogmatics that "destroys at its root the very notion of a dogmatic system. Where there is no longer a secure platform for thinking and speaking, there is likewise no system."[19]

This means that our best theological work will always be partial and fragmentary. It will always fail to do adequate justice to its subject matter, the living God. In light of that we must never grow satisfied and complacent with our findings. Instead, in constant dependence on God and the Word of God, we must cultivate the habit of open-ended theologizing that takes seriously the contexts in which we are situated. In this way we bear witness to the axiom of the psalmist (Ps 127:1 TNIV): "Unless the LORD builds the house, the builders labor in vain. Unless the LORD watches over the city, the guards stand watch in vain." Here is Barth's summation of the matter, which, from my perspective, admirably sums up the practice of theological methods that are committed to the primacy and freedom of the Word of God:

> There is no point in dogmatic thinking and speaking if in it all systematic clarity and certainty is not challenged by the fact that the content of the Word of God is God's work and activity, and therefore God's free grace, which as such escapes our comprehension and control, upon which, reckoning with it in faith, we can only meditate, and for which we can only hope. It is not from an external attack of doubt or criticism, but from its own very concrete focal point and foundation, from the source of all Christian and therefore dogmatic certitude, that all its insights and first principles, the nexus of its axioms and inferences derive; and even these statements are constantly questioned both as a whole and in detail, and their temporariness and incompleteness exposed. The focal point and foundation themselves determine that in dogmatics strictly speaking there are no comprehensive views, no final conclusions and results. There is only the investigation and teaching which take place in the act of dogmatic work and which, strictly speaking, must continually begin again at the beginning in every point. The best and most significant thing that is done in this matter is that again and again we are directed to look back to the centre and foundation of it all.[20]

---

[19]Karl Barth, *The Doctrine of the Word of God*, vol. I/2 of *Church Dogmatics*, trans. G. W. Bromiley, ed. G. W. Bromiley and T. F. Torrance (Edinburgh: T&T Clark, 1975), 868.
[20]Ibid.

8

An Interdisciplinary Theology Response

TELFORD C. WORK

From a veteran theologian's perspective, the five essays here are rich and illuminating. But from a beginning researcher's perspective, they might seem to complicate the question "Where do I start?" Academic supervisors often require a lengthy theological project to begin by stating and defending its method. That involves choosing between contested alternatives. On what basis should a researcher choose? How he or she answers is in many ways that person's *real* methodology. Do these five answers make things any clearer? I think they can. These five proposals are not a cacophony of conflicting advice for people setting out on theological projects. They reflect a bigger picture.

Hans Frei's typology of Christian theological methods helps bring some simplicity and clarity to the complicated methodological landscape. He sketches five distinct interrelationships between theology and philosophy.[1] Besides philosophy, theology relates similarly to external disciplines, cultural heritages and rivals. Frei's schema can show how a theologian is drawing on anthropological, sociological or biological categories, or informing key terms (such as *justice* or *liberation*) by the categories of another culture or discipline (such as Marxist or neoclassical social analysis or political science).

In Frei's first type, theology is entirely subsumed into the other discipline, and its claims are translated without remainder into that discipline's categories. Theology becomes dispensable allegorical language for what philosophy,

---

[1]Hans Frei, *Types of Christian Theology* (New Haven, CT: Yale University Press, 1994).

science or some other field explains straightforwardly. Its opposite is Frei's fifth type, where theology stands on its own and relies entirely on its own native language to function, rendering philosophy and every other discipline useless or worse. In both of these types, one discipline is in the driver's seat, so to speak.

Between these rather monodisciplinary extremes lie three others. In Frei's second type, philosophy supplies the controlling categories, and theology plays by philosophy's rules. Theology can make contributions, but mainly within the reigning discipline's categories: for instance, many contemporary liberal and conservative apologetics labor to demonstrate the "rationality" of Christian claims according to modern standards of epistemology. In Frei's fourth type, theological logic dominates. It employs philosophical resources eclectically and critically as they are helpful. In types two and four one discipline still occupies the driver's seat, while the other is in back—making suggestions or complaining, perhaps, but unable to do more.

In Frei's third, middle type, the two disciplines are correlated and compatible, even translatable. Here the car's two drivers must cooperate where (and because) they fundamentally agree. While no car actually works this way, a tandem kayak does. Each paddler can only go where both can go together. This arrangement may seem optimal to a moderate. But the history of liberal Christianity confirms that it is actually quite limited, and one discipline tends to acquiesce anyway. Frei's approach trains us to examine which disciplines are exercising *material* influence on the theological process, not just *formal* influence. That helps us identify subtle influences that may otherwise be overlooked. What does it reveal about our five methodologies?

CODIFICATION

Frei classifies as type two not only liberal Protestant theology but also conservative evangelical theology, since both tend to judge theological claims by the standards of modern Enlightenment epistemology. Evangelicals may protest that they have not been so shaped by modernism, but much evidence suggests otherwise.[2] Frei would likely regard Sung Wook Chung's codifying God's Word approach as subtly conforming to Enlightenment convictions, so taking a materially type two approach. Chung prefers theology merely "organizing

---

[2]See Nancey Murphy, *Beyond Liberalism and Fundamentalism: How Modern and Postmodern Theology Set the Theological Agenda* (Philadelphia: Trinity Press International, 1996).

God's Word into a system of doctrines in accordance with essential topics of biblical instruction."[3] It is one thing to treat theological topics, as New Testament Epistles naturally do; it is another to say that codifying biblical teachings according to topics is theology's "most basic and fundamental manner of instruction of divine truths."[4] Origen, Thomas Aquinas, Calvin and Philipp Melanchthon *arranged* material according to a creed, a narrative or a logical progression. To *codify*, however, is to treat the material as the kind of thing one codifies: rules, principles, facts and the like. It is a very modern inclination: Alasdair MacIntyre refers to it as "encyclopedia" in *Three Rival Versions of Moral Enquiry*.[5] While Scripture features topical treatments, no biblical writing actually does the systematic collecting and codifying of "revelation" that Chung is commending. Then is codification really the most basic and fundamental manner of teaching the Word of God?

I am not arguing against systematic topical theology! Catalogues of biblical claims organized by topic can be legitimate and very helpful indeed. The church can always use this kind of popular catechetical approach. However, the form itself, its supporting methods and its list of favorite topics do not enjoy a privileged position in either the history of theology or the life of the whole church—even in broader evangelicalism. They seem central and indispensable because of the historical circumstances that focused attention on the topics that became *loci communes*, and because a modern epistemological framework arose in which this feature of the Reformed confessional tradition was adaptable. Other traditions and eras have favored dialectical forms, narratives, sermons, disputations, commentaries and much more. So what at first appears to be a type four or five theological methodology actually approaches type two, where philosophical culture sets the agenda and theology follows it.

CONFESSION

By Frei's definition, Barth's doctrine is type four theology, and Paul Metzger's "Confessing the Faith" follows it. Calvin's *Institutes* leads with the matter of

---

[3]See p. 31 in this volume.
[4]See p. 33 in this volume.
[5]Alasdair MacIntyre, *Three Rival Versions of Moral Enquiry: Encyclopedia, Genealogy, and Tradition* (Notre Dame, IN: University of Notre Dame Press, 1990), especially chap. 8.

knowledge of God, and Barth answered liberal Protestantism's anthropo-centric account of knowledge with a dialectical (and originally Lutheran) emphasis on revelation whose origin and content was the Word of God in its threefold form. Theological resources seem to be in charge.

However, the matter may not be quite so straightforward. In Barth's theology the doctrine of revelation takes the lead in a peculiar way. In re-sponding to the questions of knowledge that his context posed to the gospel after centuries of crisis in the church over authority, Barth characterizes the three persons of the Trinity as revealer, revelation and revealedness. Barth's jointly epistemological and trinitarian focus was a great gift to a church that needed the reminder that the source, content and goal of knowledge is God. Calling this type three theology is inaccurate, because of the way theology seizes the initiative from the questioning context and instinctively seeks to overturn some of the assumptions of those questions. Yet even as I say this, I hesitate. The terms of the dialogue between Barth and his context still seem substantively influenced and even driven by that context.

For instance, Metzger notes that "the doctrine of the Trinity grounds the method for Barth, since this doctrine is foundational to all theology. All other doctrines rise and fall in relation to it."[6] Even so, why didn't his theology *lead* with the doctrine of God, as Thomas Aquinas did in the *Summa*? Why was revelation such a critical category as Barth got his the-ology under way, and why did it continue to preoccupy him? It does not seem to function that way in Scripture. While Calvin's *Institutes* prioritizes the knowledge of God, Barth is not slavishly following him here.

The reason seems circumstantial. The problem of knowledge came to preoccupy philosophers from the scholastic through the modern eras. Christians appealed to "sources" of knowledge such as natural and special revelation, experience, tradition, faith and the like. None of these episte-mological moves settled matters, so that the discussion could move on. Worse, they kept ceding ground to the less controversial kinds of natural knowledge that philosophy and science found more agreeable, until faith and reason, revelation and demonstration, and authority and justification seemed all to be pairs of very different things, at the cost of the Christian

---

[6]See p. 131 in this volume.

tradition's integrity.[7] Barth's aversion to the analogy of being was sparked and intensified in lasting ways as he saw the consequences of such concessions play out politically in Germany.

There is nothing necessarily wrong with any of this give-and-take. My point is that Barth's systematic theology is not a project in codification or simple arrangement of teachings. Its creativity and innovation show that it is not merely an explication of Christian confession. It did not operate in isolation but emerged from his cultural and theological context, engaged in often-tense dialogue with other voices, and shifted with his own thought and times. Even if we acknowledge that the Trinity did serve as the foundation in Barth's theological structure, the category of revelation was its original blueprint, and interwar European modernity the lot and its neighborhood.

As the later Barth's theology evolved, his doctrine of revelation did not stay anchored in the Trinity in the same way, but revelation remained a priority.[8] Sometimes its force could be disfiguring: to Pentecostal sensibilities, calling the Spirit "revealedness" was jarring, artificial and narrow. Trinitarian doctrine was not *simply* setting the direction of his theology, even if it did materially inform it and operated far more freely than it could in Schleiermacher's or Tillich's tandem kayaks.[9]

The challenge Barth faced is how to respond to a threat forcefully enough to extinguish it without distorting the whole tradition in the process, even just by shifting its priorities. At a number of Christian history's turning points, victors have conceded ground to challengers in this way, both subtly and unsubtly.[10] Theology *itself* is hybridized by its allies and disputants.

---

[7]William F. Abraham's *Canon and Criterion in Christian Theology* (Oxford: Clarendon, 1998) argues that a focus on authority and then epistemology ultimately replaced the more well-rounded institution of canon in ways that predated the Reformation and were particularly radicalized in modernity.

[8]Barth shifted away from trinitarian toward Chalcedonian incarnational categories to improve his career-long articulation of Christian revelation. The later Barth quietly softened his position and claimed that "alongside the first and primary Word of God [Jesus Christ], and in relation to it, there are *at least* two other true words which are distinct yet inter-related." See Karl Barth, *The Doctrine of Reconciliation*, vol. IV/3 of *Church Dogmatics*, trans. G. W. Bromiley, ed. G. W. Bromiley and T. F. Torrance (Edinburgh: T&T Clark, 1975), 114. What was once a strict correspondence became a much looser one. Barth shifted his structure's weight onto a new foundation, incarnation; so it was no longer threatening to speak of "at least" three forms of the Word of God.

[9]Ibid., 120.

[10]See Donald K. McKim, *Theological Turning Points: Major Issues in Christian Thought* (Louisville: Westminster, 1988).

Perhaps Frei's type four is more of a struggle and a compromise between two perspectives than his description suggests—or else Barth and Metzger represent another type, between types three and four, where philosophy (here epistemology), culture and context are more influential than the theologian acknowledges or even desires. Metzger's is *a* fruitful approach for *a* particular range of settings, but not necessarily a norm for evangelical theological method in every setting.

MISSION

In form, John Franke's missional method seems to be at least as intrinsically trinitarian as Metzger's, suggesting a type four or five, with theology setting the agenda and even supplying all necessary resources. Because the *missio Dei* is rooted in the love that is God's very nature rather than revelation that freely expresses it, it could be a richer point of departure for exploring the divine self-expression that entails, among other things, revelation.[11] Yet Franke's method is also more explicitly contextual, since the Father's mission sends the Spirit-led Son into the far country of rebellious humanity: not just wayward Israel but the equally wayward ends of the earth. We disciples, who are sent along the same way (Jn 20:21), learn about God and God's kingdom from wherever we are on that way, and what we say rightly reflects our particular perspectives.

What we see and say, then, is not monolithic. But that observation potentially restricts Franke's proposal's scope. Franke unsurprisingly articulates a rather free-church vision of God's will for theology: "to cooperate with the Spirit to form witnessing communities that participate in the divine mission by living God's love in the way of Jesus Christ for the sake of the world."[12] While not necessarily disagreeing, a Roman Catholic would not have put it that way. Franke would surely affirm that his portrait of missional theological method draws from a particular reading of the Scriptures, powerfully influenced by the circumstantially shaped tradition Franke refers to alongside Scripture and culture. Ezigbo's observation applies to Franke and

---

[11]The good Samaritan illustrates the distinction. He revealed his heart in the course of helping the Jewish victim (Lk 10:30-35), but his purpose was to love his neighbor. Even if they came to know each other, "love" communicates the Samaritan's fulfilled will more fully than "knowledge." And the prodigal son's father shows that he can love without being known.

[12]See p. 60 in this volume.

Metzger alike: "human contexts deeply shape our theologies and what questions we attempt to address."[13]

Franke urges that biblical narrative shapes theology's agenda "rather than reading the Bible through the assumptions of culture."[14] His chapter suggests that this is easier said than done, for all of us. Decades as a missionary in India and Britain led Lesslie Newbigin to observe that we are not very good at allowing God to set our agenda even when we try, and the gospel's power lies in the way God acts right through our failures to follow or even discern his way, above all in Jesus' cross and resurrection.

This volume's authors live in an academic culture that celebrates and highlights plurality and diversity—some varieties of it, anyway. How much does that location guide Franke's sense that plural contexts and perspectives do and should imply "a committed or 'thick' plurality" of theological conclusions about Jesus' central and unique role, the Spirit's witness and the Bible's trustworthiness?[15] Surely "missional" method does not *in itself* imply plurality. It does not imply that to Byzantine Orthodox missionaries; or if it does, Byzantine plurality differs starkly from free-church plurality. In the fifth century, St. Vincent of Lerins stressed that the truth of the Catholic faith was demonstrated in its commonality, in *quod ubique, quod semper, quod ab omnibus creditum est*: what is believed everywhere, always, by all.

Times have changed. Where once mission anticipated cultural assimilation and imperialism, today it anticipates cultural diversity and multiculturalism. Yet Newbigin counsels that when we proclaim the gospel, the Spirit tends to surprise us with the outcomes. We should be open to results that might not fit our expectations. There is raw material in the Scriptures and Christian history to support missiological outcomes of both uniformity and pluriformity. And the New Testament tends most to champion not plurality, cultural diversity, liberation from oppression, or social transformation in the present age but eternal life, unity, new personal hope in the midst of apocalyptic hopelessness, an available social alternative to the world's doomed futility, moral discipline, steadfastness under pressure and

---

[13]See p. 102 in this volume.
[14]See p. 53 in this volume.
[15]See p. 71 in this volume.

so on. God may disappoint postcolonial missionaries' multicultural expectations as much as God frustrated Constantinian missionaries' civilizing ones.

How can *any* theology be type four when human perspectives and traits play out so subtly and powerfully in our theological projects? Franke draws on Newbigin to warn that "as participants in a particular culture we are not able to see many of the numerous ways in which we take for granted and absolutize our own socially constructed cultural model."[16] That is true of Franke's own description of missional theology too, and of course the rest of ours. These observations do not invalidate missional theology, but they can alert us to subtle ways we have absolutized our locations along Christ's way.

CONTEXT

Victor Ifeanyi Ezigbo's "God in Human Context" claims that theology properly engages the questions that human life poses to the gospel. That evokes Paul Tillich's type three correlational model of theology, with context taking the initiative in posing questions and theology responding.

"Context shapes all theology."[17] Ezigbo contrasts *consciously* with *unconsciously* contextual theology, treating the former with much more favor. He consciously responds to Nigerian questions about the relationship between the human world and the spiritual world, arriving at satisfying findings that actually transfer helpfully into North American contexts. In times of need, Westernized believers turn to a similar host of powers and principalities. In America, our witch doctors wear white coats, sell therapies and homeopathic treatments, and court our votes. People all over the world run to powers and principalities in similar ways. So a local context such as his can serve as a gateway from the particular to the universal.

Yet I wonder whether the contours of his whole method, focusing as they do on identity and epistemology, are more *unconsciously* contextual. Ezigbo claims that because the Bible is a Holy Spirit–inspired collection, the Bible's role in Christian theology is to mentor and judge "the Christian identity of all theologies,"[18] and that readers should seek Jesus' vision of the "ideal" human relationship with God and fellow creatures. These claims are asserted,

---

[16]See p. 59 in this volume.
[17]See p. 102 in this volume.
[18]See p. 108 in this volume.

not demonstrated. Their key categories seem to be *identity* and *epistemology* (specifically Jesus as revealer).

Is *the* heart of contextual theological method really Christian identity, proven by fidelity to Scripture and pursued by sought-after knowledge of an ideal relationship with God and others? A modern global epistemological context seems to be subtly and decisively shaping Ezigbo's whole theological enterprise along the lines of Frei's type two.

INTERDISCIPLINARY THEOLOGY

My sketch of an interdisciplinary method seems to fit type four's description, with its metaphor of framing and painting according to Jesus' characterization of the kingdom of God and Colossians 1:15-20's cosmic Christology. But does it?

Westmont College's evangelical liberal arts environment was formative for my vision. And Westmont's beloved Colossians passage looks quite different when we start at Colossians 1:13 rather than our customary Colossians 1:15: "He has delivered us from the dominion of darkness and transferred us to the kingdom of his beloved Son, in whom we have redemption, the forgiveness of sins. He is the image of the invisible God, the first-born of all creation" (Col 1:13-15 RSV).

Paul situates things apocalyptically, in the aftermath of our deliverance from darkness and bondage. Beginning with Colossians 1:15 washes out most of the passage's apocalyptic flavor and lends the verses a more static, Kuyperian character that suggests a smoother engagement of the world through the various disciplines.

So a philosophical context, in this case a recent European Constantinian paradigm for Christian interdisciplinary education, is taming my community's interpretation of the biblical passage that we treat as foundational for our mission and uncritically influencing my vision of the structure of interdisciplinary theology. That makes my proposal more type two than I intended.

Those missing elements from Colossians 1:13-14 are not altogether absent from my treatment, so to compensate I might restore and strengthen them and refocus in their direction. In a footnote, I suggested that a skeleton and an auto frame are other "obscure frameworks" that cast framing in a more active role. They better resemble the kingdom of God in being both more obscure and more determinative. Other disciplines' "painting" would then be akin to fleshing out. A poorly framed vision would be like a misshapen or crippled body or an unsafe, unusable car.[19] That raises the stakes considerably: academic fields unframed by the kingdom remain in darkness and bondage. Framing them amounts to saving them.

Does our college—and do I—have the courage to pursue that bold a vision of our college's mission? Our environment has restrained me.

COMMON LESSONS FOR THEOLOGIANS

What can we gather from this analysis that might serve our theological efforts?

First, none of our theologies falls quite within Frei's monodisciplinary types one or five. We are not surrendering to some other discipline's way of knowledge. Nor are we treating theology as so omnicompetent that it can replace every other. We are all in various modes of engagement with traditions outside Christian theology itself. That is obvious in the case of interdisciplinary, missional and contextual theology, but it is significant that it seems unavoidable in confessional and topical theology as well. A theological project should allow for this from the outset.

Engagement can take a variety of stances in each type: proactive, reactive and dialogical. A type four theology can be reactive—a defensive driver, so to speak, such as Barth—and a type two theology a proactive backseat driver (Kierkegaard?). Missional theology tends to play offense; confessional theology tends to play defense; contextual and interdisciplinary theology tend to prefer dialogue. But these tendencies feature many exceptions. It pays to be attentive to the stance one's theology is taking and consider whether it is warranted, suits the argument and serves one's goals.

What is it about Christian theology—or perhaps human enquiry in general—that makes engagement so basic? I think it is the faith's apostolic character. The Lord's ambassadors reached us wherever we were, entrusted us with his good news and its endless implications, and sent us to proclaim and pursue it in all times and places. Types one and five are no longer apostolic.

---

[19]This bolder picture of interdisciplinary theology especially describes environments of mission and renewal, where people are being newly transferred to life in the Son's kingdom. The picture-frame metaphor might still describe environments where Christian faith is established and widespread and other disciplines already respectful.

That may be why they have not surfaced in this volume. Whatever our approach, we should expect our theology to involve some kind of wider engagement, however subtle and unpredictable, as the gospel's reach brings us into contact with others along the Lord's way.

Second, our theological engagements seem to involve an inescapable awkwardness. Whether we label Christian faith's essential content as the gospel, *fides quae creditor*, the deposit of faith, or God's Word or revelation, we all treat it as the final authority for Christian theology, *and* we all struggle to honor its preeminence in our theological projects. Our methods are not antidotes or prophylactics that guarantee our theological integrity. I think this reflects the kingdom's ongoing disruptive work. Theologians should anticipate it, consider its lessons, and watch for ways we may be compromising that essential content even as we strive to express it.

Third, our transient local contexts and the more stable catholic faith factor into every theological project, and in varying ways. Theologians frame our shots like photographers and videographers. Do you want to focus on a bigger picture, as it appears from your point of view? Use a wide-angle lens to take in a larger scene from a particular perspective? Or are you envisioning more of a close-up? Then use a telephoto lens to focus on particulars within a wider visual or narrative scene. The better we know the elements we are working with, the more intentional and effective our work can be.

Fourth, for all that we have in common, we still offer five distinct methods of theological reflection. None encompasses all or even any of the others. A method is a tool. The variety of Christian theological styles has always been rich and versatile, equipping us with a well-stocked toolbox rather than a formulaic checklist. And evangelicalism offers many more options. In thirty years, a book like this one would likely feature a somewhat different set as needs and priorities change.

Tools make great servants but poor masters. Method is indispensable in an apprentice's training and even more powerfully helpful when assimilated into a master's intuition. In a workshop, it can save lives. Nevertheless, if method and theory are focused on too slavishly, they can sacrifice insight, judgment, freedom, creativity and effectiveness. They can make our thinking tedious and sterile.

So this is not one of those volumes where contributors stake out mutually exclusive positions so readers can discern which one (if any) is right. Some tools are better made than others, but no one all-purpose method guarantees the best results. In this respect theology is an art, not a technique. It calls for judgment and discernment, not just skill. Exposure to the church's theological riches and some practice working with them develop a theologian's particular voice. Here too St. Augustine is exemplary. His projects spanned many of the approaches we have described here as he served the Lord and his church in its complex life and challenges. *On the Trinity* is dogmatic, *The Enchiridion* topical, *City of God* missional, *On Christian Doctrine* interdisciplinary, and *Confessions* contextual. A master craftsman who knew which tools to use for which jobs, he chose modes of theology that served his purposes.

Fifth, the domains of our theological methods overlap considerably, but they serve particular needs. Topical theology is especially useful for catechesis and for encouraging thorough attention to Scripture, whereas missional theology serves hospitality, evangelism and reevangelization. Interdisciplinary and contextual theology pursue matters that lie at the intersections of powerful currents that flow in and through Christian communities, while dogmatic and confessional theology respond to threatening ambiguities, oversights and errors. Christian life involves a complex interplay of "first-order" practices,[20] and theology serves and draws from each of them in distinct ways. So a project's most pertinent practical aspects of Christian life are worth pondering along with its cultural and existential location.

"Where do I start?" Start from wherever you are. Serve the Lord with humble confidence. Acquire tools and acquaint yourself with them. Shape your intuitions by following excellent exemplars. Identify an opportunity or a need and pursue it. Pay attention to the big picture and your own local surroundings. And expect the unexpected along with the familiar.

---

[20]See Franke, p. 58, in this volume, characterizing theology as an analytical "second-order" practice.

9

A Contextual
Theology Response

VICTOR IFEANYI EZIGBO

Assessing the strengths and weaknesses of a theological method brings into focus the issue of the consumers of "Christian theological products" such as doctrines, faith confessions and theological commentaries on Scripture. The genre of contextual theology I proposed aimed to bridge the worlds of two consumers of Christian theology: the world of academic theologians and the world of Christians with no formal theological education. The belief that Christian theologians' primary duty is to serve the church (and not just the academic guild) should no longer be taken for granted. Christian theology is commonly construed as a field of armchair research that ought to be grounded in the study of Christian Scripture, faith confessions, doctrines and ecclesiastical traditions. While theologians expect their theological reflections to shape the life of the church in both the private and public spheres, most continue to be preoccupied with peer-driven questions, largely ignoring the questions of the majority of Christians who do not have formal theological education. But if theology were to be construed as a field of study that should answer questions of both Christians with no formal theological education and those with formal theological education, what would it look like? This question has shaped my understanding of the nature of theology, the function of a theological method and the task of a theologian.

Christian theology may be defined as the reflection on the world (in all of its complex components—life, death, inhabitants, intricate structures, meaning and *telos*) in the light of the Christian view of God. At a glance, it is clear that theology's subject matter, namely, the God-world relation, is too complex to be studied through a single theological method. For example, a theologian should not rely on the Bible and theological literature alone when discussing what it is to be *human*. Any theological anthropology that aims to contribute to the discourse on what it is to be human in the public square should interact with the works of scholars in other fields of study (such as anthropology, sociology and psychology) that deal with human beings as well. The variegated expressions of Christianity displayed by numerous competing ecclesiastical and theological traditions should equally remind us of the difficulty of defining the term *Christian* and the futility of seeking a "one-size-fits-all" Christian theological method. Also, the field of Christian theology encompasses disparate theological genres, which require different theological methods. To name some theological genres, we have contextual theology, historical theology, political theology, dogmatic theology, systematic theology, philosophical theology, moral theology and practical theology. Although these genres of theology intersect, each has a distinguishable area of focus. For instance, systematic theology focuses primarily on the task of presenting Christian beliefs and doctrines in a holistic and coherent manner. Unlike systematic theologians, contextual theologians are concerned primarily with the construction of Christian theology that is truly relevant to the context (history, experience and culture) of present-day Christians.

Theology is not constructed *ex nihilo* but rather is created *ex materia*. Three related questions are therefore in order when exploring the issue of theological method. First, where should a theologian get essential materials (sources) for the construction of Christian theology? Second, how should a theologian understand the relationship and functions of theology's sources when constructing Christian theology? Third, what primary hermeneutics (interpretive framework or approach) should a theologian use when dealing with theological sources and theological subject matters in order to effectively accomplish a specific theological task or agenda? To illustrate these interrelated questions, imagine that a Christian theologian is given the following task: to construct a Christology that empowers Christians in the United States to tackle the social problem of police brutality and excessive use of deadly force, which the Black Lives Matter movements have brought to the fore. How should the theologian approach this theological task? The agenda, expertise and audience of the theologian ought to shape his approach to this task. Supposing the theologian is trained in both the genres of systematic theology and contextual theology, he will most likely aim to produce Christology that passes three related tests: the test of Christianness or Christian identity, the test of relevance and the test of coherence. The focus of a test of Christian identity is on a theology's faithfulness to Christian Scripture. A test of relevance is designed to assess how a theology addresses the peculiar questions generated by the context of the intended audience of the theology. A test of coherence focuses on how intelligibly and coherently a theologian has presented her or his theological reflection, axioms, claims and conclusions.

If the requirements of these interrelated tests are to be met, a theologian should exegete the contemporary context of the United States with the aim to discern the christological questions embedded in (1) America's responses to police brutality and use of deadly force,[1] (2) the history of the victims of police brutality and (3) the victims' experience—their ongoing encounter with the police. The theologian should also exegete the Scripture with the aim to draw out christological insights that are specifically relevant to christological questions she or he has identified from a careful study of the contemporary context of the United States. Theologies that are not grounded in scriptural insights and teaching may not be called "Christian" and may rarely appeal to a predominantly Christian audience. The theologian should utilize the gift of the mind to present Christology that offers an intelligible and a coherent solution that tackles the causes of police brutality and injustice wreaked on the American people. However, studying only Christian Scripture and faith confessions of Christian traditions will not bring the theologian very far in developing the Christology that tackles the peculiar causes of police brutality and its devastating impact on the United States. Theologians should discern how present-day Christians experience God and read the Scriptures in light of their daily struggles to negotiate their existence in the midst of pressure from competing religious traditions, social problems, political realities and economic states of affairs of their time. In

---

[1] Some of the responses have come in the forms of retaliatory killings of police officers and movements such as Black Lives Matter, Blue Lives Matter and All Lives Matter.

what follows, I will assess the theological methods put forward by Sung Wook Chung, Paul Metzger, John Franke and Telford Work.

Paul Louis Metzger's trinitarian method in dogmatic theology and Sung Wook Chung's Bible doctrines/conservative theology are classic examples of theologians operating with the assumption that a theologian's only task is to exegete Scripture, faith confessions and Christian doctrines. Chung sees theology as the "codification or systematization of what the Bible teaches about crucial doctrinal topics" in a logical manner.[2] Metzger's dogmatic theological method is grounded in faith confessions, which derive from Scripture's testimony about the triune God. Their theological methods and genres of theology require theologians to produce theologies that pass the test of Christian identity (faithfulness to Scripture and church traditions) and test of coherence. The theology that bears the name "Christian" ought to show how and why it merits the Christian identity. Any theology that rejects Christian Scripture will most likely fail the test of Christian identity. Christian theologians who produce theologies that are incoherent will do more harm than good to the Christian faith. Such theologies most likely will not appeal to many people (both Christians and non-Christians). Theological claims that are clearly contradictory will most likely distract people from appreciating the substance of such claims and how they may or may not contribute to their faith.

However, the theological methods proposed by Chung and Metzger fail to take seriously the role of human context in formulating theological beliefs. They do not see the human context as one of the indispensable sources of theology. Their methods will widen the gulf between the world of professional theologians and the world of Christians with no formal theological education. Theologians are encouraged to formulate armchair theologies and also to apply such theologies to Christian community. In the words of Chung, theologians should embark "on the task of formulating the doctrine of the deity of Jesus Christ on the basis of the exegetical studies of the relevant texts (grammatical/historical interpretation), theological interpretation of the texts, biblical-theological research, and the integration of historical theology. ... After formulating the doctrine of Christ's deity, the theologian can apply

---

[2] See p. 31 in this volume.

the doctrine to the life, ministry and apologetic endeavor of the Christian."[3] How could such Christology be relevant and meaningful to an audience, if it has not engaged the christological questions the audience has asked? How could theologians who write such Christology know the questions the audience is asking, if they choose neither to study nor to listen to the communities that are the audience? Presenting Christology that upholds the deity of Jesus Christ to a community whose faith in Jesus Christ is being tested by the church's silence on police brutality and killings may be praised for being faithful to Scripture. Such a Christology, however, will be ignored because it has nothing important to say about exposing police brutality, preventing such killings or empowering the American people to create a more just society, which does not allow such inhumane actions to flourish. Also, Chung's method does not seem to take seriously the fact that the Bible is not an ahistorical text. Theologians should not assume that a body of texts that were written by the earliest Jewish and Christian communities to address specific political, religious, social and economic issues of their era can always speak effectively to present-day Christian communities who do not share the same political, religious, social and economic milieu. Theologians should discern the function of Scripture as a source of theology—that is, how it is relevant and irrelevant to peculiar issues/needs of Christians of our era.

Metzger argues for a "dogmatic theology [that] uses pneumatology to resolve concerns pertaining to the revelation of Christ and Christology."[4] He develops a method that (1) passes the test of dogmatic theology as conceived by Reformed theologians, particularly Karl Barth, and (2) passes the test of a trinitarian concept of God. Such theology "works from the presupposition that God is triune and draws on the activity of the Holy Spirit in the life of Christ."[5] His theological model, which is grounded in a faith confession of "God's revelation in Christ in the power of the Spirit," will remind theologians to develop theologies that do not speculate about God's identity but seek to discern the identity of God that is consistently presented in Christian Scriptures.[6] Clearly Metzger exhibits the characteristics

---

[3]See pp. 49-50 in this volume.
[4]See p. 131 in this volume.
[5]See p. 132 in this volume.
[6]See p. 139 in this volume.

of theologians whose theological reflections focus primarily on peer-driven questions (for example, questions about Barth's Christology). One could only wonder what Metzger's study of Barth would look like if his aim were to discern Barth's relevance to the contemporary christological questions that Christians with no formal theological education are asking today. I am not suggesting that theologians should not engage peer-driven questions, but if theologians expect their theological reflections to benefit all Christians (and not just academic theologians), they should seek to develop skills and the patience required to exegete the religious, social, political, economic and cultural contexts that shape the life of Christians in their communities.

If theologians believe their task is to explain and appropriate Scripture, faith confessions and Christian doctrines (especially those approved by their ecclesiastical traditions) for the purpose of edifying their Christian communities, then they may never see the living context of Christians as an indispensable source of theology. Imagining the task of a theologian in this way has resulted in many theologians producing theological works that are based almost entirely on a rehearsal, reexamination and reinterpretation of already existing theological works.[7] Construing a theologian as one who should exegete only Scriptures, faith confessions and doctrines has led to the misconception of theology as the product of armchair research and also to the misconception of human context as mere recipient of theology. The problem here is that theologians are usually ready to force their armchair theologies on Christian communities without *listening to* and *learning from* the questions addressed to them by the daily struggles, aspirations, beliefs, hopes, doubts and social location of Christians with no formal theological education. One of the reasons the majority of Christians who do not have a formal theological education rarely care about academic theological literature is because theologians are caught up in the web of peer-driven theological questions that are most often irrelevant to the real daily experience and curiosity of the majority of Christians.

Returning to Metzger's dogmatic theological approach, he does not seem to take seriously the complex history of the doctrine of the Trinity—its origins, competing meanings and questions about its utility. Do Christians

---

[7]"Theological wars" that usually ensue focus on whose interpretation of a particular theologian is accurate.

agree on the meanings and usefulness of the terms *prosopon, ousia* and *homoousios* in their conversation about the Trinity? How many Christians with no formal theological education who confess that God is triune during worship services consciously use the term *God* for three divine persons? The earliest versions of the doctrine of the Trinity were the products of theological reflections on the identity of the Christian God, which were grounded in *particular questions* about theological/biblical exegesis, Christian praxis and ecclesiastical authority that troubled Christians from the second century to the fifth century, particularly those living in Roman North Africa and Asia Minor. The difference between the questions that twenty-first-century Christians address to this doctrine and the questions that led to its initial formulations in the early church should not be ignored. For example, how many Christians in our era who are interested in the doctrine of the Trinity focus on whether the term *true God* should be reserved for the Father and the term *God* for the incarnate Christ? In the fourth century, Libyan theologian Arius argued that the incarnate Christ should be called "God" merely as an honorific title because he was not the "true God." Arius argued that God incarnate (Jesus of Nazareth, the Christ) was created by God the Father. On the contrary, Athanasius, Arius's contemporary and opponent, contended that the term *true God* was an appropriate title for the Father and the Son.[8] One could only wonder whether Arius and Athanasius would have entertained the questions that womanist, feminist and *mujerista* theologians raise today about some traditional formulations of the doctrine of the Trinity. Also, we are left to guess whether the experience of women in the time of the early church could have informed the initial formulation of a doctrine of the Trinity. My point is that by engaging the questions and concerns of Christians with no formal theological education, theologians can serve them.

A brief word about the nature of faith confession is in order, since it is central to Metzger's dogmatic theology. Faith confessions do not fall from the sky. They are conditioned by the contexts of the initial community that proposed them. Since faith confessions are developed through theological reflections, should we assign the status of irrevocability to them? To illustrate my point, consider water baptism, which Christians once believed washed

---

[8]See Athanasius, *Four Discourses Against the Arians* 1.2.6, in *Nicene and Post-Nicene Fathers*, ed. Philip Schaff and Henry Wace (repr., Grand Rapids: Eerdmans, 1957), 4:309.

away the condemnation associated with the original sin without much question or doubt. The theological war that broke out between Augustine and Pelagius in the fifth century, which was fought on many theological fronts (particularly in the areas of theological anthropology and soteriology), planted a seed of doubt in the consciousness of many Christians that forced them to rethink the function of water baptism. As a result, today many Protestant Christians reject the confession or belief that water baptism washes away or neutralizes the penal consequences of the original sin.

In contrast to Metzger's and Chung's theological approaches, John Franke's missional theology is attentive to the concerns of both academic theologians and Christians with no formal theological education. Franke emphasizes theology's duty to the church. He writes: "Because the very purpose of missional theology is to assist congregations to participate faithfully in the mission of God, it is inherently focused on life and practice rather than merely on an intellectual articulation and appreciation of the mission of God."[9] Franke's missional theology also belongs to the genre of contextual theology. For him, "Theology always emerges from a particular set of circumstances and conditions that serve to give it a particular shape."[10] Regarding how theologians are to determine a course of action when they respond to the theological questions embedded in the lived situations of Christians, Franke contends the Bible "is the principal means by which the Spirit guides the church, and hence the Bible is theology's norming norm."[11] The version of "missional theology" proposed by Franke will guide theologians to produce theological works that pass the three tests I have discussed in this essay. However, Franke does not quite discuss concretely *how* to bring the "christological yield [from reflection on Scripture] into conversation with the particular cultural context of the Christian community."[12] How does a theologian's context shape her reading and interpretation of Scripture? What is at stake here is how to guard against the temptation to superimpose an armchair theology on a particular community.

My contextual theology approach differs from Franke's missional theology on one key point. While Franke understands the relationship between

---

[9]See pp. 57-58 in this volume.
[10]See p. 58 in this volume.
[11]See p. 61 in this volume.
[12]See p. 67 in this volume.

theology's sources from a primary-secondary perspective, I interpret the relationship between theology's sources from a functional perspective. Franke's concern about "allowing the narrative of Scripture to shape the theological agenda rather than reading the Bible through the assumptions of culture" only arises when the relationship between the sources of theology is construed in terms of a primary-secondary mindset.[13] The question that Franke is asking is: Should the Bible or culture set a theological agenda? But should this question arise? As I have argued, Christian Scripture and context (of which "culture" is a part) perform different functions in theological construction. Unlike context, Scripture may not tell us about the actual push and pull factors that inform the life of many Christians today. For example, how much can Scripture tell us about the actual causes of police brutality and excessive use of deadly force in the United States? Appealing to original sin as the root of all sinful acts in the world neither fully takes into account nor is it helpful in identifying the history, assumptions, fears, racial prejudices and tensions that inform mutual suspicions of white American police and African American communities. Other disciplines can help Christian theologians to discern correctly the socioeconomic, religious and political currents that condition how Christians practice their faith.

Telford Work's interdisciplinary method, which argues for doing Christian theology that is "consistent with the canon and with resources from across disciplines," is therefore really important to theological discourse.[14] Work contends that Christian "theology's unique role . . . is to frame" knowledge gathered from other fields of study.[15] But why does Christian theology qualify for such a role? And how can Christian theology perform such a role? To Work, theology "is not just another discipline with a scope and tool set that transfers to any other academic field, even philosophy. The kingdom of God penetrates every other domain of human inquiry. In every one it manifests signs of Christ's present reign and identifies their connections with all others."[16] Work's claim is grounded in the assumption that all genuine knowledge about the world is within the

---

[13]See p. 53 in this volume.
[14]See p. 75 in this volume.
[15]See p. 73 in this volume.
[16]See p. 77 in this volume.

domain of God's kingdom. For Work, then, theologians can be likened to "framers" because their field of study (theology) functions as the "frames" for knowledge produced in other fields. He writes,

> Christian theology . . . explicates the kingdom's *framework* for old creation. This framework is doubly *obscure*: unveiled rather than ordinary, and eschatologically new rather than protologically old. *What* it frames is knowable through many and varied other disciplines, from natural and behavioral sciences to social sciences and humanities—even philosophy and religion.[17]

He contends that theology frames knowledge from other disciplines because the field of theology deals with God's kingdom and also with Jesus Christ, whose reign is identifiable in other disciplines.

One may ask: How exactly should Christian theology *frame* other disciplines? Work's response is,

> Just as a frame does not cover or dominate the painting it surrounds but presents and perfects it, so Christian theology cannot teach us everything and is not meant to. An artwork's mount board and frame hold its shape, protect it, interpret it and enhance it. Christian theologians perform the similar service of displaying the true shape and significance of all things in the kingdom's domain.[18]

To illustrate his claim, Work focuses on how Christian theology, particularly Christology, can frame the issue of homosexuality. A way Christology can frame what other disciplines are discovering about homosexuality is to place them within the broader context of the Christian understandings of the eschaton. Work argues that Christian theologians may engage the issue of homosexuality by asking "*How are our bodies readied (or not) for the eschaton? In light of the biblical witness, is homosexual activity (perhaps in our context, perhaps in every context) problematic for present and future Christian service?*"[19]

While Work's interdisciplinary method demonstrates the value of Christian theology to other disciplines, it does not show if Christian theology can learn from other disciplines. The metaphors of framers and painters are not entirely helpful. His usage of these metaphors does not promote genuine dialogue and

---

[17]See p. 78 in this volume.
[18]See pp. 78-79 in this volume.
[19]See p. 86 in this volume.

mutual learning and critique between Christian theology and other disciplines. For instance, if Christian theology's role is merely to frame—that is, to "protect . . . interpret . . . and enhance"—knowledge about homosexuality gained from other disciplines, can Christian theology learn something new from other disciplines? Should Christian theologians be ready to change their doctrinal statement on homosexuality on the basis of new knowledge gained about homosexuality from other disciplines? Work also fails to show if the theologies of other religions (e.g., Islamic theology) should also frame other disciplines. The special status he gives to Christian theology needs to be justified vis-à-vis the uniqueness of other religions' theological traditions, some of which compete with Christianity on some crucial points.

By way of conclusion, should theologians continue to give to Christians with no formal theological education the theological products that are designed to meet only the peculiar needs (concerns and questions) of academic theologians? The answer, in my judgment, is no. Such theological products can rarely bridge the unwarranted gulf between the worlds of Christians with formal theological education and those with no formal theological education. Christian theologies should promote and enable the spiritual well-being of the church. Spiritual well-being in this sense is really about Christians living a healthy life of thanksgiving to the triune God who calls them into both a relationship and participation in God's providential work as embodied by Jesus Christ. It will be nearly impossible for theologians to know why and how Christians with no formal theological education are not living a healthy life of relationship with God and also participating in God's salvific work if they do not study them, listen to them and learn from them.

10

A Trinitarian Dogmatic Theology Response

PAUL LOUIS METZGER

INTRODUCTORY REMARKS

Theologies often function without paying homage to the accompanying or ruling methods that shape them. One of the important dimensions of this volume is its aim to make explicit methodological determinations that are operative in various kinds of theology. There is more, however. Not only do methods give shape to theologies, but also theological, philosophical and historiographical judgments shape methodological considerations. Future treatments of method will need to give greater consideration to these various theological, philosophical and historiographical factors.

With these opening lines in mind, I would go so far as to claim that all forms of theological method and prolegomena to theology are themselves theological or confessional in nature. At the outset of his prolegomena to *Systematic Theology*, volume one, *The Triune God*, Robert Jenson writes, "The most prolegomena to theology can appropriately do is [*sic*] provide readers an advance description of the enterprise. Even this cannot be a pre-theological beginning, for every attempt to say what sort of thing theology is implies material theological presuppositions, and so is false if the latter are false."[1] The foundation stones one puts in place at the outset of a theological enterprise, including the method, are theological in nature. In fact, they are confessional.

---

[1] Robert W. Jenson, "What Systematic Theology Is About," in *Systematic Theology*, vol. 1, *The Triune God* (New York: Oxford University Press, 1997), 3.

For example, all of the essays in this volume operate in some manner from realist convictions. Each of the authors included herein maintains that God and the world exist outside the theologian's head. While we do not have a God's-eye point of view (*critical* realism), there is some level of correspondence between the way God thinks and the way we think (critical *realism*). Even as we attend to the impact of our cultural contexts and theory-laden lenses for viewing the world, as well as the impact of sin on our noetic structures, we hope to think God's thoughts after God with the aid of Scripture and the Spirit. Not everyone is a realist. Not everyone maintains that there is a God who reveals God's self to us and who helps us experience and know God. Moreover, anyone doing *Christian* theology starts out from the assumption that Jesus Christ is somehow of pivotal importance to the development of theology and that one's theological method must account for his significance in some vital manner. Again, this is a theological or confessional conviction that shapes each of the essays in this volume.

REFLECTIONS BEARING ON PROPOSITIONAL OR CODIFYING APPROACHES

All prolegomena to theology, including methodology, are biblical in nature, if they are attending to God's revelation in Jesus Christ. After all, the Bible is the locus for disclosures of him. From a methodological standpoint bearing on the range of doing theology, the question is not so much "Does one frame theology or doctrine biblically?" but "How does one use Scripture?" Does one construe biblical texts as propositional teachings about God and the world, religious symbols with polyvalent import, narrative depictions of divine and human agents, accounts of historical events, including God's mighty acts on behalf of Israel and the church?[2] The list goes on.

The emphasis given to knowing God revealed in Jesus Christ in the essay on codifying God's Word is important. Doctrinal formulation is always secondary to knowing the triune God in a deeply personal manner. As Sung Wook Chung notes, the ultimate aim of theology is to assist in knowing and walking with God rather than to be an intellectual exercise, no matter how important. While Chung's use of such terms as *systematic theology* as applied

---

[2]See, for example, David H. Kelsey, *The Uses of Scripture in Recent Theology* (Philadelphia: Fortress, 1975).

to Calvin can be debated,[3] I would rather focus on what appears to be an overly optimistic sense of the theologian's ability to encapsulate all data into a theological framework.

Chung equates a confessional or dogmatic approach with post-Reformation theologies that "privileged" their particular theological traditions; however, such privileging has taken other confessional forms throughout the history of the church, including today. Although Chung appears to affirm critical realism and seems to distance himself from what is taken to be a commonsense realistic approach to acquiring and systematizing data, his particular topical approach does not account sufficiently for the confessional proclivities of all theologians. Chung takes special exception to the confessional enterprise, which he associates with the Protestant scholastics. While acknowledging the danger of faulty presuppositions in doing theology according to the topical approach, is not Chung's topical or thematic model itself a latent confession? Moreover, the claim that late medieval Catholic thought incorporated alien philosophical categories—whether Aristotelian or neo-Platonic—does not do justice to how theology has always interacted with and has been influenced more or less by reigning philosophical notions, including Augustine and the Reformers with neo-Platonism and nominalism respectively.[4] We cannot remove ourselves from the philosophical frameworks that shape our eras but must constantly engage them constructively and critically, as we seek to submit our theologies daily to being reformed by the Word, as Karl Barth maintained.[5] Barth's posture before the Word was part of his confessional orientation, bound up

---

[3]Lewis Ayres claims that "The origins of systematic theology lie in German Protestant theological shifts in the eighteenth and nineteenth centuries, building on the development of dogmatics since Melanchthon's *Loci communes* in the mid-sixteenth century" (*Nicaea and Its Legacy: An Approach to Fourth-Century Trinitarian Theology* [Oxford: Oxford University Press, 2004], 392-93). A great deal of water had passed beneath the bridge in dogmatic reflection involving Scripture's authority and the reframing of knowledge according to distinct disciplines from the time of the Reformation to the Enlightenment period; the designation that Calvin was doing systematic theology appears anachronistic and lacks consideration of the various developments from his time to modernity.

[4]For consideration of philosophy's impact on theology in the medieval period, see Etienne Gilson, *History of Christian Philosophy in the Middle Ages* (New York: Random House, 1955). Of special interest here is his discussion of neo-Platonism's impact on Augustine's thought throughout his career (70). For consideration of Luther as a nominalist, see Heiko A. Oberman, *Luther: Man Between God and the Devil* (New York: Image Books, 1992), 119-23. On the influence of voluntarism on Calvin's thought, see Alister E. McGrath, *A Life of John Calvin: A Study in the Shaping of Western Culture* (Oxford: Blackwell, 1990), 37, 46.

[5]Karl Barth, *The Doctrine of the Word of God*, vol. I/2 of *Church Dogmatics*, ed. G. W. Bromiley and T. F. Torrance (Edinburgh: T&T Clark, 1956), 682.

with his view of the dialectical and actualistic nature of God's Word. All theologians frame their topics confessionally, whether explicitly (as in the case of Barth) or implicitly.

TRANSITIONAL STATEMENT TO REFLECTIONS BEARING ON OTHER APPROACHES

Chung's statement regarding post-Reformation Protestant confessions serves well as a transition to my reflections on the other essays in this volume. For Chung, the aim to preserve particular confessional dogmatic traditions involving proof-texting methods may have eclipsed *sola Scriptura* in some cases, leading to what he terms "ossified and reified dogmatism."[6] Here I call to mind Peter Harrison's work *The Territories of Science and Religion.*[7] For Harrison, the basis for the Protestant confessions functioning like proof-texting, propositional, objectifying frameworks was the search for solidarity and cohesion in a post–religious wars world involving the separation of religious communities according to political territories. Such separation of religious groups bound up with political domains led to a separation of "religion" and "science." Whereas the two had operated together up until this period by and large as a unified whole in pursuit of virtue as a way of life, "science" (previously known as natural philosophy) and "religion" (previously framed as theology or metaphysics) were now set forth as systems of thought presented as distinct or separate bodies of knowledge or disciplines that were often pitted against each other through codifying and objectifying language.

REFLECTIONS BEARING ON INTERDISCIPLINARY APPROACHES

This discussion bears on consideration of independent disciplines in the interdisciplinary essay, which Telford C. Work assumes are separate without specifying clearly the respective boundaries, however porous. As with

---

[6]See p. 35 in this volume.

[7]Peter Harrison, *The Territories of Science and Religion* (Chicago: University of Chicago Press, 2015). For insightful reflections that address historiographical themes, including those like Harrison's work, and their bearing on theology, see my colleague Derrick Peterson's blog, *A Greater Courage*, www .agreatercourage.blogspot.com (accessed July 22, 2017). I have found our exchanges on historiographical themes quite instructive, including their relevance for theological method.

various theological classification systems that developed in the eighteenth and nineteenth centuries, including systematic theology (in contrast to other theological subcategories), the sciences developed separately or autonomously from theology in the modern period. All too often, exchanges between these subjects have been expressed in the modern world as shots across the bow rather than as multifaceted conversations that involve informed respect in the pursuit of wisdom and the common good. We will return to this point shortly.

While there is merit in highlighting the importance of interdisciplinary work in theology, all prolegomena to theology are conversational or interdisciplinary in nature. While some theologians seek to build their theologies on the right metaphysical frameworks offered by this or that philosophical or ideological system, Barth did not seek to copy philosophers, or scientists, for that matter, not for the sake of ignoring them or keeping them at bay with a shot across the bow, but because he believed he needed to take up the shared pursuit of truth from his own vantage point, though in conversation with them. Jenson puts the matter well:

> Barth did not declare independence from "the philosophers" because philosophy is something so different from theology that it must be kept at arm's length. His reason was exactly the opposite: he refused to depend on the official philosophers because what they offered to do for him he thought he should do for himself, in conversation with them when that seemed likely to help. The *Kirchliche Dogmatik* [*Church Dogmatics*] is an enormous attempt to interpret all reality by the fact of Christ; indeed, it can be read as the first truly major system of Western metaphysics since the collapse of Hegelianism.[8]

Each discipline involved in the conversation has something to offer, but what? And what are the limits to each discipline? I would have liked to see more attention given to this subject in the interdisciplinary essay. Take for example the case study of homosexuality. It would have proven helpful to develop specifically what theology can contribute to the theme, as well as the natural and social sciences. Does science deal with "What is?" and theology and ethics deal with "What ought to be?" a distinction

---

[8]Jenson, *Systematic Theology*, 1:21.

made by David Hume that is often applied to science and ethics? Attention to David Bebbington's evangelical quadrilateral (conversionism, activism, biblicism and crucicentrism) is helpful but hardly sufficient. Along similar lines, consideration of Ian Barbour's models of how religion and theology interface with science would prove instructive. Are they enemies, strangers or partners, for example?[9] The emphases of "the integrity and interconnectivity of the disciplines" is certainly suggestive of an approach to the subject, but elaboration would help to make the enterprise more concrete.[10] In fact, it will prove beneficial in the future for theologians accounting for connections and distinctions between what we call "religion" and "science" to consider the import of Harrison's work noted earlier, namely, that the categories of science and religion are rather modern in formation, and that they do not have "some unitary and enduring essence that persists over time."[11]

Harrison might have difficulty with Ian Barbour's well-traveled categories of "conflict," "independence," "dialogue" and "integration," as they appear intellectualist in orientation. For Harrison, in the ancient world, natural philosophy (which later evolved into science in the early modern Christian West) is a necessary stepping stone (with mathematics) to theology, which together aim at virtue—the happy or blessed life in which one achieves one's ultimate end or *telos* before God. The lines of demarcation today between the various disciplines are horizontal in nature; in contrast, for the ancients and medievals—pagan or Christian—the separation (or better, porous distinction) between natural philosophy (including the various disciplinary pursuits) and theology was vertical and progressive in nature. In view of Harrison's groundbreaking historiographical work, it will be important for theologians in the future to frame theological method, including the relation of science and theology, in a way that accounts more for virtue and morality—the end or goal of life—and not feature exclusively or primarily intellectual considerations. The interdisciplinary essay's emphasis on homosexuality is a pressing topic that helps readers account more for the importance of ethics in doing theology but could benefit from such

---

[9]Ian G. Barbour, *When Science Meets Religion: Enemies, Strangers, or Partners?* (New York: HarperCollins, 2000).

[10]See p. 78 in this volume.

[11]Harrison, *Territories of Science and Religion*, 6.

clarifying and expansive remarks on the relation of "theology" to "science" for the sake of theological method.[12]

REFLECTIONS BEARING ON CONTEXTUAL APPROACHES

In addition to the biblical and interdisciplinary nature of confessional theology broadly conceived, all prolegomena to theology are contextual, including dogmatic or confessional theology. Jenson goes so far as to say,

> Every theological effort is involved in the church's conversation with some surrounding religious culture. . . . Recent clamor for "contextual theology" is of course empty, there never having been any other kind. A chief mark of the religious culture of Western modernity is historical self-consciousness. Thus theological proposals in the modern West typically not only converse with a particular religious and intellectual situation but describe their interlocutor.[13]

While I agree in large part with Jenson, one (of several) context that theology in the West does not often account for is racialization—how the reality of race bears on every domain of life, including education, employment, health care and beyond. "Regular" theology may or often will account for various philosophical locales, but not often the concrete considerations pertaining to ethical matters, such as race. While perhaps best classified as "irregular," some theologians in the States might go so far as to view black theology as "abnormative" theology, since they are blind to the racial or racialized context in which they themselves are located.[14] Confessional

---

[12]I should add here that I appreciated Work's note suggesting that one might approach theology as providing the skeleton for a body of work. For all the differences, here I call to mind T. F. Torrance's use of geometry in Einstein's thought to reflect on Barth on natural theology: geometry serves to order physics, not from without but from within, where it becomes a form of natural science. For Barth, natural theology operates within the system of nature as an organizing framework similar to geometry within physics. Thomas F. Torrance, preface to *Space, Time and Resurrection* (Edinburgh: T&T Clark, 1998), ix-xi.

[13]Jenson, *Systematic Theology*, 1:ix.

[14]Barth discusses "regular" and "irregular" dogmatics in *The Doctrine of the Word of God*, vol. I/1 of *Church Dogmatics*, trans. G. W. Bromiley, ed. G. W. Bromiley and T. F. Torrance (Edinburgh: T&T Clark, 1975). See for example pp. 277-80. Both "regular" and "irregular" dogmatics have their place, one for instruction in a particular school and aiming at completion (regular), and the other aiming at addressing issues arising in the context of church proclamation apart from a particular school or educational institution and without seeking after completion (irregular). For Barth, both aim to serve church proclamation through the scientific exploration of the church's subject of study, namely, the reporting of the event of God revealed in Jesus Christ, rather than a closed system of thought.

theology must account for such ethnic and racial locations, even as a part of its content and with a bearing on its missional ends. All too often, apart from attention to intellectual, philosophical constructs that often shape theological method, theology operates blindly in a racialized world.

With this point in mind, it is not always what a theologian says but what one does not say that signifies racialization.[15] Theology must account for what goes on under the hood of the theology, so to speak, that is, accounting for what makes the theological engine run, including the underside of culture, those often discounted by the privileged classes. There is no such thing as an amorphous or acontextual theology in the States or abroad, a point that I believe resonates with Victor Ifeanyi Ezigbo's essay, "God in Human Context."

Here I am reminded of great missional theologian Lesslie Newbigin's point on the culturally embedded reality of gospel witness: "The idea that one can or could at any time separate out by some process of distillation a pure gospel unadulterated by any cultural accretions is an illusion."[16] Kanzo Uchimura, a Japanese Christian intellectual operating at a time when European powers, including Christian missions, were forcing themselves on Japanese culture, brought the point on cultural embeddedness to bear on race: "A Japanese by becoming a Christian does not cease to be a Japanese. On the contrary, he becomes more Japanese by becoming a Christian. A Japanese who becomes an American or an Englishman, or an amorphous universal man, is neither a true Japanese nor a true Christian."[17] Uchimura then argues that the apostle Paul, Martin Luther and John Knox "were not characterless universal men, but distinctly national, therefore distinctly human and distinctly Christian," adding that Japanese people saved as "'universal Christians' may turn out to be no more than denationalized Japanese, whose universality is no more than Americanism or Anglicanism adopted to cover up their lost nationality."[18]

---

[15]See for example "Theologians and White Supremacy: An Interview with James H. Cone," in *America: The National Catholic Review*, November 20, 2006, http://americamagazine.org/issue/592/article/theologians-and-white-supremacy; see also James Cone's *The Cross and the Lynching Tree* (Maryknoll, NY: Orbis, 2011).

[16]Lesslie Newbigin, *Foolishness to the Greeks: The Gospel and Western Culture* (Grand Rapids: Eerdmans, 1986), 4.

[17]Kanzo Uchimura, "Japanese Christianity," in *Sources of Japanese Tradition*, ed. Ryusaku Tsunoda, William Theodore de Bary and Donald Keene (New York: Columbia University Press, 1958), 2:113.

[18]Ibid., 113-14.

For their own part, Karl Barth and Dietrich Bonhoeffer accounted for their ethnic context, including the oppressed, as they identified with the Jewish people during the Nazi reign of terror. Barth's Barmen Declaration,[19] as well as his doctrine of election in *Church Dogmatics* II/2 (with its emphasis on Jesus of Nazareth—the Jew—as the electing God and elect human),[20] serves as a frontal assault on Aryan supremacy. Or as Barth argues in his doctrine of the Word—which is by no means amorphous or "Germanic"—we cannot ascend to God through race or culture, or give spiritual significance to "Nordic blood,"[21] though we cannot ignore race's impact on theological formulations either. For his own part, Bonhoeffer, who was shaped by the African American community's struggle in the States, claims that "only those who cry out for the Jews may sing Gregorian chants."[22] No doubt, the same would go for doing theology in any missional context across the globe where people groups experience oppression.

REFLECTIONS BEARING ON MISSIONAL APPROACHES

Just as all prolegomena to theology are contextual, so, too, all prolegomena to theology are missional, whether explicitly or implicitly. The question is "Which mission?" Hopefully, it is a mission that flows from the biblical narrative and that accounts for God's missional being in fact being narrated in Christian Scripture. As John R. Franke reasons, the triune God is by nature missional; so, too, this God's church is missional. Or as Bonhoeffer puts the matter, Jesus is the man for others, and the church is the community for others.[23] The problem presents itself in our day that "missional" can function as a buzzword that is all too readily employed to justify a theological or ministry venture, yet without careful consideration of what Franke and others delineate as appropriately "missional." One of the key issues to consider here is: What kind of

---

[19]Douglas S. Bax, trans., "The Barmen Theological Declaration, A New Translation," *Journal of Theology for Southern Africa* 47 (June 1984): 78-81. The Barmen Declaration was written in 1934.

[20]Karl Barth, *The Doctrine of God*, vol. II/2 of *Church Dogmatics*, ed. G. W. Bromiley and T. F. Torrance (Edinburgh: T&T Clark, 1957). The German edition was published in 1942.

[21]Karl Barth, *Church Dogmatics*, I/1, xiv.

[22]See Eberhard Bethge, "Dietrich Bonhoeffer and the Jews," in *Ethical Responsibility: Bonhoeffer's Legacy to the Churches*, ed. John D. Godsey and Geffrey B. Kelly, Toronto Studies in Theology 6 (New York: Edwin Mellen, 1981), 71.

[23]See Bonhoeffer's discussion of these themes in *Letters and Papers from Prison*, enlarged ed. (New York: Touchstone, 1997).

missional thrust does a theology give rise to—one that is hegemonic or humble? This question has import for the present volume, as mention has been made in different essays about the need for becoming more sensitive to various ethnicities and religions across the globe.

All too often, mission has operated in a way that prejudices one concept of deity over against others as part of a larger colonializing campaign in service to Euro-American universalism.[24] The fragmentation of theology and natural philosophy into separate domains that could be objectified according to beliefs and practices in a Europe divided according to various political territories led to the fragmentation of religion across the globe (Harrison). In place of true religion and false piety, the move was made to separate out different religions with the aim of privileging Christianity over all others in competitive terms, as was the case with the emerging conflict between "science" and "religion." Such objectification was the result of political forces separating out and conquering territories in both cases—science versus religion and religion versus religions.[25] All too frequently, the privatizing of religion through "codified sets of beliefs and specific practices"[26] aided and aids political empires that would propagate those beliefs as having universally binding authority elsewhere in the world in service to imperial, colonizing ambitions,[27] and often to devastating effect.

The only theology that is truly missional from a Christian vantage point is one that traces the footsteps of the prodigal son's God, who goes off into the far country in pursuit of us as a humble, decentered deity:

---

[24]See for example Tomoko Masuzawa, *The Invention of World Religions: Or, How European Universalism Was Preserved in the Language of Pluralism* (Chicago: University of Chicago Press, 2005), 19-20.

[25]Harrison, *Territories of Science and Religion*, 97-103.

[26]Ibid., 98.

[27]Here it is striking to note the historical point that the Japanese had no word to signify "religion" until Commodore Perry with his warships representing the United States government demanded that the Japanese government open its ports and establish trade with the United States in 1853. Perry called on the Japanese to promote the freedom of religion. The European and American governments objectified religions in service to their political and economic aims at expansion. Japan navigated this imposition in such a manner as to build its own empire in a global context of increasing secularization. See Jason Ānanda Josephson, *The Invention of Religion in Japan* (Chicago: University of Chicago Press, 2012). Here I call to mind the point in Harrison that "the 'other religions' were thus constructed as interior versions of the territorialized Christian religions of Europe" (Harrison, *Territories of Science and Religion*, 99). See also William T. Cavanaugh's discussion of the British Empire's reign in India, where religion was privatized so that Indians could be Hindus as British citizens: *The Myth of Religious Violence: Secular Ideology and the Roots of Modern Conflict* (Oxford: Oxford University Press, 2009), 88-90.

God shows Himself to be the great and true God in the fact that He can and will let His grace bear this cost, that He is capable and willing and ready for this condescension, this act of extravagance, this far journey. What marks out God above all false gods is that they are not capable and ready for this. In their otherworldliness and supernaturalness and otherness, etc., the gods are a reflection of the human pride which will not unbend, which will not stoop to that which is beneath it. God is not proud. In His high majesty He is humble. It is in this high humility that He speaks and acts as the God who reconciles the world to Himself.[28]

A CONCLUDING WORD

Theology is a global conversation. *Global* here is taken in a twofold sense: an all-inclusive accounting for various approaches to doing theology and the global climate of the geopolitical and religious landscape. We cannot think of theology as a monologue, but as a dialogue—one that involves Christian Scripture and the various theological subdisciplines, the "sciences," people of diverse contexts, including ethnic backgrounds, and the various "religions." Over the coming decades, it will behoove theologians in our polarized global climate to center our confession on the decentered deity of humble glory revealed in Jesus Christ. My hope is that this volume serves as a conversation to this end.

---

[28]Karl Barth, *The Doctrine of Reconciliation*, vol. IV/1 of *Church Dogmatics*, trans. A. T. Mackay et al., ed. G. W. Bromiley and T. F. Torrance (Edinburgh: T&T Clark, 1956), 159.

What Have We Learned Regarding Theological Method, and Where Do We Go from Here?

TENTATIVE CONCLUSIONS

*STANLEY E. PORTER AND
STEVEN M. STUDEBAKER*

Questions of method are nothing new in the field of theology, including not being new in that more specialized area that is sometimes still called systematic theology. In fact, questions regarding theological method have been at the forefront of much discussion within serious theology for centuries, as has been indicated in the introductory chapter and in several of the essays by our contributors to this volume.[1] In that regard, this volume—for all of its uniqueness in placing various theological methods in face-to-face contact—is part of a continuing and developing discussion regarding the foundations, assumptions, scope, materials and other determining factors in how to do theology. Because of this previous tradition, it comes as something of a surprise that matters of method

---

[1]A good case in point is found in the work of John Calvin. For example, in the introduction to the subject and how he treats it in his *Institutes*, found in the French edition published in 1560, Calvin lays out what we might well call a theological method. He describes the fundamental importance of Scripture, he recognizes the need for interpretation to make it relevant to his contemporary audience, he attempts to contextualize his work, he places it in the context of other disciplines such as philosophy, and he relates it to the field of Christian dogma. Readers will note the similarities of many of these points to the theological methods in this volume. See John Calvin, *Institutes of the Christian Religion*, trans. Ford Lewis Battles, ed. John T. McNeill (Philadelphia: Westminster, 1960), 1:6-8.

have continued to be difficult to nail down in theological discussions. No doubt some of this is because theological method is not of the same type as is found in some other disciplines. In some other disciplines, methods are more precisely defined and formulaically applied in ways that are not typical of the theological enterprise. However, even if there is recognizable difference between theological and other methods used in related disciplines (such as biblical studies), this is not a sufficient explanation of the continuing debate over theological method. There seems to be something inherent to theology that both begs for an acute awareness and use of proper method and resists its clear formulation and application. This is seen to some extent in the methods that are presented in this volume, in that we suspect that some of the proponents in this debate find it difficult to believe that others of the methods presented here are even appropriate methods for theology and, if they are appropriate, they can easily be seen to be either similar to or even subsumable within other approaches.

Method in theology continues to be a matter of discussion because theological method is undeniably complex, and the essays in this volume give good evidence of this complexity by the various factors that they introduce. This volume has brought together five evangelical scholars to discuss theological method, and, whatever similarities they may have in common, they are sufficiently distinct to warrant the kind of discussion found herein. The extent of this complexity is evidenced in both the positional essays by each scholar and their responses in this same volume. Even within the broad rubric of evangelical theology, there is sufficient diversity—and this could be multiplied by drawing on still other methods—to raise legitimate concerns regarding the entailments of theological method. They are here given labels that are an attempt to be descriptive of their orientation and task: Bible doctrines (codification), missional (practical), interdisciplinary, contextual and dogmatic.

Even though these various methods often speak to similar issues, one can see from their brief descriptors that they envision the theological enterprise as differing in nature. The Bible doctrines approach clearly focuses on the Bible, but on the Bible in a particular way in which the various portions of Scripture are seen as providing material for a codified and systematized presentation of it. Whereas this first approach is explicitly concerned with the fundamental source of theology, the missional approach is focused on its aims and outcomes, including the practice of theology. Even if the aims are grounded in Scripture, an overriding narrative is seen to be operational that is captured in the mission of God in the world. The interdisciplinary approach is no more modernistic than the other approaches but perhaps more explicit in recognizing the role that other methodological orientations may play in the theological enterprise. Contextual theology focuses not on the source or purpose or tools of theology but on its situation in life, explicitly recognizing that theology does not emerge from places other than those where theologians reside, both figuratively and literally. Finally, dogmatic theology is the most clearly historical of the methods in that it draws on historical formulations of theology, including the possibility of various creeds and their interpretations within the course of Christian history. If one were simply to categorize these approaches to theology on the basis of their fundamental orientations, we might well conclude that theology can be many things: a biblical study, an applied discipline, one discipline among many, a contemporarily situated enterprise or a historical discipline. Such a reformulation is no doubt reductionistic, but it serves to illustrate that, whatever commonalities these various theological methods may claim to have, they all have distinctive features that set them apart from one another by means of their points of emphasis and orientation.

This state of play raises a number of questions for the discipline of theological method. Among these are, is it possible or even desirable to find a singular method that might encompass all of the major features of these methods? If so, why has this not been done? If it is not possible, what are the implications of this for questions of method in theology and the nature of evangelical theology itself? Why is it that method is so difficult within the field of systematic theology? Why can't it be like some other disciplines where, even if the methods themselves might have technical complexity, there is greater explicitness regarding what they are and how they are used? Why, despite all of this, do some theologians appear either to avoid methodological questions or to be willfully unaware that there are debates surrounding such issues going on around them?

We cannot attempt to answer all of these questions, certainly in this conclusion or even in a volume such as this. In some ways, the individual responses are indicators by the various proponents of how they see their theological method in relationship to the others. Some wish to be inclusive, while others wish to be separatist; some see overriding compatibility, while others are content with diversity. Instead of addressing these questions raised above, which in fact this volume is designed to address at least in part, we wish to concentrate on two important questions that a conclusion such as this should raise at the end of a volume such as this. The questions are: What have we learned regarding theological method? and, Where do we go from here?

WHAT HAVE WE LEARNED REGARDING THEOLOGICAL METHOD?

There are a number of observations that may profitably be made in light of the collection of essays—both positional papers and responses—found in this volume.

One of the first is to recognize the complexity of questions of method. Questions of method are always complex, because they force the interpreter to confront fundamental issues in a given discipline. These questions include such important matters as: what exactly is the nature of the theological enterprise, what are the presuppositions of theology, what is the role of the theologian in doing theology, what are the sources of theology, what is the relationship of theology to the worlds in which we live and do theology, what are the limits of theology, how does one decide for a given method, and how does one implement it? And the list could go on. The five essays in this volume all recognize the complexity of questions of theological method, even if their proposed solutions to them are varied and they sometimes might come across as advocating a simple method for the sake of making clear the distinctives of their approach.

The Bible doctrine approach, for example, appears to make theological method something relatively routine, in which, at least according to some of its practitioners, it can be reduced to a few simple steps that are applied to the Bible, out of which clearly emerge theological conclusions. In the hands of some theologians, this might indeed become a matter of programmatic theology,[2] but our proponent of such an approach, Sung Wook Chung, does not let himself be drawn into such simplistic thinking. He not only draws on Scripture as the source of his theology but he recognizes the role that is played by biblical and historical theology and the need for practical application. Some may still think that this method skates too quickly over many of the complexities involved—such as assuming a unity and univocal view of Scripture, utilizing grammatical-historical exegesis that itself is the product of its time (and an earlier time than now), attempting to find acontextual meanings of historically situated texts, among others—but by recognizing these other important areas, historical and contextual elements are brought into the methodological formulation. Even though each of the other positions can also be accused of having a blind spot that mitigates such complexity, each of the proponents either at the outset or inevitably recognizes that theology is not just complex but multiplex, and their particular orientation to it must recognize and respond to other factors.

John Franke's missional approach may assume the missional narrative of Scripture, but he also recognizes the precariousness of theology that brings the gospel and culture into dialogue. Hence he describes theology as a second-order discipline because it is always contextually situated. This recognition means that it is dependent on a number of first-order disciplines, which themselves must be scrutinized (in a way that is not done in this volume) for their sufficiency as foundations for such second-level construction.

Telford Work reveals the complexity that he envisions in theology by his use of a number of different metaphors as ways of conveying his approach. He uses such metaphors as building, framing, painting and even skeletons, all in an attempt to come to terms with the way in which theology is interdisciplinarily related to other fields. However, even though he advocates an interdisciplinary approach, he sees theology not simply as one of the disciplines but as the one that pervades all else. This is indeed a complex picture.

Victor Ezigbo recognizes that the history of theology is one of contextual theology. All theologians, from those of the early church to the present, have

---

[2]We were going to use the term *slide-rule theology*, but we realized that many of our readers might not be familiar with the slide rule, or even its replacement, the calculator. Hence we use the term *programmatic* with invocation of language of the computer age in which we currently live. Future generations will need to find their own, new metaphors.

been culturally and contextually embedded. However, Ezigbo means more than that—that the human being is one of the major sources of theology. The human is not just the author but the human situation is the context of theology. Ezigbo thereby recognizes the complexity of making any kind of theological statement that can find a location other than within its human context.

Finally, Paul Metzger takes a dogmatic approach that draws on the tradition of the church and specifically a trinitarian theology and more particularly trinitarian theologian Karl Barth. The doctrine of the Trinity is itself notoriously complex, and so use of it as a theological method instills complexity within the entire already complex system. Drawing specifically on the formulations of Barth, regardless of what one thinks of his contribution to Christian theology and especially to evangelical theology, endorses a particular formulation and definition of this trinitarian theology. The complexity is compounded by the question of whether such a theological method is more historical than systematic or even theological.

The second observation to make regarding these theological methods is the role that the interpretive subject plays in such formulations. The question of the role of the subject in theological method raises a number of epistemological questions that rightly should have their place in discussion of systematic theology but that take us beyond the scope of this volume.[3] We must content ourselves with saying simply that one of the major accomplishments of much modern philosophy has been the recognition of the role of the subject. The subject has become the focus of discussion because of its importance for defining the self and thereby the self as a knowing, involved and active entity in relation to the world, with important questions being raised regarding the role of the subject in not just perceiving and responding to but its being involved in and even creating and formulating its world.

All of the approaches to method represented in this book appear to have the implicit belief that the subject, here defined as the theologian as subject, is perceiving phenomena in the world around itself (Work refers to how the

---

[3]The field of epistemology, not discussed in systematic theology as it perhaps should be, is a major area of investigation and concern. Some helpful works are: A. D. Woozley, *Theory of Knowledge: An Introduction* (London: Hutchinson, 1949); Roderick M. Chisholm, *Theory of Knowledge* (Englewood Cliffs, NJ: Prentice-Hall, 1966); David L. Wolfe, *Epistemology: The Justification of Belief* (Downers Grove, IL: InterVarsity Press, 1982); and Laurence BonJour, *Epistemology: Classic Problems and Contemporary Responses* (Lanham, MD: Rowman & Littlefield, 2002).

proponents in this volume are critical realists—a subject that itself merits debate and discussion).[4] This may well be true, but this is an epistemological position that is being assumed or asserted by the various proponents. There are other positions that might be assumed or asserted as well. Nevertheless, even if we grant this view of the subject in relation to the world, we may well still ask how it is that the subject determines its approach to theology. In other words, we may wonder what are the warrants or proofs that the subject draws on to affirm the particular theological method that is being endorsed. The importance of this question is seen by the fact that all five of the proponents align themselves with an evangelical approach to theology. If they are all evangelicals in orientation, what are the factors that have resulted in their endorsing these varied, complex methods? There are a variety of reasons for why various positions are endorsed. These might include anything from preferences to extended arguments purportedly based on various types of evidence. As mentioned above, this is not a book on epistemology, so we would be asking too much for the contributors to outline their view of reality, how we perceive it and the role of the subject within it. However, we cannot help but note that none of the contributors offers a robust defense of the epistemological assumptions that motivate their particular theological method. Nevertheless, we see that the role of the subject remains important in each one of them.

For the codified approach, the subject must make choices regarding which scriptural passages to interpret, the method of interpretation, the systematization of these exegetical results and so on. The missional theologian must first assert that the fundamental conviction is that God is missional. The biblical account may provide support for such an assertion, but the assertion must apparently be made first to justify finding it in the text. Similarly, the interdisciplinary approach finds that, despite the various other disciplines, the theological discipline is not merely first among equals but pervades all others. The contextual approach makes a necessity into a virtue and is probably the most explicit in finding the place of the human subject as the focal point of

---

[4]There are a number of philosophical problems with standard definitions of critical realism, especially as typically used in contemporary theological discussion. The major shortcomings concern the nature of warrants of belief. This topic is outside the scope of this volume. An excellent place to begin such discussion is Alvin Plantinga, *Warrant: The Current Debate* (New York: Oxford University Press, 1993), and Plantinga, *Warrant and Proper Function* (New York: Oxford University Press, 1993).

theology. Finally, the trinitarian dogmatic approach appeals to the fact that Barth rejuvenated trinitarian theology as warrant for his being the model of theological method. Readers will no doubt recognize the clear endorsements of these methods by their proponents but may also wonder regarding the underlying bases for these orientations. As mentioned above, theology is (at least in the words of Franke) a second-order discipline, and there may well be first-order questions that are still unanswered and that merit further examination before one takes up any of the methods presented here.

The third observation to make is that, despite all of the above statements, there is a recurring indication in all of the essays, even if in some of them it is subtle, that Scripture is fundamental to the theological enterprise and hence must feature largely in an appropriate theological method. One might well claim that this is entirely appropriate for an evangelical theological method as part of an evangelical theology, but these essays make clear that there is far more to this role of Scripture than a perfunctory nod to a theological tradition. The basis of these methods in Scripture is perhaps the fundamental warrant or unstated assumption of all of them and the foundation of their approach that they have in common.

This basis in Scripture is clearly seen in Chung's codified approach, which promotes Bible doctrine as its fundamental orientation. To a large extent—even with recognition of the complexity of biblical and historical theology—this method is fundamentally reliant on Scripture and the interpretation of numerous individual biblical passages. Franke's missional approach grounds its orientation on what it sees as the overriding scriptural story, in particular John 20:21 with Jesus' words "As the father has sent me, so I send you" (NRSV). The gospel message that forms an axis with culture is an encapsulation of the message that is found in the Scriptures. Work's interdisciplinary approach situates his theological explorations in the context of teaching at a liberal arts college whose motto is based on Colossians 1:18, regarding Christ having preeminence in all things. Even though Work describes Scripture as "a product of 'evangelical method,'" he looks to both Testaments as reflecting and grounding the kind of interdisciplinary work that he envisions as the task of theology. Ezigbo's contextual theology is somewhat opaque regarding Scripture, but even he wishes to find the source of his theology in God and God's revelation, which includes Scripture (along with what he calls "human context, ecumenical ecclesial theological tradition and reason"), even if he emphasizes the human context. For Metzger's trinitarian dogmatic theology, because he relies on Barth, he also includes, if not so much Scripture, at least the Word of God in its diverse ways as defined and conceived by Barth. Metzger's theological method is the least dependent on Scripture, except that one might well argue that the notion of the Trinity, even if not explicitly stated in the Bible, is a rightful interpretation of the biblical testimony regarding the threefold person of the Godhead. If the last two methods are not as biblically explicit as the other three, it is hard to conceive of any of the five theological methods being proposed without at least an implicit reliance on a notion of the foundational importance of Scripture. However, we find it hard to believe that any Christian systematic theology could be formulated that did not have at least a minimal role for Scripture—although perhaps stranger things might be seen.[5]

The fourth observation is that, even though Scripture is important to all of the theological methods, it is not the only consideration. In other words, there are other major factors to consider in theological method besides the Bible. Because the methods are complex and not oriented to the question of method in the same way, not all of these factors are of the same type. Besides Scripture, some of the factors to consider are context, history and tradition. But even these are considered in varying ways and in varying degrees within the several different theological methods.

The first, context, is probably the most important of the three to consider. Despite the various orientations of the theological methods, each one of them has a place for context, whether this is an originating context (such as that of Scripture) or, more importantly, one's contemporary context. Contextual theology, as represented by the work of Ezigbo, is clearly formulated around the need for understanding context. He defines the notion of contextual theology, distinguishing the idea that all of theology is contextual from the more specialized sense in which the human factor is paramount. On the other end of the spectrum is the Bible doctrine approach of Chung. This

---

[5]Even Paul Tillich's systematic theology—one of the most philosophically oriented systematic theologies—occasionally cites a biblical passage, although admittedly not many of them. These occasional citations, however, are a far remove from indicating that Scripture is fundamental to Tillich's theological method, even if he writes within the Christian theological tradition.

method takes into consideration the original context of Scripture—even if it wishes to move from contingency and particularity to generalization and universals in a quick interpretive move—but more importantly includes several other types of context. These include the context of previous and other interpretations, such as are found in biblical and historical theology, and the context of contemporary application. Even if it does not appear to do so, this codification approach to theology has contextual understanding underlying much of its approach, even if the notion is not pronounced or defined in a robust way (Ezigbo claims that it lacks it, as does the trinitarian dogmatic approach). Between these two apparently (even if not really) opposed approaches lie the others. The missional approach of Franke builds context into its formulation, so that it stands in the middle, with gospel and context forming an axis of orientation. Franke emphasizes that the missional approach is a practical and hence contextual approach to theology, in which the missional orientation is reflected in the culturally specific—read this as contextually sensitive—ways in which this is expressed. Mission and context thus go hand in hand. The interdisciplinary method of Work is probably less explicitly contextual but finds itself nevertheless thoroughly contextually oriented by virtue of its incorporation of interdisciplinarity. This method draws itself, even if it itself remains at the forefront, into relationship with other contextually sensitive approaches that help to inform theology. The trinitarian dogmatic method of Metzger, with its focus on two central theological notions, finds itself implicitly as contextually bound as the contextual approach, in spite of its appearances. Trinitarianism itself and Barth in particular are contextual applications of theological method and reflect specific places and times in which expressions of Christian theology were made. Thus all of the approaches, regardless of how they may prima facie present themselves in relation to context, find themselves as contextually dependent.

Similar statements may be made about history and tradition. There are historical and traditional elements to each of the methods as well. We might even reasonably differentiate between the Bible doctrine and trinitarian dogmatic approaches, on the one hand, as being explicitly historical and traditional in orientation, and the missional, interdisciplinary and contextual approaches, on the other hand, as representing themselves as less overtly historical and traditional. However, we would be mistaken to think that the latter group are not attentive to both history and tradition. The missional approach looks to the biblical narrative to find its support for a missional approach. The interdisciplinary approach finds itself following the biblical traditions and walking in the footsteps of the apostles, both attempts to ground the interdisciplinary approach in history and tradition. The contextual approach also is dependent on its own notions of history and tradition. In particular, it is concerned with what it means to be human and to be human within various contexts with their own histories and traditions, especially those other than Western theology.

In some of the responses to the essays, the contributors have identified a number of the common features of the several approaches. Chung does this by finding commonality among all of the theological methods, while Work uses Hans Frei's typology of methods to show that all five cluster around two basic approaches that have much in common. Franke also finds much to commend in the varying methods and invokes Barth as part of his endorsement. Thus, even if the Bible plays an implicit if not explicit foundational role in theological method, there are other dimensions of thought that play more or less explicit roles in the varieties of theological method found in this volume.

The fifth and final observation is that the essays here represent healthy inquiry into the nature of theological method. However, even if we agree on the various factors that should be taken into account in formulating a theological method (e.g., Scripture), there are a variety of ways in which they may be construed and related to one another. Several of these multifaceted models have been mentioned in the essays above. These include the Wesleyan quadrilateral and David Bebbington's formula for defining evangelicalism, used here as an example of balancing competing factors. The history of interpretation also has a long tradition of tripartite formulations of understanding, also intimated here in various formulations of the factors involved in theological method.

As indicated above, most of the methods defined in this volume have chosen to characterize themselves as primarily oriented to one overriding or governing principle, even if the underlying method itself is a complex assemblage of various factors. This is all to say that there is not only no agreed number of major components in construction of a theological method—including Scripture, context, history, tradition and other factors—but also no agreed way that these are to be placed in relationship to one another. The few multifactor approaches mentioned in the essays offer hints but not clear formulations of how such systematic theorizing is to occur. As a result, there is legitimate debate among the five methods here represented over such matters as the foundations, scope and materials of theology and with them the methods by which they are discussed. In that sense, this volume has been a singular success in that it has brought to the fore different theological methods that provide suitable contrasts to one another on the basis of their varying foundations, how they conceive of the scope and extent of theology, and the various materials that they draw on in formulating their methods.

There is no doubt much more that could, and perhaps even should, be said about what we have learned from these five theological methods. Each reader, depending on his or her own assumptions, background and context, will no doubt view each of them differently—favorably or unfavorably—and find ways of engaging with them in various ways as a result.

WHERE DO WE GO FROM HERE?

Having identified a number of observations about these five theological methods, we might legitimately turn from them as instantiations of the varied approaches to contemporary expressions of systematic theology and ask the question of where we go from here regarding questions of method in systematic theology. The asking of this question positions us, as the editors of this volume, to turn from being chroniclers to prophets. We are no doubt more comfortable describing what is than what ought to or might be. Nevertheless, having surveyed the various approaches, we are now perhaps in a position to think about what the future of evangelical theological method might entail. Several considerations come to mind.

The first is to consider what level of increased interaction among these methods might occur in the future. To our knowledge, this is the first such book to bring these varying methods into this type of constructive and interactive interplay. We have been offered brief but significant presentations of these methods by active and convinced proponents of the varied positions, along with their critical responses to one another's work. Although none of the authors has overtly or even covertly (to our knowledge) repented of his position and been convinced by one of the others, we have seen that some of the authors are more willing to see accommodation and rapprochement among the methods than others. Sometimes, as in the case of Chung, this rapprochement occurs on the foundation of the method being endorsed by the one proposing the closer relationship, while in others there is a healthy recognition of similarity and difference, without necessarily any attempt either to bring them closer together or to force them further apart, as in the classificatory scheme of Work. For the most part, however, each seems as fully convinced now, at the end of the exercise, as when we all began—arguably, we hope, with a greater understanding of the areas of need within their own method and of the previously unrealized and underappreciated strengths of the other methods.

Without necessarily predicting the outcome—and certainly not in an attempt to put pressure on the proposers—we would not be surprised to see future accommodation on the part of the various authors involved, as they recognize that these various theological methods have individual strengths that are worth considering and even possibly making a part of their own approach to theology. What this might look like we find difficult to say. However, we suspect that such movement will involve the greater appreciation of context, understood in its various forms—whether that means original context of the Bible or the context of contemporary theological formulation and even application. This may well also result in the increased realization that any theological formulation is in fact only for the occasion and not meant to be a timeless set of propositions devoid of interpretive or applicational context. With some cautious optimism we can perhaps look forward to such results.

The second consideration for the future is to weigh whether other methods might have an impact on these evangelical approaches, especially those methods that are located outside evangelicalism. For an example (and others could be chosen), the correlative theological method has had a major impact on theology, especially nonevangelical theology, over the last sixty or so years. Correlational theology is roughly defined as "a mutually critical dialogue between theological thinking and other forms of critical thinking."[6]

---

[6]Werner G. Jeanrond, "Correlational Theology and the Chicago School," in *Introduction to Christian Theology: Contemporary North American Perspectives*, ed. Roger A. Badham (Louisville: Westminster John Knox, 1998), 137. This article provides a useful introduction of correlational theology, drawn on in our comments.

In other words, this is theology that positions itself on an equal footing with other intellectual and academic disciplines and modes of thought. Correlational theology was first formulated by the neo-orthodox and existential theologian Paul Tillich in the first volume of his *Systematic Theology*[7] but has come to be associated with what some have called the Chicago school of theology, including Tillich (who spent most of his career at Union Theological Seminary, from 1933–1955, then Harvard University from 1955–1962, and finally the University of Chicago Divinity School from 1962 until his death in 1965) and the two well-known Chicago professors David Tracy and Langdon Gilkey, but also other theologians such as Hans Küng (who spent three months at the University of Chicago in 1981) and Edward Schillebeeckx, each with his own perspective on the theological enterprise.

Correlational theology does not feature in a significant way in any of the positive essays in this volume, but it is mentioned by Work in his essay with reference to Ezigbo's contextual theology (and among his five types of theology based on Hans Frei, it is type three). However, there is an appreciable gap in approach between Ezigbo's use of context and what Tillich does in his systematic theology. One needs merely to read the two treatments to see that Ezigbo's notion of context, which is the important place of realization of theology, is significantly different from Tillich's invocation of the humane disciplines. This merely serves to illustrate our point. The correlative theological method continues to exercise influence, especially in a multidisciplinary world in which religious truth is not privileged but must compete alongside other posited realities. However, having said that, we recognize that contextual theology—and especially theology that makes contextual connections with the surrounding society—will no doubt continue to develop and have a role to play within both contemporary theology and especially contemporary society, a society that seems to favor plurality and complexity as well as downgrading the significance or uniqueness of theology.

A third consideration is to assess the future of each of these methods and to contemplate whether there is room for development of them and of other such methods within evangelicalism. This volume has provided an opportunity for dedicated authors to lay out their current positions. These positions

---

[7]Paul Tillich, *Systematic Theology* (Chicago: University of Chicago Press, 1951), 1:67-73.

have also been criticized by those who, if not holding to the same positions, are at least sympathetic to the evangelical theological task and purpose. I think that we have learned something about some of the major methods in evangelical systematic theology that provides avenues for us to move forward with further refinement in our methods.

For example, the codified view might incorporate more of an overt recognition of the contextual nature of all theology. Even if we agree that the Bible provides the basis or final court of appeal for our theology, we may wish to have greater humility and even temerity in the forcefulness with which we state that such and such a position is a definitive conclusion of our theology. We might do this because we recognize that our interpretation is based on our contemporary interpretive context (e.g., issues regarding Christology are important at least in part because of disputes over them; the same could be said regarding such issues as gender roles, women in the church, the nature of atonement, etc.) and done by interpreters who themselves are firmly and ineluctably embedded in contexts. A duly instructed and chastened form of codified theology might provide a more convincing theological method for those who are not already attracted to it.

We could make similar kinds of observations regarding others of the theological methods included within this volume. Missional theology may benefit from critique regarding its reductionistic stance toward its own self-evident (at least to its practitioners) foundation. A more thorough grounding in Scripture, a willingness to be open to other forms of intellectual discourse that have proved insightful even in Christian theology through the centuries, and its own greater contextualization could create a more robust missional theology. Missional theology in such a context might be more serviceable in a greater variety of theological venues, without appearing to fit all of theology into a single narrative.

Interdisciplinary approaches to theology are probably rightly accused of being ambivalent about the final arbiter of their theological stances: is the ultimate basis Scripture, a particular discipline or a complex of disciplines drawn on in ways that easily elude those who do not necessarily understand the method? A clearer definition of foundations might help this method to sort through the complexity of competing disciplines to arrive at an interdisciplinary approach that is itself driven by estimable principles.

Contextual theology clearly offers much in recognizing that all theology is indeed contextual (and humanitarian). If, however, all theology is contextual, and contexts change, then it is very difficult to determine what is the fundamental core or the stable middle of Christian theology. Contextual theology perhaps needs to make clearer how, why and on what basis it maintains the central tenets of Christian theology, and how it arrives at them when context is determinative.

Dogmatic theology probably runs the greatest risk of being the furthest removed from contemporary theological concerns, because it places its emphasis on particular dogmas. These dogmas might appear to be contextless, formulated in a previous era out of now incomprehensible or even irrelevant concerns, and asserted to audiences who find the language used to be irrelevant to the present. Dogmatic theology, however, that recognizes its need to rethink dogma in the light of contemporary theological concerns, even while keeping one's relationship with the past, might have promise of effectively bridging the gap from the past to the present.

In the course of our discussion, some of these theological methods have mentioned various other theological perspectives that merit further consideration (e.g., Franke mentions Reformed, Lutheran, Wesleyan, Pentecostal, feminist, womanist, black, Hispanic and Asian, to which might be added ecotheology and liberation theology, among still others), but few if any of these reflect a unique method. Most of them utilize methods that are already being employed in the field of systematic theology, but they provide a new body of evidence or a new set of issues (usually of a contextual nature) or a different set of presuppositions for further consideration. But what would it mean to develop a genuinely new theological method? What would it mean not simply to refine those methods with which we are already familiar but to develop a new approach to how to do theology? What we have in mind here is not simply repeating previous methods applied to new material but thoroughly reconceptualizing the notion of method. How would we go about doing this? How do we do this and remain faithful to the Christian theological tradition? How do we balance our previous theological knowledge and the changing contexts and realities of our contemporary contexts? How do we hold in tension traditional beliefs with new formulations and reformulations? This raises the question of whether this even constitutes a legitimate task for theology. We have no doubt that further theological reflection will result in the development of further theological methods. Rather than simply welcoming or disparaging them, we must evaluate how they meet the varied criteria that we have set for what constitutes a legitimate theological method. We trust that this volume will serve a useful purpose in this continuing discussion as readers read and react to the essays and their responses.

Contributors

Sung Wook Chung (DPhil, University of Oxford) is professor of Christian theology at Denver Seminary. He is the author of *Admiration and Challenge: Karl Barth's Theological Relationship with John Calvin* and other books on trinitarian theology, eschatology and apologetics. He is also the editor of several books, including *Karl Barth and Evangelical Theology: Convergences and Divergences.*

Victor Ifeanyi Ezigbo (PhD, University of Edinburgh) is professor of systematic and contextual theology and chair of the Biblical and Theological Studies Department at Bethel University. He is the author of *Re-imagining African Christologies: Conversing with the Interpretations and Appropriations of Jesus in Contemporary African Christianity* and *Introducing Christian Theologies: Voices from Global Christian Communities* in two volumes.

John R. Franke (DPhil, University of Oxford) is professor of religious studies and missiology at the Evangelische Theologische Faculteit in Leuven, Belgium; theologian-in-residence at Second Presbyterian Church in Indianapolis; and general coordinator for the Gospel and Our Culture Network in North America. He is the author of numerous articles and several books, including *Beyond Foundationalism: Shaping Theology in a Postmodern Context; The Character of Theology: An Introduction to Its Nature, Task, and Purpose; Barth for Armchair Theologians;* and *Manifold Witness: The Plurality of Truth.*

Paul Louis Metzger (PhD, King's College London) is professor of Christian theology and theology of culture and the founder and director of the Institute for Cultural Engagement: New Wine, New Wineskins at Multnomah University and Seminary. His books include *The Word of Christ and the World* *of Culture: Sacred and Secular Through the Theology of Karl Barth*; *Consuming Jesus: Beyond Race and Class Divisions in a Consumer Church*; *Exploring Ecclesiology: An Evangelical and Ecumenical Introduction* (with Brad Harper); and *Connecting Christ: How to Discuss Jesus in a World of Diverse Paths*.

Stanley E. Porter (PhD, University of Sheffield) is president and dean, professor of New Testament, and Roy A. Hope Chair in Christian Worldview at McMaster Divinity College. He is the author of twenty-eight books on various topics in New Testament and related subjects, including *Hermeneutics: An Introduction to Interpretive Theory* (with Jason C. Robinson), and has edited more than eighty volumes, including *Biblical Hermeneutics: Five Views* (with Beth M. Stovell). Porter has also published over three hundred articles, chapters and related writings.

Steven M. Studebaker (PhD, Marquette University) is the Howard and Shirley Bentall Chair in Evangelical Thought and associate professor of systematic and historical theology at McMaster Divinity College. He is the author of *A Pentecostal Political Theology for American Renewal: Spirit of the Kingdoms, Citizens of the Cities* and *From Pentecost to the Triune God: A Pentecostal Trinitarian Theology*, as well as several other books on Jonathan Edwards's trinitarian theology and Pentecostal theology.

Telford C. Work (PhD, Duke University) is professor of theology at Westmont College. He is the author of *Living and Active: Scripture in the Economy of Salvation*; *Deuteronomy*; and *Ain't Too Proud to Beg: Living Through the Lord's Prayer*.

Author Index

Subject Index

activism, 89-91
actualism, 117-19, 133, 162-63
aggression, 86-88
Aquinas, Thomas, 5, 18, 33, 167-68
Arianism, 49, 74, 205
Arius, 49, 183
Athanasius, 33, 49, 90, 183
Augustine of Hippo, 5, 18, 33, 75-77, 79, 83, 176, 184, 190
Augustinian theology, 75-77
authority of Scripture, 3, 6, 15, 16-17, 20-21, 31, 45, 65-66, 73-75, 98-100, 107-11, 151, 156
Bebbington's quadrilateral, 80-81, 85, 89-90, 193, 209
Bethel University, 3
biblical canon, 71, 73-75, 99, 169
Calvin, John, 20, 34, 38-39, 84, 160-61, 167-68, 190, 199
canonical-linguistic theological method, 16-17, 157
Chalcedon, Council of, 27, 100, 114
Christendom, 25, 52-53, 62, 67
Christian identity, 84, 99-100, 108, 110-11, 112-13, 180
church history, 5, 75
communities of faith, 62-63, 72
conservative Christology, 46-51
conservative theology, 24, 30-51, 145
Constantinople, Council of, 100, 114
contemporary theological method, 12-19
contextual Christology, 111-15
contextual theology, 26, 63, 93-115
    history of contextual theology, 95-98
conversion, 3, 54-55, 85-86, 88
correlational theology, 11, 172, 211-12
critical realism, 43, 189, 190, 204-6
critique of conservative theology, 155-58, 166-67, 180-82, 189-91, 203, 213
critique of contextual theology, 148-51, 172-73, 194-96, 203, 214
critique of interdisciplinary theology, 145-48, 158-60, 173-74, 185-87, 191-94, 203, 213

critique of missional theology, 144-45, 170-72, 184-85, 196-98, 203, 213
critique of Trinitarian dogmatic theology, 151-53, 162-64, 167-70, 180-84, 204, 214
cultural embeddedness of the gospel, 15, 55, 58, 160, 195, 204, 213
cultural engagement, 17-19
ecclesiology, 27, 52-54, 57-58, 62-63, 67-69, 71-72, 82, 90, 127, 132-33, 138-39, 143-45, 151-53, 160, 162, 168, 170-71, 177, 184, 196
eisegesis, 46, 51
emerging church, 4
eschatology, 3, 22, 85-86, 89-90
evangelical beliefs, 3
evangelical diversity, 4
Evangelical Theological Society, 3, 156
evangelicalism, 2-4
exegesis, 40-41, 47-49
feminism, 13, 26, 155, 183, 214
Foursquare Gospel, 26, 80-81, 83, 85, 89
Fuller Theological seminary, 3
Graham, Billy, 3
Harvard University, 212
Heilsgeschichte, 33
historical/grammatical interpretation, 47-49
history of evangelical method, 7-12
historical positivism, 117, 124, 128, 131-34
Holy Spirit, 4-6, 21, 27, 31, 38, 42, 44, 46, 49-50, 54, 56, 60-61, 63-64, 68-69, 71, 73, 80-84, 88-90, 99, 108, 117, 119-20, 124, 126-27, 130-39, 143, 145, 149, 151, 169-72, 181, 184, 189
homoiousios, 49
homoousios, 49
homosexuality, 80-92, 158, 186-87, 192-93
human context, 26, 95, 100-104, 112-15, 149-50, 180
Hume, David, 193
individualism, 62
integrative theology, 42-43, 153
interdisciplinary Christology, 80-92
interdisciplinary theology, 25-26, 73-92
Irenaeus of Lyons, 33, 136

Scripture Index

Finding the Textbook You Need

The IVP Academic Textbook Selector
is an online tool for instantly finding the IVP books
suitable for over 250 courses across 24 disciplines.

---

ivpacademic.com